Naturalists on the Isthmus of Panama

A Hundred Years of Natural History on the Biological Bridge of the Americas

STANLEY HECKADON-MORENO

D0982273

SMITHSONIAN TROPICAL RESEARCH INSTITUTE

PANAMA 2004

This book is an edition of the Smithsonian Tropical Research Institute, Panama.

First Spanish edition: 1998
First English edition: 2004

ISBN 9962-8901-0-1 for the Spanish edition
ISBN 9962-614-07-4 for the English edition

Editor: Hans Roeder
Image editing: Lina Gonzalez and Diego Heckadon

Printed in Colombia by Imprelibros S.A. Cali.

This publication was possible in part due to the support of Dr. David Cofrin.

The photo on the front cover of early naturalists on Barro Colorado Island, Panama, taken in 1924, shows from left to right: G. S. Dodds, James Zetek, Ignacio Molino, Nathan Banks, George Wheeler, Graham Fairchild, Frederick Burguess, David Fairchild, and William Morton Wheeler.
Photo: Archives of the Museum of Comparative Zoology, Harvard.

Contents

Presentation

It is a pleasure to present to English speaking readers *Naturalists on the Isthmus of Panama* by Stanley Heckadon-Moreno, a researcher at the Smithsonian Tropical Research Institute.

Readers might like to know the genesis and importance of this work. For nine years, Stanley has been writing a monthly article for *Epocas*, the cultural and historical supplement of the Panama City's daily *La Prensa*, aimed at promoting a greater interest among the larger community toward science by reconstructing the history of natural sciences in the Isthmus during the XIX and the XX centuries. Given the interests shown by teachers, students and the public who collected these supplements as a source of information, he gathered them in a book published by STRI in 1998. The book the reader has in his hands now is a revised and enlarged version of the Spanish original, including new information of expeditions that long ago explored Panama's forests.

Readers will find here an account of some of the most important scientific milestones of a century that helped to broaden our knowledge on the magnitude of the diversity of plants and animals of the Isthmus. Most of the information presented in this book was unpublished, gathered painfully and laboriously from library archives and research centers in different countries. These include the field notes, publications long forgotten, newspaper items and photos of some of these pioneers of tropical studies.

This book, not only is an extremely valuable contribution to our knowledge of the history of natural sciences in this strategic region of the tropics, but also outlines the early history of STRI and of other outstanding research centers who have worked in Panama such as: the American Museum of Natural History, the Missouri Botanical Garden, the Field Museum of Natural History and Harvard's Museum of Comparative Zoology.

5

It is most meaningful that this publication coincides with the celebrations of the Centennial of the Republic of Panama, for this book also rescues parts of the country's intellectual history: the consolidation of a tradition, a scientific tradition spanning three generations of naturalists. Thus it is my pleasure to acknowledge here the generous hospitality of the people of Panama, a country that has hosted STRI since the Smithsonian's famous led expedition: the Biological Survey of the Panama Canal, carried out between 1910-1912, during the construction of the inter-oceanic waterway.

Frequently we forget that the achievements of present day scientists are built on the work of their precursors. By rescuing the stories of early plant explorers as Berthold Seemann, Henri Pittier and Paul C. Standley; of students of bird life as Frank Chapman and Alexander Wetmore; or mammologists as Edward A. Goldman or such outstanding pioneers of tropical fishes like Seth E. Meek and Samuel Hildebrand, Stanley Heckadon-Moreno helps us to understand and appreciate the place that in tropical biology worldwide has been played by Panama and the Smithsonian Tropical Research Institute. Through their work and others of their generation locations in Panama such as Barro Colorado Island and the Soberanía National Park have become the best studied areas in the New World. Nevertheless, we still keep finding many new species, particularly among the arthropods of the forest canopy, as much as 60% of the species that exist still remain undescribed by science. Much remains to be done by today's pioneers.

I hope that this book, with the examples on the work and adventures of some pioneers of tropical research, would be a source of inspiration to today's generation, and a sincere acknowledgement to the vital role played by them in helping to establish the basis for our intellectual vantage points we enjoy today.

Ira Rubinoff
Director
Smithsonian Tropical Research Institute

In Memory of
Dr. Martin H. Moynihan, Naturalist (1928–1996)

Photo by Olga F. Linares, Portugal.

Born in Chicago in 1928, and brought up in France, Martin H. Moynihan completed his Ph.D. in biology at Oxford University in 1953, under the tutelage of Nobel laureate Niko Tinbergen. As an associate researcher at the Harvard Museum of Comparative Zoology, he arrived in Panama in 1957 to become the "resident naturalist" for the Biological Station on Barro Colorado Island.

Thanks to his vision, and to his scientific and organizational skills, he transformed the tiny field station on the island into the Smithsonian Tropical Research Institute, STRI. Today, STRI is a leading center for the advanced study of marine and terrestrial biology in the tropics. It is one of the greatest legacies that the U.S. presence left in Panama during the 20th Century.

Martin H. Moynihan was a great field biologist, specializing in the study of the behavior of avian, terrestrial, and marine animals in their natural environments. His research program, initiated in Panama, took him around the world. Among the organisms that particularly drew his attention were birds, New World monkeys, and squid.

A true gentleman, with a gifted sense of humor, Martin had many intellectual interests, among them a passion for history. He was graced with many talents. A skilled artist, he illustrated his books with his own exquisite drawings and paintings of the animals he studied.

After retiring in 1973 from his role as founding director of STRI, Martin continued to serve as one of the Institute's outstanding scientists. He and his wife, Olga F. Linares, lived in an old, exquisitely restored mansion in the *barrio* of San Felipe, the walled colonial quarter of Panama City, with a view of the Pacific Ocean which he so loved.

S.H.-M.

".... and he who has traveled the wilderness of the Indies, if it only be the ten or eight leagues between Nombre de Dios and Panama, will well understand the nature of the vast forests that are in the Indies. As winter which brings cold never comes, and the humidity of the air and the soil is so high, it comes to pass that the mountains produce infinite trees, and the plains, that they call *savannas*, infinite grasses. Therefore, for pastures, grasses; and for buildings, lumber; and for the hearths, firewood; are never wanting. To tell the differences and appearances of so many wild trees is impossible for most of them, not even their names are known."

Joseph De Acosta, SJ
Natural and Moral History of the Indies, 1590

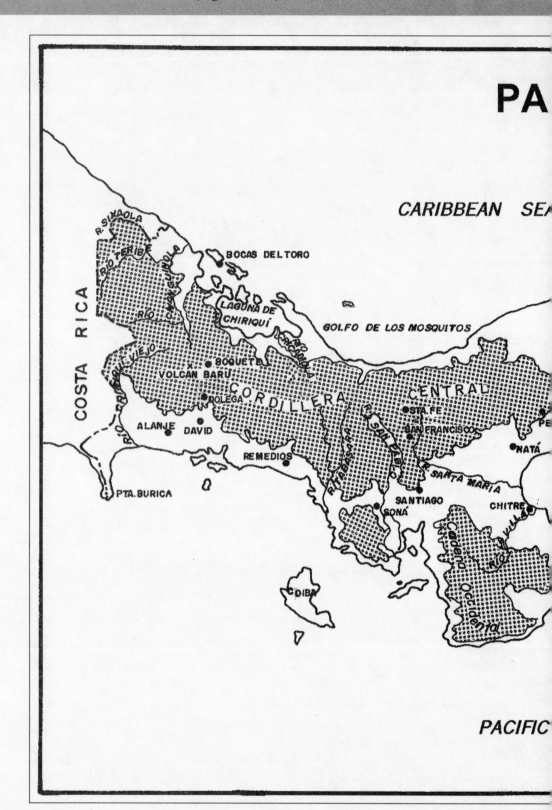

MA

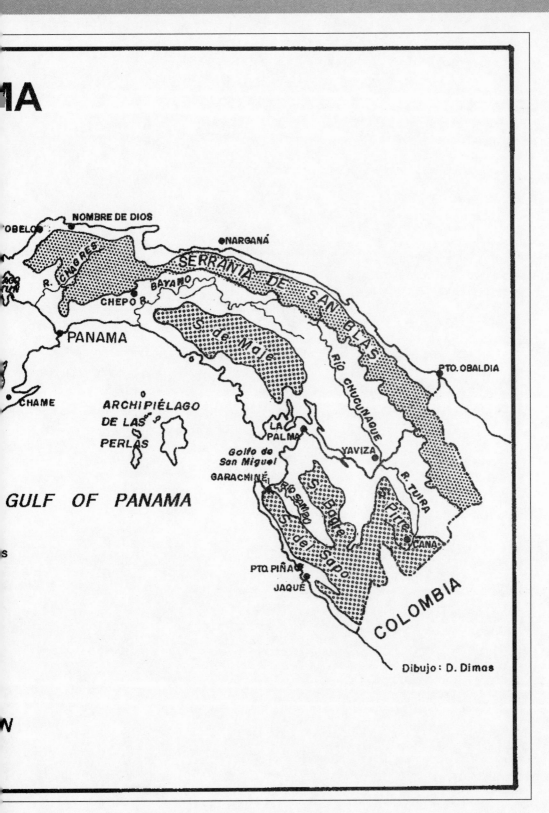

NOMBRE DE DIOS

OBELO

NARGANÁ

R. CHAGRES

SERRANÍA DE SAN BLAS

BAYANO

CHEPO R.

PANAMA

PTO. OBALDIA

S. de Maje

CHAME

ARCHIPIÉLAGO
DE LAS
PERLAS

Río CHUCUNAQUE

LA
PALMA

Golfo de
San Miguel

YAVIZA

GARACHINÉ

GULF OF PANAMA

R. TUIRA

S. Bagre

Río Sambu

S. Pirre

CANA

S. del Sapo

PTO. PIÑA

JAQUÉ

COLOMBIA

Dibujo: D. Dimas

W

A Note to the English Reader

The original version of this book was published in Spanish in 1998. Since then, several people interested in the course taken by natural history on the Isthmus have asked for an English translation. It is my pleasure to comply with such a request, particularly in 2003, the year when Panama celebrates its centennial as a republic. This book is thus a part of STRI's contribution to the 100th anniversary celebrations of the country that has hosted it for most of the 20th Century. It is also homage to the 80th birthday of the biological laboratory in Barro Colorado Island.

Since 1998 additional information has come to light on some of the early naturalists who explored Panama. Some of these new facts, including old unpublished photos, have been incorporated into the English version.

This work includes abundant excerpts from the field notes and publications made by these early students of Panama's tropical nature. These quotes have been left in their original form. At times readers might find their grammatical construction and expressions somewhat quaint. One reason is that some naturalists were not native English speakers. Berthold Seemann, for example, was a German, and Henri Pittier, a French speaking Swiss. Not uncommonly for the times, some of them lacked a formal education, not having attended a university. They were either gifted, self taught amateurs who became specialists, like the great orchidologist Charles Powell, or had learned the trade during hard long years of field work as assistants under a master, such as the zoologist Edward A. Goldman.

I would like to recognize my debt of gratitude to those people and institutions who have made possible this English version. to Dr. David Cofrin, a member of the Smithsonian Associates, for his kind and crucial donation toward the translation expenses; to Ana Luisa Sanchez, Beth King, and Malena Sarlo, who undertook the painstaking work of translating the book from Spanish; to my dear friends and colleagues Dr. Olga F. Linares and George Angher, who kindly took precious time from their busy schedule to revise the entire manuscript and turn its prose into a more elegant English; to Dr. Neal Smith, for sharing his historical perspectives on the role of the naturalists of the American Museum of Natural History in Panama; to Rebecca Rissanen, a STRI volunteer from the University of Panama, for her cheerful and effective support in innumerable details of the research; to Lina Gonzalez, of the Digital Imaging Laboratory at STRI, and Diego Heckadon whose constant willingness and skill guaranteed the quality of the numerous images that enrich the text; to Vielka Chang-Yau and Angel Aguirre of the Earl S. Tupper Library, always supportive in the seemingly endless quest for new documents.

Pam Hansen and Vyrthis Thomas, at the archives of the Smithsonian Institution, were selfless in looking up innumerable manuscripts, letters and images from the biological expeditions conducted long ago by members of this great institution.

My thanks also go to Douglas Holland, archivist at the Missouri Botanical Garden, for his superb and friendly help in tracking down photographs, letters, news items, and documents from the explorations of the MBG along the first half of the 20th Century; to Nina Cummings, head of the photo archives of the Field Museum, Chicago, for photos of the field work done by Seth Meek and Samuel Hildebrand in Panama from 1910 to 1912; and finally, to the Library of the American Museum of Natural History, New York, and in particular to Tom Moritz and Mathew Pavlick for their help with information about the studies of Frank Chapman in Panama during the 1920s and 1930s.

To the personnel at Imprelibros in Cali, Colombia, in particular to Fernando Orozco, for the care and attention to detail given to this work.

Stanley Heckadon-Moreno
Panama, Ancón, January 2004

Acknowledgements to the Spanish Edition

This book has been possible thanks to the generous assistance of several people and institutions to whom I owe an enormous debt of gratitude. Mario Lewis Morgan, in 1995, offered me the pages of *Epocas*, the historical and cultural supplement of Panama City's daily newspaper, *La Prensa*, for a monthly article on the naturalists who have explored Panama. Over the next two years my old friend Francisco Herrera gave generously of his time to revise these manuscripts, while Olga Barrio translated many of the unpublished documents and manuscripts from English to Spanish.

Crucial was the assistance from the Smithsonian Institution, Washington, D.C. First, I would like to thank the Women's Committee, whose kind donation supported the printing of the Spanish version. Lucy Dorick and Lisa Barnett played a key role in preparing the funding proposal submitted to the Women's Committee.

Thanks also go to Pamela Henson and William Cox from the Smithsonian Archives; to Phil Angle; Dr. Michael Braun, of the Molecular Systematic Laboratory; Ruth Schallert, of the Botanical Archives; Dr. Robert Fisher, of the Mammals Division at the National Museum of Natural History, and Storrs Olson, a dedicated student of Panama and the province of Bocas del Toro.

In Panama, my thanks go to the Smithsonian Tropical Research Institute (STRI), and its director, Dr. Ira Rubinoff, for his interest and granting me time away from my other duties. The Volunteer Program at STRI, managed by Georgina de Alba and Adriana Bilgray, provided a group of motivated young students who did not dismay during the grueling task of searching the archives: Marissa Colburn, Danielle Steward, and, especially, Alma Perez. Angel Aguirre, Vielka Chang-Yau, and Elizabeth Sanchez, of the STRI library staff, were extremely helpful. Also thanks to María Luz Calderon; Alejandro Caballero, at the Digital Imaging Laboratory; Marcos Guerra, at the photo laboratory; and Raineldo Urriola, for his logistical support. Numerous comments were received from my colleagues Drs. George Angehr, Mireya Correa, Noris Salazar, Klaus Winter, Neal Smith, Paul Colvinaux, Olga F. Linares, and Nelida Gómez.

Many thanks to Christopher Wallace, from the Panama Canal Commission, for historical data on Charles W. Powell.

Dr. Belisario Betancur, ex-president of Colombia and a friend of Panama, who, at the Coronado meetings (at which the future of the Canal under Panamanian administration was decided), helped me to establish contacts with the Fundación Santillana para Iberoamérica, over which he presides. At the Editorial Santillana, I am grateful to Marissa Montesano de Talavera, from the Panama office, and to Guillermo Polanco, Ana Lorena Orozco, and Wagner Solorzano of the Costa Rican office.

The cover is graced by a beautiful, prize-winning oil painting from the private collection of Dr. Eloy Alfaro, Panama's current ambassador to the United States, by Panamanian painter José Inocente Duarte. My thanks go to the late Irene Escoffery, who provided the contacts and made all necessary arrangements.

To Sonia, my wife, and our children, Diego and Monica, for their moral support and patience, vital for attempting these enterprises of the spirit.

Stanley Heckadon-Moreno

Introduction

❖

This book recounts the histories of some of the pioneer naturalists who have contributed towards building our knowledge of the magnitude of diversity of Panama's plants and animals, and their relationships with other life forms in the two great American continents.

Panama is a narrow isthmus that emerged from the sea some three million years ago, thus becoming a land bridge linking the flora and fauna of North and South America, and a barrier separating the marine species of both oceans. Physically small, with only 77,000 km² in area, Panama is extraordinarily rich in biological diversity. It is said that "Panama" meant "abundance of fishes" in the language of the Cueva people who inhabited the isthmus when the Spaniards arrived. But Panama could also signify abundance and diversity of mammals, birds and plants.

The articles gathered in this volume were originally published between 1995 and 1997 in *Epocas*, a monthly cultural and historical supplement of *La Prensa*, one of Panama's leading newspapers. Not directed at specialists, these writings were aimed at a growing sector of the community interested in knowing more about the country's natural history. A well-informed public, one that values its natural heritage, is one of the best guarantees toward the intelligent use and conservation of natural resources. These are currently being threatened by a destructive pattern of economic development which, in the long run, is unsustainable.

These monthly essays were started without a preconceived plan, not intending to be gathered into a book. It was impossible to anticipate where the quest would lead, for the author, as a social scientist, is a layman in natural sciences. It has been a harsh learning process, rife with uncertainties, dead ends, and elusive leads; but also the cause for myriad satisfactions as little known sources of information were discovered. As data emerged which allowed me to reconstruct the explorations of these early pioneers and their contributions to tropical biology, the articles painfully took shape one by one.

When these articles appeared in *Epocas*, diverse readers across Panama—teachers and professors, students and professionals, businessmen, colleagues—encouraged me to compile them into a book. This idea gathered strength in 1996 due to a double scientific commemoration: the 150th anniversary of the Smithsonian Institution in Washington, dedicated to the advance and diffusion of knowledge, and the 50th year since the creation of the Smithsonian Tropical Research Institute (STRI) in Panama.

In a real sense this work benefits from one of STRI's most valuable assets: its fertile intellectual environment. Here, scientists from many nationalities and disciplines meet to create an extraordinary center for research on tropical marine and terrestrial environments.

Paradoxically, Panamanians have shown scant motivation to study their own natural heritage. About the only local author who delved into the theme of naturalists who explored the Isthmus was professor Novencido Escobar. His book *El Desarrollo de las Ciencias Naturales y la Medicina en Panama*, (The development of the natural sciences and medicine in Panama), was published in 1987 by the Biblioteca de la Cultura Panameña, at the University of Panama.

Most of the information that I consulted was in English, dispersed in archives from different research institutions around the world. A very serious problem that affects developing countries is their weak interest in sciences reflected, for example, in the lack of specialized libraries. In this sense, Panama is privileged in that it can count on the excellent Earl S. Tupper Library at STRI, where our search for the literature first began. Gradually, the search extended to other archives within the Smithsonian Institution in Washington, and to scientific and academic centers in North America and Europe, a task made much easier by those marvellous tools, the e-mail and the Internet.

From the vast *corpus* of documents used in preparing these writings we relied not so much on those in which naturalists gave detailed accounts of newfound species, but rather on their general sketches about Isthmian nature and culture. This data, taken mostly from their personal diaries, field reports, and letters, allowed us to see, through the eyes of these explorers, the Panamanian landscape —the forests and savannas; the uses, customs, and beliefs that people held towards the local flora and fauna; the conditions of towns, villages and roads; the ways of gaining a livelihood; the political and administrative systems; the demographic and ethnic composition of the population.

Some travelers were very terse in their comments. Others left priceless observations about Panama, drawing attention to traits not usually perceived by the common traveler. As a rule, it seems that those interested in plants were more communicative than those who studied insects.

**From Berthold Seemann to
Eugene Eisenmann Brandon**

The period under scrutiny encompasses a little over a hundred years, from the middle of the 19th Century to the mid 20th Century. Hence this book could be subtitled "a century of natural history on the biological bridge of the Americas," a time span during which the role of the Isthmus as a bridge joining the flora and fauna of the Americas, and as barrier separating the oceans, gradually became evident.

This book presents articles on sixteen naturalists in chronological order. The story begins in Panama in the decade of the 1840s, with German botanist Berthold Seemann (1825-1871), a naturalist on board the HMS *Herald*, a research vessel sent between 1846 and 1851 by the British navy on a scientific expedition around the world. The narrative concludes with Eugene Eisenmann Brandon (1906-1981), a Panamanian who as a student of the birds of Panama and Central America was closely associated with the history of the famous Biological Station on Barro Colorado Island in the Panama Canal. Throughout these hundred years the world at large, and Panama in particular, underwent major changes.

The 19th Century

Many Panamanian plants are named after Berthold Seemann, who explored previously unstudied regions of the Isthmus, collecting more than a thousand specimens of local plants during several trips he made between 1846 and 1849. Returning to London, he published two books in which the Panamanian data appeared prominently: in 1853, *Narratives of the Voyage of the H.M.S Herald during the Years of 1845-1851 under the Command of Captain Henry Kellett*, in two volumes; subsequently, in 1852-1857, *The Botany of the Voyage of the H.M.S. Herald during the Years 1845-51*, a work in four parts, one of which, *The Flora of Panama*, was profusely illustrated with drawings of tropical plants.

The other 19th Century naturalist to be presented here is the Pole Josef von Warscewicz (1812-1866), a pioneer collector of orchids, hummingbirds, and reptiles for European museums and botanical gardens. Warscewicz traveled through Panama in 1848 and 1851. In 1848, he proceeded from David, on the dry Pacific slope, climbed Volcán Barú, near the continental divide, and ended his trip at Chiriquí Grande Lagoon, on the rainy Caribbean side of the Isthmus. His biographical data is scarce.

The explorations of Seemann and Warscewicz coincided with a period of rapid changes in Panama, at that time a Department of the Republic of New Granada (now Colombia). It was the early days of steam navigation and the construction of the Panama Railroad, linking the Atlantic to the Pacific (1850-1855). The steamship and the train facilitated trade and the work of naturalists. The population of the Isthmus stood at about 130,000, and Panama City, its walled capital, barely had 5,000 souls. The Department was divided into two provinces, Panama and Veraguas, and one territory, Darién.

The 20th Century

We begin the 20th Century with the explorations of Wilmot W. Brown, Jr., an American, who, from 1900 to 1904, collected birds and mammals for the Museum of Comparative Zoology at Harvard University. These were troubled times, marked by the War of a Thousand Days, Colombia's most violent civil conflict, and by Panama's separation from Colombia, which initiated the United States' effort to build the canal. Brown collected along the Interoceanic Railway and along the Pacific coastal savannas, extending westward from Panama City to Chiriquí. Here he climbed Volcán Barú, Panama's highest point (3,450 m). He also explored the Archipelago of Las Perlas in the Gulf of Panama.

Since the French attempts to build the Panama Canal (1880-1890), the international scientific community had been calling, unsuccessfully, for intensive studies on the plants and animals of the Isthmus. All this changed in 1910 with the construction of a huge dam across the Chagres River giving birth to Lake Gatún, the largest man-made body of water known until then. Suddenly, the imminent flooding of hundreds of kilometers of tropical forests by the biggest engineering project ever made, the study of the narrowest and lowest portion of land in the Americas became a scientific priority.

Opposite page: "Tropical Scenery". The bewildering diversity of plant life in a tropical forest near the village of Chepigana on the Tuira River, challenged pioneer nature photographer Timothy O'Sullivan.
Here, an early image taken by him in 1870 during the expedition led by T. O. Selfridge, seeking a route for an interoceanic canal across Darién.
Source: Smithsonian Institution, National Anthropological Archives. Washington, D.C.

The Panama Railroad, built between 1850 and 1855, linked the Atlantic and the Pacific for the first time. It facilitated international commerce and tropical studies.
Engraving from: F. N. Otis, *Illustrated History of the Panama Railroad*, New York, 1862.

The Smithsonian Institution and the Panama Biological Survey

In this unprecedented saga in the quest for knowledge about the tropics, the Smithsonian Institution played a leading role by carrying out, between 1910 and 1912, the great biological survey of the Canal Zone and Panama. Four naturalists participating in this important scientific expedition are portrayed here: the Swiss botanist Henri Pittier (1857-1950); Edward A. Goldman (1873-1946), a zoologist, and Seth E. Meek (1859-1914) and his assistant Samuel F. Hildebrand (1883-1946), who studied sea and freshwater fishes.

These naturalists would be among the first to document their tropical field studies using the photographic camera. Almost like children with a new toy, they delighted in taking pictures of what they saw, leaving us a unique legacy of the flora and fauna of the Isthmus in the early 20th Century, and of its people, their practices, and their customs.

Henri Pittier was a naturalist in the broadest sense of the word: botanist, climatologist, geologist, cartographer, and a man with a passionate interest in indigenous cultures. From 1910 to 1912, he investigated the forests along the axis of the canal works and surrounding areas, including the Chagres River. He also explored the Atlantic coast, from Colón to Puerto Obaldía on the Colombian border. In 1911, he visited Chiriquí three times. He also studied the forests of the Bayano River and Darién, and conducted detailed field work on the vegetation of the natural savannas of the Pacific side of the Isthmus: in Chepo and Pacora, east of Panama City, and the country west of Panama City, from Punta Chame to Chiriquí Province. In 1915 and 1916, Pittier founded and directed the first experimental station for tropical agriculture in Panama, located on the banks of Matias Hernández River, on the outskirts of the capital city.

At the same time, zoologist Edward A. Goldman organized two expeditions to collect birds and mammals. In the first, he visited Lake Gatún, the savannas of Chepo, and the highland forests of Cerro Azul on the continental divide, as well as Portobelo and Nombre de Dios on the rainy Atlantic coast. On his second trip, he collected specimens along the canal works, then eastward into Darién, along the Tuira River and the Cana valley and, finally, in the highlands of Cerro Pirre.

Goldman would bequeath us his priceless *The Mammals of Panama*, richly documented with photos and one of the first ever maps on the country's life zones. The Smithsonian Institution published this book in 1920.

It could be said that the modern study of fresh and salt-water fishes of Panama began with Seth Meek and Samuel F. Hildebrand; both ichthyologists came with the Smithsonian expedition. Their fieldwork was intensive; they collected specimens on Lake Gatún and its many tributaries, from rivers near the Pacific and Atlantic entrances of the canal, along the Gulf of Panama, the Tuira River and the valley of Cana. They produced many scientific articles and a memorable book, *The Marine Fishes of Panama*, published in three volumes by the

Field Museum of Chicago between 1923 and 1928. In this work, they supported the theory that the Isthmus had played a vital role when, upon rising from the sea, it became a barrier separating fish in the Pacific Ocean from those in the Atlantic. From 1935 onwards, Hildebrand investigated how the canal facilitated the movement of fish between both oceans.

The Barro Colorado Biological Station

The creation of Barro Colorado Island Biological Station in Lake Gatún plays a prominent role in our understanding of the tropics of the New World. During the first decades of the 20th Century, this tiny field station became one of the world's most famous research centers for the study of tropical biology.

A leading figure in this history was an entomologist, James Zetek (1886-1959). Initially, Zetek came to Panama under the command of the legendary Colonel William C. Gorgas to study one of humanity's greatest scourges in the tropics, the mosquito. From 1923 to 1953, Zetek would be the Island's first manager and a vital force during the laboratory's heroic years.

Panama owes a huge debt of gratitude to Frank M. Chapman (1864-1945) of the American Museum of Natural History in New York, who visited Panama every year between 1925 and 1935 to study the birds of Barro Colorado Island and the forest in which they dwell. He published two books about the island, which became the first best sellers on the tropics to be written by a naturalist. In these works, aimed at English speaking audiences living in temperate climates, he describes the astonishing diversity of life forms inhabiting the tropical forests and the fascinating relationships between plants and animals.

The first book appeared in 1931 under the title *My Tropical Air Castle: Nature Studies in Panama*. His second book, *Life in an Air Castle: Nature Studies in the Tropics*, came out in 1938. These works would make Barro Colorado as famous for naturalists around the world as the Panama Canal is among engineers.

Researchers Working on Plants

Included in this book are the profiles of four key plant researchers working in Panama during the early part of the 20th Century: Charles W. Powell (1854-1926); Paul C. Standley (1884-1963), a botanist at the Smithsonian Institution and the Chicago Field Museum of Natural History; Paul Allen (1911-1963), from the Missouri Botanical Garden, and George Proctor Cooper from Yale University.

During the 1910s and 1920s, Panama's most important tourist attraction, after the canal, was the orchid garden at Cerro Ancón, owned by a dispenser of quinine pills of the Isthmian Canal Commission. His garden was unique in the world; it held some 7,000 plants, representing 400 different species of orchids, most found only in Panama. His name: Charles Wesley Powell. Powell's case is exemplary for several reasons. First, it shows how a botanical layman can become a leading collector and an expert on orchids, the most aristocratic and temperamental of tropical plants. Secondly, his garden helped to attract the Missouri Botanical Garden to the Isthmus, which led to a series of expeditions being organized and, finally, to the publication of the monumental work, *The Flora of Panama*, begun in 1943 and finished in 1981. This compendium of isthmian flowering plants is more than 6,000 pages in length.

To the great botanist Paul C. Standley we owe two valuable works on local plants, both published by the Smithsonian Institution: in 1927, *Flora of Barro Colorado Island*, the first complete catalog of plants in the Island, and, in 1928, *Flora of the Panama Canal Zone*. Standley collected more than 7,500 plant specimens from the Canal area, Taboga Island, and from most of the gallery forests along the rivers of Panama City and its eastern environs. Today, these streams have become sewers as a result of the city's uncontrolled urban growth. To prepare his last book, Standley also analyzed thousands of plant specimens from the Isthmus gathered since the 19th Century by other collectors, a monumental task indeed.

Paul Allen was one of the great students of the flora of Central America and Panama. Between 1934 and 1947, he made 17 expeditions across Panama under the auspices of the Missouri Botanical Garden. After Pittier, he probably collected in more Panamanian regions than any other naturalist. Orchids were his specialty, but he also paid great attention to palms, and especially to a group he considered one of the noblest contributions of the American tropics: the *pifá* or *pixbae* (*Bixia orillana*).

Between 1926 and 1928, George P. Cooper from the Yale School of Forestry, to-

gether with George Slater, from the United Fruit Company, organized the first in-depth expedition to carefully study the vegetation and potential contribution of timber trees in Western Panama. Until then, the flora of Bocas del Toro was hardly known. The only person to study its flora previously was J. H. Hart, who sailed from Jamaica in 1886, and explored the islands of Bocas del Toro and the Guariviara River on the mainland. Cooper and Slater conducted detailed studies of the forests along the coasts of the Almirante and Chiriquí Grande Lagoons, and on the islands of the Bocas del Toro Archipelago. In Chiriquí, on the drier Pacific side, their expedition conducted the first survey to be made of the plants growing in the middle and lower courses of the Chiriquí Viejo River valley.

Bird Researchers

The diversity of birds in Panama is truly awesome. More than 950 species have been identified from the Isthmus, far more than occurs in the vastly larger territories of the U.S. and Canada combined. From among numerous ornithologists whose studies have built Panama's reputation as a paradise for tropical birds, we have chosen to talk about three: Ludlow Griscom (1890-1959), from Harvard University; Alexander Wetmore (1886-1978), from the Smithsonian Institution, and Eugene Eisenmann Brandon (1906-1981), a Panamanian lawyer and a passionate ornithologist. Well connected to the American Museum of Natural History in New York, Eisenmann was one of the outstanding figures in American tropical ornithology in the mid 20th Century.

A member of the Smithsonian Biological
Survey of Panama in the highlands of Cerro
Azul, on the continental divide between the
Atlantic and the Pacific, 1912.
Photo by E. A. Goldman. Source: Smithsonian
Institution Archives. Washington, D.C.

In his time, Ludlow Griscom was considered to be the dean of bird watchers for
South and Central America. In 1917, 1924,
and 1927, he embarked on three great expeditions to study the birds of the Isthmus.
During these journeys he explored most of
the Pacific coast, from Darién and Chimán
in the east, to the Serranía del Tabasará, in
Chiriquí, the coast of Soná and the Gulf of
Montijo, in Veraguas to the west. In his
publications, Griscom analyzed over 16,000
bird specimens from Panama, many that he
obtained himself, others by his collectors,
and still others by researchers responsible
for making the principal collections of Panamanian birds held by the great natural history museums of the U.S. and Europe. Griscom was fascinated by the role the Isthmus
played as a bridge in the distribution of birds
throughout the Americas.

There was practically no region in the country that Alexander Wetmore did not visit in

his expeditions to study the birds of Panama during the 22 years stretching from 1944 to 1966. He traveled from Bocas del Toro and Chiriquí provinces on the Costa Rican border to Darién and San Blas on the frontier with Colombia. He explored the islands of the archipelagos of Bocas del Toro and San Blas in the Caribbean, and those of Las Perlas and Coiba, in the Pacific. His methodical observations and the field specimens he collected, allowed him to produce a monumental work, *The Birds of the Republic of Panama*, published in four volumes by the Smithsonian Institution between 1965 and 1984. Wetmore considered the narrow and forested Isthmus of Panama to be one of the most interesting geographical areas in the world, primarily because it connects the Northern and Southern portions of the Americas.

Periods of Scientific Investigation

In the historical journey pursued in this book, we shall see how scientific interest in Panama has peaks clearly related to the great advances in interoceanic transportation: the dawn of steamship navigation in the 1840s, the construction of the interoceanic railroad in the 1850s, and the two periods of Canal construction, the first by the French from 1880 to 1890, and the second by the U.S. from 1904 to 1914. Less known is the major stimulus that these great engineering works provided in the development of tropical biology. On the other hand, major world conflagrations and economic depressions worked in the opposite direction, diminishing scientific interest about the Isthmus.

The Origin of the Naturalists

During the 19th Century, most explorers visiting the Isthmus were Europeans, reflecting the strong ties that existed between Latin America and Europe at the time. Panama, then a Department of New Granada or Colombia, was no exception. Nineteenth Century U.S. naturalists still spent their energy studying the vast hinterlands of their own country. Their presence in Panama began in earnest during the 20th Century, with the construction of the Canal, a gigantic engineering feat. The Canal was inaugurated in August 1914, the year and month when the First World War exploded. This conflict affected relations with Europe, further weakened by the great economic depression of the 1930s, followed by the hecatomb of the Second World War.

The Areas of Intensive Studies

In the century under consideration, studies of Panama's flora and fauna were concentrated in some regions and not others. The region most thoroughly scrutinized comprised the forests of the central sector of the Isthmus, the narrowest and lowest point in the New World, specifically along the Chagres River, the river of interoceanic communication and one of the main arteries of world commerce. The first interoceanic railroad in the Americas was built along the Chagres River valley; later, the damming of its waters would make the construction of the Canal possible.

Other regions that drew the naturalists' attention were the highlands on both ends of the Isthmus: to the west, the mountains of

Chiriquí and Veraguas, and to a lesser degree those of Bocas del Toro, all bordering Costa Rica, and contiguous with the ranges of Central America; to the east, the mountainous jungles of Darién, on the frontier with Colombia, which are linked to the Andean ranges. A key question raised by these naturalists was that of how many life forms existed on the Isthmus; and of the nature of their relationship to those of North and South America, continents whose floras and faunas were so different.

Here, it should be noted how little attention naturalists paid to the dry areas of the Azuero peninsula in the provinces of Los Santos and Herrera, which are the most deforested and cultivated regions in the Isthmus. Even today, large areas of Panama are ill explored, particularly on the Atlantic side, including San Blas, the coast of Colón, Veraguas, and a good portion of Bocas del Toro. The map on page XX shows that until the 1940s the areas explored by scientific expeditions covered only a small part of the country.

Generalists and Specialists

Many of the pioneers who explored Panama during the first half of the 19th Century and the early 20th Century were not specialists, but naturalists in the broad sense of the word. Everything about the tropics seemed new to them, so they wanted to know about both plants and animals. Inevitably, their writings reflected the prevalent ideas as well as the prejudices of their societies of origin and of the international scientific community at that time.

The parents and teachers of these early students of the tropics, whether they were specialists or serious amateurs, played a key role in awakening their scientific vocations; from an early age, they caught a passionate spark for the wonders of nature.

Paradoxically, the biological wealth of the Isthmus seems to have dampened, rather than stimulated, a national interest in studying and managing it so that it would be useful to successive generations. National investment in science and natural sciences has remained almost nonexistent. Hardly any presidential candidate has included the role of science in his political platform. The country, for example, has denied its vocation for forestry. Thus, it lacks schools and universities for training foresters; public and private forestry research is almost nil. Surrounded by oceans it has no school of marine biology.

Naturalists and Conservation

At the turn of the 20th Century, naturalists such as Pittier described the Isthmus as a vast carpet of forests covering almost three-fourths of the land. The other fourth consisted mostly of natural savannas and Pacific dry forest. People had then modified only 5% of the country for their subsistence.

As we approach the end of the 20th Century, this situation has changed radically. Of these magnificent forests, perhaps only a third is left. Great social and economic advances have been accompanied by an appalling environmental destruction. Most of the forests have vanished, converted into pastureland for the extensive rearing of

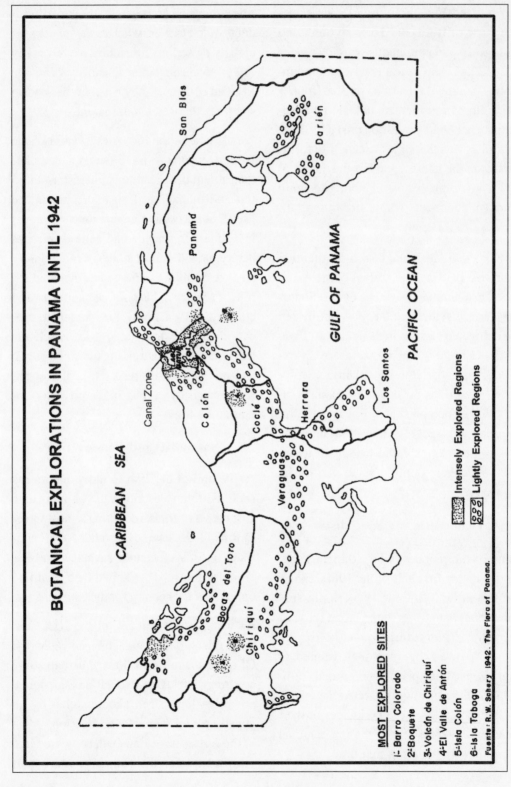

Botanical Explorations in Panama until 1942. Map from R. W. Schery: *The Flora of Panama*, 1942.

cattle. About half of the surviving forests are located inside the *comarcas* (indigenous reserves) and the other half are within the national park system.

Naturalists such as James Zetek, Alexander Wetmore, and Eugene Eisenmann Brandon, who dedicated their lives to the study of Panama's tropical habitats, witnessed this dramatic transformation of the landscape, which became more intense in the 1940s, after the Second World War. The rapid extinction of the flora and fauna encouraged them to plant the first seeds of environmental awareness and conservation in the Isthmus. To these pioneers we owe the first popular articles and calls to the urgent need to manage and use wisely Panama's irreplaceable natural heritage.

According to some of these enthusiastic student's of Panama's tropical nature, such as Eugene Eisenmann, the natural heritage should be used to promote a healthy self-esteem and sense of national pride among the citizenry. Unfortunately, Panama, a country dedicated to trade and commerce, and afflicted by an ancestral inferiority complex toward the outside world, continues to ignore what it possesses in abundance: its incomparable biological diversity. Furthermore, these early naturalists visualized the potential of such awesome biological wealth as the bassis of a new industry of nature tourism. In the future, this activity could benefit all regions of the country and generate more jobs and revenue than the Canal yields.

To conclude, it is essential to note that the naturalists who explored Panama in the 19th and 20th Centuries had predecessors. Such honor roll is headed, in the early 16th Century, by the chroniclers of the Indies, amongst whom we must mention Gonzalo Fernández de Oviedo (1478-1557). Fernández de Oviedo arrived in Santa María La Antigua, in Darién, in 1514, a year after the discovery of the South Sea by Vasco Núñez de Balboa and stayed there for many years. Although he was *veedor* or overseer, that is a mine inspector, at heart he was a great naturalist. His masterpiece, *Historia General y Natural de las Indias* (The natural and general history of the Indies), published in 1535, contains several chapters describing in detail to an amazed world audience the diversity of plants and animals encountered in the first governorship and diocese of the Spanish Main, Panama.

Berthold Seemann and the Expedition of the HMS Herald to Panama (1846-1851)

On September 22, 1846, a promising 21-year-old German botanist arrived in Panama after crossing the Isthmus via the Chagres River. He had come to join the HMS *Herald*, a British exploration vessel whose scientist had died as a result of a gun accident in Ecuador. From 1846 to 1851, the young man explored the Pacific Coast of the Americas. He traveled extensively and repeatedly through Panama, studying in depth its tropical wildlife and its people. He holds the honor of publishing the first book on the Panamanian flora. His name was Berthold Carl Seemann. Born in 1825 in Hannover, Germany, Seemann died of fever in Chontales, Nicaragua, in 1871, at 46 years of age, while managing a gold mine. His studies of Panama coincided with a period when great changes ocurred in the Isthmus as a result of steam navigation and the construction of the Panama Railroad, the first interoceanic railway in the Americas. The California gold rush brought the era of travel by train and steamer to the then Department of the Isthmus, a backwater of New Granada or Colombia.

Thanks to his instructors at the lyceum in Hannover, Seemann developed a keen interest in plants at a very early age. He showed a precocious talent for observation and writing. At the age of 17, he published his first scientific article. In the *Journal of Botany* of London, he was described as a keen observer, with a great memory, energetic and persistent. His short and prolific life was characterized by a struggle between his committment to science and his thirst to do things that were useful to mankind. Although he would have wanted to remain within a great scientific institution pursuing a research career, his attraction for the tropics and development projects finally won out.

Deep down, Seemann was a gypsy, driven by an intense desire to know the world. In 1844, at age 19, he traveled to England, to Kew Botanical Garden, to become a botanist. There he met W. J. Hooker, who recommended him to the British Navy. The Navy needed a naturalist for the expedition of the HMS *Herald* to replace Edmonston, its deceased scientist.

Naturalist of the HMS *Herald* Expedition

The *Herald* and its support ship, the *Pandora*, left England on June 25, 1845, to explore and chart the Pacific coast of the Americas, and to investigate the flora and fauna of countries along it. After anchoring in Rio de Janeiro, the expedition went around Cape Horn and sailed along the coasts of Chile, Peru, Ecuador, and Colombia. On March 23, 1846, they sighted the Las Perlas Archipelago in the Gulf of Panama, and two days later the ships anchored at Flamenco, a small island in the bay of Panama City. For the next five years this would serve as the main anchorage point for the expedition.

As J. W. Mowicke pointed out, one of the greatest achievements of the British Navy in the 19th Century was the successful execution of important scientific expeditions. The most famous of these voyages, usually baptized under the name of its flagship, was that of the HMS *Beagle*, whose naturalist was Charles Darwin. Lesser known were the voyages of the HMS *Sulphur* (1836-1842) and the HMS *Herald* (1845-1851) to the Pacific Coast of the Americas.

One of the British Navy's great contributions to geography was the elaboration of the 19th Century's most precise maps of

some 4,000 miles of Pacific Coast in the New World. Because of its strategic location, Panama received much attention from these naval expeditions. The first mission was in 1828, when the HMS *Chanticleer*, under the command of Henry Foster, mapped the Atlantic side of Panama.

The hydrographic charting of the more extensive Pacific shoreline was begun by the

Sir Edward Belcher, commander of HMS *Sulphur's* scientific expedition, from 1836 to 1842. Engraving from Pierce & Winslow (ed.): *HMS* Sulphur *on the Northwest and California Coast, 1837 and 1839*. Ontario, Canada, 1979.

HMS *Sulphur* and *Starling* (1837-1839), and concluded by the HMS *Herald* and *Pandora*. The Pacific coast of Panama, then a part of New Granada, was very extensive. It stretched from Punta Burica and the Chiriquí Viejo River on the Costa Rican border to the mouth of the San Juan River, in the Choco.

In contrast to the excellent cartography made of the coasts, no maps of similar quality were produced for the mainland until the 20th Century. Except for the charting of the course of the Chagres (the river of interoceanic communication), the location of rivers and mountains in the maps of Panama remained extremely imprecise.

The Difficulties of Mapping the Tropics

These days, map-making seems easy. In the 19th Century, however, drawing even the smallest map was a costly, slow and at

Berthold Seemann (1825-1871).
Born in Hannover, Germany, Seemann died in Chontales, Nicaragua. He explored Panama between 1846 and 1851. Illustration from a lithograph made in Paris, 1863.

times dangerous task. Seemann, a natural-ist, learned to respect and admire the skills and dedication of the cartographers. He tells us that, for them, the hardest area to map was the coastline extending from Panama and Darién to the Choco. A hot land and among the rainiest in the world, mile after mile of this unexplored shore was covered by vast, impenetrable mangrove swamps re-plete with huge crocodiles.

During the day, the crew endured incessant bites from clouds of mosquitoes and sand flies. At night, heat made sleep extremely difficult. Furthermore, the men had to con-quer their deep fears of the swampy and rainy tropical forests. At the time, people firmly believed that the cause of mortal tropical fevers were the "miasmas," poison-ous gasses said to rise from the rank jungle vegetation as mist, when a sudden down-pour was followed by a very hot sun.

When Seemann arrived in Panama City, the *Herald* had already sailed for Canada. While awaiting its return, he traveled through Panama and Veraguas, the two provinces of the Department of Panama. On January 17, the *Herald* and the *Pandora* re-turned, anchoring at Flamenco Island. See-mann went on board, and, in April 1847, the expedition began mapping the Gulf of Panama. It rained so heavily that they were forced back to Flamenco. On May 1, 1847, they stopped at Coiba, the biggest island in the Central American Pacific, gathering food, water, and firewood. The expedition repeatedly visited Coiba Island, which See-mann considered among his favorite places for botanical exploration. On May 6, they were at Isla Iguana, at the tip of the Azuero

peninsula, from which they set off for Peru, Ecuador and Colombia. They returned to Flamenco on November 14, 1847.

Exploration of the coast of the Darién started on December 1, covering a territory extend-ing from Punta Garachiné to the San Juan River. On December 3, Seemann went ashore at Punta Garachiné. He would also study at Piñas Bay, Cupica, Bahía Solano, and Cabo Corrientes.

From the end of February until April 1848, while the ship charted the coast to the west, from Punta Mala to Coiba Island and the mouth of Boca Chica, Chiriquí, our natu-ralist explored the savannas of the Pacific. Seemann trekked from the Cantón of Chor-rera, through Natá, Santiago and up to Alan-je, the most remote canton in Panama, now part of the Province of Chiriquí.

Upon returning to Flamenco, the *Herald* received orders from the Admiralty to aban-don the exploration of the coast of Veraguas and proceed to the Arctic, in search of Sir John Franklin's shipwrecked expedition. This desolate and little known frozen land was then a priority for England, which re-peatedly sent expeditions in search of the Northwest passage, a shortcut between the Atlantic and the Pacific. Many of them failed. On May 9, 1848, a becalmed day, the *Herald* had to be towed out from Fla-menco by the steamer *Sampson*. Once at sea, the ship set sail for the Behring Straits to begin the dangerous quest of rescuing sur-vivors of the Arctic shipwreck—but the ships of the Franklin expedition were never found. The *Herald* returned to Flamenco in January 1849.

Panama and the California Gold Rush

By 1849, news of the discovery of gold in California was spreading fast. Seemann left the following impressions of the human avalanche that began crossing the Isthmus on its way to the gold deposits:

> We arrived at Panama on the 19th of January, 1849, after an absence of nearly nine months; but pleasing though it was to see a place again so familiar to us, the state of the country was little calculated to allow any further intercourse than was absolutely necessary. The accounts of the newly discovered gold mines of California having reached the United States, had brought such a number of adventuring emigrants to the Isthmus for embarkation, that the usual conveyances, food, lodging. . . . failed. The emigrants, disregarding the rainy season of a noxious climate, had tried to overcome these obstacles by walking across [the Isthmus], sleeping in the woods, eating quantities of fruit, and exposing themselves, unprotected by proper clothing, to the powerful rays of the mid-day's sun,—a sun that not unfrequently raises the temperature to 124 F, forming a striking contrast to the snow-clad fields of Pennsylvania and Ohio, which they had just left. These causes tended to produce a cholera of the worst description, and it was for this reason that the 'Herald' communicated with Panama merely through the Consulate, and that botanical excursions on my part became impracticable.

During these days, Seemann met the Polish botanist von Warsewicz, who, sponsored by Alexander von Humboldt, had been investigating the provinces of Panama and Veraguas for seven months. Seemann recounts:

> Not being able to remain at Panama, we spent several days at Taboga, the most delightful island in the Bay. In its center rises a hill about 1,000 feet high, cultivated with useful fruit and vegetables nearly to the summit, sending down little streams to the valley, where between palms and tamarind trees, the habitations of the natives are almost hid. Walking amongst the Mammee and orange groves, seeing the Nispero, the Alligator-pear, and the Mango-trees, loaded with fruit, or admiring the extensive Pineapple plantations on the side of stony hills, fancy transports the stranger into the garden of the Hesperides; but however gratifying to the senses such a place appears, a collector is little benefited by it, and I was therefore glad to exchange Taboga for the coast of Veraguas, a more profitable field for botanical investigations.

Restocked with water, firewood, and fruit from Taboga, the vessels sailed toward the vast coast of western Panama, a region then collectively known as Veraguas. The Spanish Crown had granted the duchy of Veraguas to the descendants of Columbus as a prize for the Admiral's discovery of the New World. Seemann's first inland trip was in the neighborhood of the old Spanish settlement of Nuestra Señora de los Remedios, established in 1589. Afterwards, he traveled along the Camino Real, the rugged old trail that connected Panama City with Cartago in Costa Rica and thence to Central America.

Remedios

While the ships took soundings, Seemann disembarked on Aguacate Island and traveled in a dugout canoe or *cayuco* to the coast of Chiriquí. He recounts:

> I disembarked at Remedios, a large village, and the first thing I saw there were some men making ropes. The cordage generally used in the Isthmus is obtained from different plants belonging to Columniferae. The best and whitest rope is made of the fiber of "Corteza" (*Apeiba petoumo*). A brownish-looking

During its voyages in Panama, 1837, the *Sulphur* explored the Gulf of Panama,
the Archipelago of Las Perlas, and Coiba Island.
Engraving from Pierce and Winslow (ed): *H.M.S. Sulphur on the Northwest and California Coast 1837
and 1839.* Ontario, Canada, 1979.

rope, easily affected by damp (probably because the tree it is taken from contains much saline principle) is manufactured of "Majagua de playa" (*Hibiscus arboreus*); and a third kind is obtained from "Barrigon", an undiscribed tree, which I have called *Bombax barrigon.* The *Xylopia sericea* also yields a fiber fit to be made into ropes. It is on that account named "Malagueto hembra" by the natives, to distinguish it from "Malagueto macho" (*Xylopia grandiflora*), which is destitute of such a quality.

Chorcha

From Remedios [continues Seemann] my road led to an immense virgin-forest, the Montaña de Chorcha. It was here that I discovered another new species of *Pentagonia*, with leaves like those of *P. pinnatifida*, so that we now know three species of this interesting genus. They are equally distributed over the Isthmus. *P. pinnatifida* occupies the province of Darien; *P. macrophylla* that of Panama, while *P. Tinajita*, as this third species might be called, is indigenous to Veraguas. The native name, "Tinajita", is taken from the fruit, which resembles the water-jars (tinajas) used in the country. . . .

This tree grew 10 to 14 feet in height, under the shade, along the banks of rivers and streams. In the exuberant forests of the Chorcha mountain Seemann found another very common tree "whose bark is employed against fever and toothache, and is known by the Indian name of 'Corpachi'."

Boquete and the Chiriquí Volcano

Seemann arrived at David, capital of Chiriquí, on February 14, 1849, departing the next day for Boquete, "a farm situated on the Volcano of Chiriqui, four thousand feet above the level of the sea, from whence I made excursions in the neighborhood."

Seemann had visited Boquete a year earlier. This time he found quite a few unknown plants, and regretted not being able to stay longer. The vegetation on the Chiriquí Volcano, whose altitude he incorrectly estimated at 7,000 feet, appeared to him similar to that of the Mexican highlands. He discovered new species of herbaceous plants and "a tree very common in these regions, vernacularly termed 'Saumerio', which produces a resin that is used in churches as incense. To obtain it the tree is felled, and when in a state of decay the balsam is found collected in the branches—the stem itself does not contain any."

On March 1, 1849, Seemann joined the *Herald* at the mangrove-covered estuary of Boca Chica, the seaport of David. They head towards the Paridas Islands and Burica Point, where the expedition completed the nautical survey of the coast of Panama. On March 19, they sailed for Central America and Hawaii. From Hawaii they went towards "the land of Eskimaux," as Seemann liked to call the Arctic. During autumn and winter of 1849-50, the *Herald* explored the Gulf of California and northwestern Mexico. In the summer of 1850, the expedition payed its last visit to the Arctic. On October 30, it started its trip home via Hong Kong and the Cape of Good Hope, arriving in England in June 1851.

Publications of the Expedition

The plants collected by Seemann in Panama added up to more than a thousand specimens. The Admiralty requested that he write the accounts of the history of the voyage, which he published in London in 1853,

THE BOTANY

OF THE

VOYAGE OF H.M.S. HERALD,

UNDER THE COMMAND OF

CAPTAIN HENRY KELLETT, R.N., C.B.,

DURING THE YEARS 1845-51.

Published under the Authority of the Lords Commissioners of the Admiralty.

BY

BERTHOLD SEEMANN, Ph.D., F.L.S.,

MEMBER OF THE IMPERIAL LEOP.-CAROLINE ACADEMY CURIOSORUM, AUTHOR OF 'THE NARRATIVE OF THE VOYAGE OF H.M.S. HERALD,' 'POPULAR HISTORY OF THE PALMS AND THEIR ALLIES,' ETC. ETC.,

Naturalist of the Expedition.

WITH ONE HUNDRED PLATES.

"A TRAVELLER SHOULD BE A BOTANIST, FOR IN ALL VIEWS PLANTS FORM THE CHIEF EMBELLISHMENT."
Charles Darwin.

LONDON:
LOVELL REEVE, 5, HENRIETTA STREET, COVENT GARDEN.
1852–1857.

Cover of Berthold Seemann's book *The Botany of the Voyage of the H.M.S. Herald, under the Command of Captain Henry Kellett during the years 1845- 51.* It was published in London between 1852 and 1857 in four parts, one of which is "The Botany of Panama."

in two volumes entitled *Narratives of the Voyage of the H.M.S. Herald, During the Years 1845-1851, under the Command of Captain Henry Kellett.*

Between 1852 and 1857, Seemann published the *Botany of the Voyage of H.M.S. Herald under the Command of Captain Henry Kellett during the Years 1845-51.* This book is divided into four parts: "Flora of the Western Eskimaux-Land," "Flora of the Isthmus of Panama," "Flora of North-Western Mexico," and "Flora of the Island of Hong Kong."

In February 1868, the *Star and Herald*, a bilingual Panama City daily, began to run a series of articles by Seemann under the title "History of the Isthmus of Panama," spanning from the discovery of the Isthmus to the start of the construction of the Panama Railroad in 1850.

His accounts of the explorations of the HMS *Herald* brought Seemann great renown. The Göttingen University in Germany granted him a doctorate, and the Imperial Academy of Sciences made him a member. In 1859, at the request of the English Government, he studied the Fiji Islands for eight months, compiling an extensive report on the conditions of this colony.

From the 1860s onwards, circumstances forced him to stray away from science. In 1864, Dutch and French capitalists hired him to study the natural resources of Venezuela. In 1865, he traveled to Nicaragua, employed by English entrepreneurs, to explore and exploit gold mines. What was good for the mining company was a blow to science. Seemann set up El Javali gold mine, in the department of Chontales. In 1868, the *Star and Herald* published several of his letters on conditions in Nicaragua. He visited Panama frequently, where he also administered a sugar mill near the interoceanic railroad. During one of his trips to the mine, he fell ill and died on October 10, 1871. He was buried near his house at the mine, surrounded by both the tropical forest he loved so much and by the gold extraction equipment he helped to install.

Berthold Seemann
and the Flora of Panama (1848)

The Bridge between the Flora and Fauna of the Americas

When, in 1848, Berthold Seemann pointed out that "the Isthmus of Panama, that part of New Granada which, like a bridge, connects the two great continents of America, their Flora, Fauna, and races . . . ," he became perhaps the first to describe the role of Panama as a biological bridge for the Americas. He emphasized that the small Isthmus held an unimaginable plant diversity.

Seemann described the vegetation zones of the Isthmus as seen by a traveler; one who, after landing on the Sea of the South, goes up a jungle river, crosses the mangrove, savanna and dry forest belts of the Pacific, then crosses the foothills of the Central Cordillera to finally reach the very humid lowlands on the Atlantic side. He also noted the endless number of trees and plants used by Panamanians in the 19th Century.

The Vegetation of the Rivers

According to Seemann:

A country so much visited by heavy rains naturally abounds in rivers; their number cannot fall short of 200, and during the wet season not a mile of land can be traversed without crossing at least five or six periodical streams. Most of the rivers have deltas, which, in many instances, assume the appearance of islands. Their vegetation is a curious mixture of littoral and inland plants, and often presents species from the higher mountains. . . . Wild fig trees form great bowers over the bed [of these rivers], evergreen *Pithecolobius* emit a delicious perfume, Bamboos, the most gigantic of grasses, show their feathery tops, groves of vegetable ivory palms display their foliage; to whatever spot the eye is directed it meets fresh beauties, new charms. The canoe is pushed for miles along the silent forests, where only pumas, jaguars, and monkeys

Splendid mangroves of the lower Tuira River, Darién. From Lucien N. B. Wyse: *Le Canal de Panamá.* Paris, 1886.

40

have taken up their abode. Suddenly, the sylvan scene is interrupted by a cleared piece of ground, a few huts. . . .

The aspect of the flora is much more diversified than the uniformity of the climate and the surface of the country would lead one to expect. The sea-coast and those parts influenced by the tides and the immediate evaporation of the sea, produce a quite peculiar vegetation, which is generally characterized by a leathery glossy foliage, and leaves with entire margins. In all muddy places, down to the verge of the ocean, are impenetrable thickets, formed of Mangroves, chiefly *Rhizophoras* and *Avicennias*, which exhale a putrid

miasmata and spread sickness over the adjacent districts. Occasionally extensive tracts are covered with the Guagara de puerco (*Acrosticum aureum*), its fronds being as much as ten feet high. Myriads of mosquitoes and sandflies fill the air; huge alligators sun themselves on the slimy banks, lying motionless, blinking with their great eyes, and jumping into the water directly any one approaches. To destroy these dreaded swamps is almost impossible. . . . Rivers, as far as they are subjected to the influence of the ebb and flow, are full of Mangroves, and the highest *Rhizophoras*, which, growing always on that side where there is the deepest water, assist the natives

Savannas and dry forests, the typical
landscape of the Pacific side of the Isthmus,
near the town of Chorrera. Cerro de Cabras
is in the background. From Armand Reclus:
Panama et Darien. Paris, 1881.

in conducting their canoes through the mud-
banks. . . . Higher up, where the ground is
firmer, are groves of Cocoa-nut Palms. . . .

The vast, wild coconut groves found along
the coast of Darién lead Seemann to support the idea of Martius, that from Panama
the coconut tree spread to the rest of the
American tropics.

Savannas and
Dry Forests of the Pacific

Seemann pioneered the study of the savannas of the Pacific, which covered perhaps a
third of the Isthmus: "The districts of the
coast of the Pacific Ocean, especially the
cantons of Nata, Santiago and Alanje,
abound in grassy plains ('llanos') of great
extent, which, in affording pasture to numerous herd of cattle, constitute the principal rich of the country. . . ."

The savanna landscape changed considerably from the rainy to the dry season. This
is his account of the savannas in the wet
season of 1848:

Far different is the vegetation of the savanas.
The ground, being level or slightly undulating, is clothed during the greater part of the
year with a turf of brilliant green. Groups of
trees and bushes rise here and there; silvery
streams, herds of cattle and deer, and the isolated huts of the natives, tend to give variety
to the scene, while the absence of Palms and
Tree-ferns imparts to the whole landscape
more the appearance of a European park than
of a tract of land in tropical America. The
turf is almost as dense as in an English gar-

den, and contains, besides numerous kinds of
grasses, many elegant *Papilionaceae*, *Poly-
galeae*, *Gentianeae*, and *Violaceae*; the sensitive plant (*Mimosa pudica*) prevails in many
localities, shutting up its tender leaves even
upon the approach of a heavy footstep. The
clumps of trees and shrubs, over which the
Garumos and Pavas are waiving their large
foliage. . . . *Orchideae* are plentiful in the vicinity of the rivers, where the trees are literally loaded with them. The Vainilla (*Vainilla*)
(a vine) climbs in abundance up the stems of
young trees, and often increases so much in
weight as to cause the downfall of its sup-
porters. The Chumicales, or groves of Sand-
paper-trees (*Curetella americana*), form curious features in the landscape; they extend
over whole districts, and their presence indicates a soil impregnated with iron. The trees
are about forty feet high, have crooked branches. . . . and their paper-like leaves, if stirred
by the wind, occasion a rattling noise, which
strongly reminds one of the European autumn,
when northerly breezes strip the trees of their
foliage.

The Rainforests

According to Seemann, in 1848:

forests cover at least two-thirds of the whole
territory. The high trees, the dense foliage,
and the numerous climbing and twining plants
almost shut out the rays of the sun, causing a
gloom, which is the more insupportable as all
other objects are hidden from view. Rain is
so frequent, and the moisture so great, that
the burning of these forests is impossible; a
striking difference to those of the temperate
regions, where a fire often consumes extensive woods in a very short space of time.
Flowers are scarce in proportion to the mass
of leaves with which the places are crowded
. . . . The Espavé and the Corotú are amongst
the most gigantic trees, attaining a height
of 90 to 130 feet, and a circumference of from
24 to 30 feet; and no better estimate can be
formed of their size, than by an inspection
of the port of Panama, where vessels of

The lowland forests and mangrove swamps of the Caribean coast of Panama
at Manzanillo island, now the city of Colón.
From F. N. Otis: *Illustrated History of the Panama Railroad.* New York, 1862.

twelve tons' burden, made of a single trunk, are riding at anchor. The forests occasionally consist of a single species of tree; but generally they are composed of different kinds. . . . Mountains, exceeding 2,000 feet in elevation, situated principally in Western Veraguas, posses a vegetation which resembles in many respects that of the Mexican highlands; one in which the forms of the torrid region are harmoniously blended with those of the temperate. . . .

Medicinal Plants

The Isthmus is rich in medicinal plants, many of which are known only to the natives, who have ably availed themselves of their properties. As febrifuges, they employ *Chicoria*, *Corpachi*, *Guavito amargo*, *Cedron,* and several *Gentianeae*, herbaceous plants that are known by the name of *Canchalaguas*. As purgatives are used *Niño muerto* or *Malcasada*, *Frijolillo*, *Cañafistola de purgar*, *Laureño*, *Javilla* and *Coquillo*. Emetics are obtained from *Garriba de peña* and *Frailecillo*. As vulneraries they use *Chiriqui*, *Guazimillo* or *Palo del soldado* and *Cope chico de suelo*. Antisyphilitics are *Cardo santo*, *Zarzaparilla*, and *Cabeza del negro*. Cooling draughts are prepared from the Ferns, *Calahuala* and *Doradilla de palo*. Antidotes for the bites of snakes are found in the stems and leaves of the *Guaco* and the seeds of the *Cedron*. Cutaneous diseases are cured by applying the bark of the *Palo de Buba* and *Nanci* and the leaves of the *Malva*.

In a land of abundant rainfall and insects, skin diseases are common. These were treated with an astonishing array of local medicinal plants. The leaves of the malva, a plant common to both coasts, were boiled and applied to skin irritated by insect bites or other diseases. The bark of the nance and buba trees also helped heal cutaneous eruptions.

Since there were many and diverse species of poisonous snakes, snake bites were frequent. Of the many remedies used by Isthmian peoples the preferred one was Cedron, a shrub growing on the edges of forests and rivers in Darién, Panama, Veraguas, and Coiba Island. Since ancient times the Indians had used its bitter seeds to cure the bites of snakes, scorpions, tarantulas, and other poisonous animals. Poor people would tie a seed around their neck in a string. The rich would carry them in wallets and cigar holders. Powdered cedron was mixed with water and then applied to the wound. A potion was also made by mixing cedron and liquor. Another forest medicinal plant was the guaco, from which a highly prized drink for snakebites and cholera was made. The people from Cruces, Arraijan, and Capira used its pulp as a laxative.

Neighbors of small towns such as Gualaca and David, in Chiriquí, used copaiba balsam to paint the frames of doors and windows. They also appreciated its medicinal properties, paying from 4 to 5 *reales* for a bottle of balsam.

For insomnia, they recommended placing a handful of the *sensitiva*, a savanna plant, under the pillow. The men of Panama City thought very highly of the amorous powers of a plant brought by the Indians from Darién, known as *amansa mujer*, literally, "woman tamer." It should be given to a woman without her knowledge. Such were the plant's erotic powers that it would turn the most reluctant female into a submissive romantic soul.

Edible Fruits

Seemann describes with astonishment how:

many indigenous plants bear eatable fruits, some of most delicious flavor. Principal are: *Algarrobo, Boca vieja, Cañafístula, Cerezo, Coco, Coronillo, Espavé, Fruta de Pava, Granadilla, Guayabo de savana, Guayabo, Guavo, Icaco, Jagua, Jobito de puerco, Marañon, Madroño de comer, Membrillo, Nance, Níspero, Panama, Papayo cimarron, Pita de zapateros, Sastra, Tinajita* and *Zarzamora.*

Of dessert probably no country can exhibit a greater variety. Besides, many indigenous ones, there are to be found the *Aguacate, Anona, Aqui, Chirimoya, Granadilla, Jobo, Lima, Limon, Mammey de Cartagena, Mango, Melon, Naranja agria, Naranja dulce, Palo de Pan, Papaya, Piña, Pomarosa,* different species of *Ciruelas* and *Toronjil.*

The natives also grew lots of plantains, he noted, which were one of the most important items in their diet, as well as root crops such as *ñame, yuca, batata,* and *otoe.* People also cultivated *chayote,* bananas, peanuts, cucumbers, squash, and several types of *aji* or chilies. Home gardens commonly contained *guandu* or *frijol de palo.* In the savannas there grew numerous trees of *guayaba* and *ciruelo,* whose fruits were eaten by the people and their domestic animals. There were three classes of *ciruelos* or plums: *ciruelo de puerco*, San Juan, and Nicoya. The seeds of the huge *corotú*, a large tree flowering in March and April, and known as *guanacaste* in Central America, served as cattle fodder in the dry season.

Culinary Plants

Several spontaneous productions are used as culinary vegetables. *Marathrum foeniculaceum* a plant resembling some of the finer seaweeds, and growing in most rivers of Veraguas, is esteemed so highly by the inhabitants that they have called it "pasa carne", i.e. excels or surpasses meat; and, indeed, its young leaf-stalks, when boiled, have a delicate flavor, not unlike that of French beans. The leaves of *Ñaju de espina* are eaten as salad, either raw or boiled, like the young branches of several *Opuntias* in Mexico; and in a country where, from the nature of the climate, the rearing of lettuces is attended with difficulties, they form a tolerable substitute. The foliage of the *Col de Nicaragua* affords another culinary vegetable, losing, apparently, as do most *Euphorbiaceae,* its poisonous qualities by boiling. The seed of the *Chigua* . . . after having been boiled and reduced to a mash are mixed with milk and sugar and thus eaten. A kind of bread is also prepared from them. As condiments for esculent purposes, divers plants are used. The red berries of the *Malagueto chico* or *Malagueta hembra* are substituted for pepper, especially by the negroes. The fruit of the *Vainilla* and *Vainilla chica* are species employed in flavoring sweet-meats, chocolate and puddings. The leaves of the *Toronjil*, a common herb, are chopped and serve to replace our Parsley. The most important, however, of all the aromatics . . . . is the *Culantra;* it imparts a flavor difficult for a foreigner to relish; but the inhabitants consider it indispensable, and are quite distressed when in the soups and sancoches their favorite condiment has by some accident been omitted.

Lumber for Construction and Making Furniture

Excellent timber for building, and wood for cabinet-makers' purposes, abound. Particular notice is due to the *Acabú, Algarrobo, Amarillo, Carbonero, Cedro cebolla* (a tree botanically unknown), *Cedro espinoso, Caoba, Espavé, Guachapali, Guavito cansaboca, Guayacan, Guazimo colorado, Laurel, Macano, Maria, Nance, Naranjo de monte,*

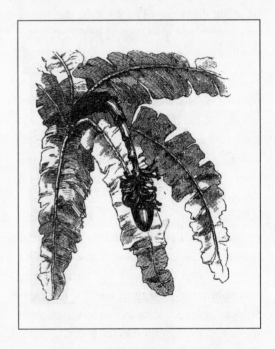

Banana in Blossom.
From Oran: Tropical Journeying en Route for California. *Harpers Monthly Magazine,* No. XCVII. June 1858, New York.

Nispero, Peronil, Quira, Roble, Terciopelo and *Corotú.* From the *Roble* and *Guayacán* the most durable wood is obtained. The *Nazareno*, a beautiful bluish fancy wood, the produce of a scientifically unknown tree, would fetch a high price in Europe. The *Quira* is remarkable for its black and brown streaks. The *Corotú* and *Espavé* supply the natives with materials for canoes.

In the central region of the Isthmus there were great stands of membrillo, a tree whose wood was used in construction. In Río de Jesús, Seemann became acquainted with the tree of paradise or granadillo; this tree, 60 to 80 feet in height, was according to the natives, only found here. The twisted *madroño* was very abundant in the forests of Veraguas, its wood highly esteemed by Panama City carpenters. Between Tolé and David, in the savannas and forest edges, the *rasca* tree proliferated; it reached 60 feet in height, and its durable wood was highly valued for construction work. Carpenters also used *cainillo*, a species commonly found between Panama and Tolé. The *balsa* tree was very useful, its light wood used in making bottle caps, and cotton from the flowers used to stuff pillows. A primitive but effective way of writing was on the large leaves of the *cope*, a tree from the savannas between Panama and Natá. With a pencil or a little stick, country people would write short messages, which would not vanish under humidity or rain and could last up to four weeks, as long as the leaves remained fresh.

The *tuna* tree was employed in making fences and healing wounds. The fruit from the *palo de vela* served to fatten cattle. Live fences for pasturelands and house patios, were made from plants such as *ortiga, poroporo, pitahaya*, and *piñuela*. In Coiba, Seemann found a lovely tree, sixty feet high, with beautiful yellow flowers which people called *tecla*.

Plants Used for Dyeing

The country produced many dyes of botanical origin: yellow from the bark of the *macano* tree; scarlet from the leaves of the *hojita de teñir*; blue from the foliage of the *añil silvestre*; violet from the *jagua* fruit; red from the pulp of the *bija* or *achiote*. Black was extracted from the seeds of the *ojo de venado* and it also served as writing ink. A savanna plant called *clava* gave a brown tint. The pink color of the hammocks from Veraguas came not from snails but the leaves of a plant known as *arribidea chica*. In the savannas of Panama and Veraguas, the *jagua* tree grew abundantly and its sap gave a violet color.

Plants for Other Domestic Uses

After grating the coconut meat using the thorny roots of the *zanora*, it was mixed with rice, the favorite isthmian dish. The large, round fruit of the calabash tree provided drinking cups or *totumas*, as well as spoons, strainers, and several other useful household items. Papaya leaves served as a substitute for soap.

From the great varieties of palm trees people would avail themselves of cooking oils, medicines, wines, vinegar, construction materials, and bark cloth. Sandpaper was obtained from the very rough, large leaves of the *chumico* tree and the *chumico* vine. Their leaves served to polish iron and wood.

Among plants cultivated for their perfume were: *buenastardes, caracuchas, copecillo oloroso, dama de noche, guabito cansaboca, jazmin de monte, ñorbo*, and *manglillo*. Isthmian washerwoman planted *flor de aroma*, whose flowers gave a most pleasant fragrance to clothing.

Tagua or Vegetable Ivory

In the second half of the 19th Century, Panama's most economically important non-timber forest product was *tagua* or vegetable ivory. The palm, named after Seemann, is scientifically known as *Phytelias seemanii*. In the rainier areas of the Pacific, from Darién to the Choco, and in Portobelo on the Caribbean side, Seemann found vast *taguales* or ivory palm groves. The nuts were in great demand in Europe for making useful articles such as walking stick handles, buttons, and toys. The Indians of Darién call it *antá*. It grew along the banks of rivers and streams. Its pleasantly scented flower attracted swarms of bees and insects. Each palm, according to Seemann, produced six to eight fruit bunches, each with up to 80 seeds. The Indians did not use the fruit, but they thatched their houses with the palm fronds and ate the soft palm heart.

According to Seemann, people from Panama City ignored the existence of this valuable palm, and even when told that the wild *tagua* groves of Darién could provide many shiploads of nuts that could be exported at a handsome profit, no one took the initiative to harvest the seeds. That would change after the 1870s, when *tagua* nuts and rubber became one of the most important exports of the Isthmus.

Natural Abundance and Material Backwardness

To Seemann it was a paradox that, while nature lavished so many useful plants on Panama, facilitating the livelihood of its people, it deprived them of the spirit for bold enterprises.

In a country like the Isthmus, where nature has supplied nearly every want of life, and where the consumption of a limited population is little felt, agriculture, deprived of its proper stimulus, cannot make much progress; it is therefore in the most primitive state. . . . A spade is a curiosity, the plough has never been heard of, and the only implements used for converting forest into fields are the axe and the machete. A piece of ground intended for cultivation is selected in the forests, cleared of the trees by felling and burning them, and surrounded with a fence. In the beginning of the wet season the field is set with plants by simply making a hole with the machete and placing the seed or root in it. . . . The same ground is occupied two or three years in succession; after that time the soil is so hard. . . . that a new spot has to be chosen. In most countries this mode of cultivation would be found impossible, but in New Granada all unoccupied land is common property of which anybody may appropriate as much as he pleases. . . . As long as the land is enclosed it remains in his possession; whenever the fence is decayed the land again becomes the property of the republic. Colonial produce, such as sugar, coffee, cacao. . . ., which require more attention than the inhabitants are wont to bestow, are merely raised for home consumption; and although the provincial government has tried to encourage this branch of industry by offering premiums for growing a certain number of plants, and the soil and climate are favorable, yet no one, except a few enterprising foreigners, have taken a prominent part in the cultivation.

Seemann emphasizes the existence of other obstacles hindering the development of isthmian agricultural exports. With barely 130,000 inhabitants, labor was scarce and wages were high. Furthermore, with ample access to free land and a very prodigal nature, people did not feel the need to seek employment.

Berthold Seemann's Notes on the Panamanian Fauna (1848)

Zoological Zones

Seemann was a botanist, and his zoological knowledge was empirical. His notes on Panamanian fauna are sparse in comparison with his accounts of local plants. He says little about the great number and diversity of birds, limiting himself to descriptions of the beauty of the plumage of hummingbirds, macaws, and parrots. Nevertheless, his narratives are useful. He describes the incredible abundance of a number of animals, nearly extinct today, the state of the isthmian habitats 150 years ago, as well as the uses, customs, and popular beliefs about the fauna.

The Isthmus as a Bridge for American Fauna

Seemann proposed that America should be divided into two zoological provinces: North and South America, separated by the mountainous barrier of the high Mexican plateau, but connected by the Isthmus of Panama. "The Isthmus therefore, in connecting the American continent, promotes not only the distribution of plants, but also offers facilities for the migration of animals, and without this passage many genera and species now common to both countries, would probably have been confined to one." It was self-evident to him that the isthmian route was used by diverse species: in North America one found South American species and vice versa. On the other hand, Seemann puzzled over the reasons why some species that crossed the isthmian land bridge did not settle here but continued on.

Mammals

Mammalia are represented by a variety of forms. Hosts of monkeys, including the white-headed chapolin (*Cebus hypoleuca*) inhabit the woods. Bats are numerous: a kind of vampire is common, causing dangerous wounds in cattle; *Diclidurus freyreisii*, seems to be a bat peculiar to the Isthmus. The jaguar, or, as the native call it, tigre (*Felis onca*, Linn.) and the puma (*Felis concolor*, Linn.), vernacularly termed lion, are destructive to cattle, but seldom attack man. A gray opossum (*Didelphis*), called Gato solo, from its solitary habits is frequent. Several kinds of conejos and squirrels. . . . Rats and mice in the Isthmus, as everywhere else, are the plague of dwellings. The *Gato de pachorra*, here and there observed, is a sloth (*Bradypus didaclilus*, Linn.). Sajinos (peccaries) are frequent, but merely eaten by the dogs. Pigs (wild) wander in herds about the forest, and are dreaded by the natives, who, when they meet them, seek safety in flight or by climbing a tree. The tapir (*Tapirus americanus*, Linn.), the *Macho de Monte, Danta,* and *Gran bestia* of the Panamanians, is the largest terrestrial animal of the Fauna, though in comparison with the Asiatic species (*Tapirus Indicus*) a mere dwarf. Its flesh is eaten, but is insipid; medicinal virtues are ascribed to the hoof, which is administered for paralysis, and a decoction of it is taken by women after childbirth.

Deer

The only ruminant animal is the *Venado,* a species of deer (*Cervus* sp.), met with in herds in the savannas. Its horns are not simple, like those of *Cervus rufus,* Cuvier, a common Peruvian animal, but branched and divided. The venado is about three feet high, and when young spotted with white dots; this colour however soon changes into a light brown. The meat, very tough when fresh, becomes tender if kept awhile or boiled with papaya; the hide is converted into soft yet durable leather, well adapted for boots in so hot a climate. The animal is easily domesticated: Mr. J. Agnew, a gentleman in David, had one which had been reared by a bitch and possessed the habits of a dog, eating meat, running about the house, and following its master. The people of Veraguas have a curious mode of hunting the venados. The bones of a pelican's wing at one end with a peculiar kind of cobweb, which forms an instrument that will imitate the cry of a young deer so closely that the old ones, in the belief that some mishap has befallen

their kid, repair to the place whence the sound proceeds, and are shot; the hunters frequently return with twelve or fifteen of them after one day's sport.

Reptiles

Reptiles abound. The scales of the turtle form an article of commerce. At the time of the discovery of the country the Spaniards evi-

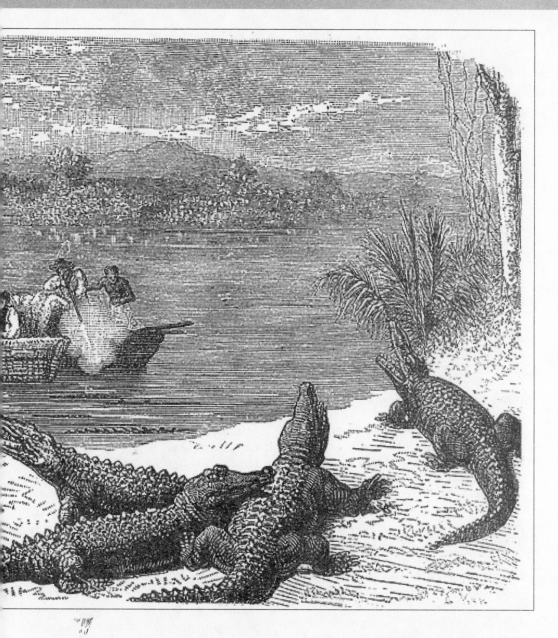

Crocodile-hunting.
Illustration from A. Reclus: *Panama et Darien.*
Paris, 1881.

denced a great repugnance to the iguanas (*Lacerta iguana*, Linn.), and expressed disgust at beholding the Indians eating them; this feeling is now overcome, and the eggs as well as the flesh of these animals are considered as delicacies. It is not the only instance in which such a change has been effected; the use of tobacco, another Indian practice, was equally disliked, now no people indulge more in it than the Spaniards and their descendants.

Alligators are numerous on the mouth of rivers, where they are found sunning themselves on the muddy banks; it is amusing to see how motionless they lie, listening to any noise and blinking their great eyes, but immediately anyone approaches them they jump into the water. Some of these animals are from four-teen to eighteen feet long. Their eagerness to attack man has often been asserted, but there is reason to believe that they are cowards, like most animals belonging to the lizard-tribe. I have only heard of a single instance of a person having been bitten, and that happened during the night, when he was wading through a rivulet. In the Rio Grande de Panama children may be seen bathing when around them there are numerous alligators; if the animals were as rapacious as they are represented, such risks would undoubtedly be avoided.

Snakes

Both land and sea snakes occur; the former are sometimes eighteen feet long. The Coral, zonated scarlet and black, the Vívora, varie-gated black and brown, and the Voladora, or flying-snake, of a lively green color, are con-sidered the most venomous. The voladora lives in trees, darting with rapidity from branch to branch, which having the appear-ance of flying, has given rise to the vernacu-lar nam. Before the *Cedron* was known many deaths occurred from the bite of snakes. The people used to wear—and in some parts of the country still wear—suspended round their necks or legs an alligator's tooth as a charm against them. I saw once a boy who had ex-pired two hours after having been bitten, and in the afternoon the body was swollen to at least double its former size, presenting a frightful appearance: great caution is there-fore necessary. Fortunately, the presence of a snake is generally known before the animal is seen or heard: this the natives attribute to a smell peculiar to these reptiles, but as the smell is not perceived by Europeans, and yet the presence of the snake is known by them, it must be ascribed to some cause yet to be ex-plained.

Toads and Frogs

Toads, and other frog-like animals, are most numerous during the wet season. A very minute species, beautifully spotted with black and red, is said to be used by the Indians to poison arrows. The abundance of toads about Portobelo has often been noticed. "So prodi-gious is their number after rain," says Mr. Lloyd, "that the popular prejudice is that rain-drops are changed into toads (*"de cada gota viene un sapo"*)"; and even the more learned maintain that the eggs of this animal are raised with the vapour from the adjoining swamps and, being conveyed to the city by the rains, are there hatched. The large size of the ani-mals however,—many of them being from four to six inches in breadth—sufficiently at-tests their mature growth in more favourable circumstances. After a night of rain the streets are almost covered with them, and it is im-possible to walk without crushing some.

Poisonous and Bothersome Insects

Spiders and scorpions are frequent, the bites of the latter producing the utmost pain, great swelling of the wounded part, and, in some cases, slight fever. Garrapatas or ticks (*Ix-odes* sp.), which swarm in the woods, are a great annoyance to both men and animals: they adhere firmly to all parts of the body, and can only be removed by scraping them off with a knife or washing the skin with spir-its. The dry season is most favourable for their development; during the wet they are not so frequent, but are more than replaced by the coloraditas, very minute red insects which exist in the grassy plains in prodigious num-bers, and the pain they cause by introducing themselves into the skin is of such an irritat-ing nature that they may justly be considered as the greatest plague of the Isthmus. The nigua or jigger (*Pulex penetrans*, Linn.), an-other annoying insect which enters the ten-der parts of the feet, under the nails, between the toes, etc., is met with principally on the higher mountains; its congener, the common flea (*Pulex irritans*, Linn.), and most other vermin common in cooler regions, are fortu-nately rare.

Beetles, Fireflies, and Glowworms

"Beetles are not numerous," said Seemann mistakenly,

but those that occur are very beautiful. The carrion-feeding beetles are scarce, while those that subsist on vegetable substances are more numerous, probably a natural consequence of the rapid decomposition of animal matter. Some are phosphorescent. The cocullo gives so brilliant a light that one may read by it; the women collect them in the sugar-plantations for the purpose of decorating their hair in the evening, when these beetles have the appearance of diamonds. Myriads of fireflies swarm in the forest. . . . One cricket, the *Cigarro* of the natives, attains a length of six inches, and is probably the largest of these creatures in existence. The *Gorgojo* (*Cicada* sp.) has the peculiarity of making a sound not unlike the hissing of snakes, for which strangers are apt to mistake it. The arriero (*Atta* sp.) is about an inch long and very destructive to plantations: it forms regular roads, occasionally from one to two miles long, and is always seen carrying portions of leaves, flowers, and other substances, mostly exceeding its own weight. A honey-bee is frequently met with, which, being stingless, may be robbed of its stores without difficulty; another species of bee produces a black wax, which is used for candles. Butterflies appear in great numbers in the beginning of the wet season, but, though some are of exquisite beauty and large size, the generality are small, and do not display that brilliancey of colours to which the eye is accustomed in the Tropics. Mosquitoes and sandflies are the scourge of the sea-coast, but they are not so numerous in the interior. One of the most annoying animals is the Gusano del monte or Guineaworm (*Filaria* sp.). Entering the flesh, especially near the knee, as a very minute being, it grows in about six weeks to length of an inch and the thickness of a good-size quill [pen]. . . . Unluckily it is seldom discovered before it has obtained a considerable size, as the generality of people look upon the wound as a mere sore, and apply every remedy but the right one.

Fish and Marine Animals

The quantity of fish, especially in the Bay of Panama, early gave rise to the name of "Panama," or "place where fish abounds." The market of the capital is well stocked, particularly with rock-cod, snappers, yellow-bellies, dolphins, whiting, soles, catfish, bonitas, al-

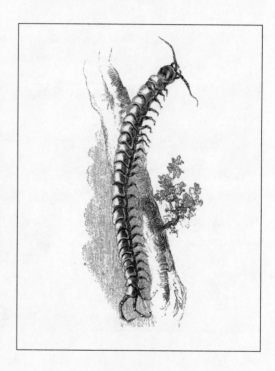

Centipede.
From ORAN: "Tropical Journeying en Route for California."
Harper's Monthly Magazine, No. XCVII, June 1858. New York.

bicore, and young sharks. Devilfish, sharks (some measuring thirty feet), and various other kinds, infest the sea-coast. The rivers also abound in fish. The Indians, in order to procure them, form parties, and after spreading a net across a shallow part of a river, drive the fish towards it by beating the water and

Mouth of the Rio Grande River, today the entrance to the Panama Canal on the Pacific side of the Isthmus. Illustration from Lucien N. B. Wyse: *Le Canal de Panama*. Paris, 1886.

by loud shouts; the captives are killed by a blow, and thrown upon a raft anchored for that purpose in the middle of the stream. A more simple method is that of stupefying the fish with the juice of the *Manzanilla* (*Hippomane Mancinella*, Linn.), the bark of *Espavé* (*Anacardium Rhinocarpus*.), or the leaves of *Barbasco* (*Ottonia glaucescens*.). A net is stretched from bank to bank, and these substances thrown into the river. The effect is surprising: the fish instantly appear on the surface, and are driven without resistance against the net, where they are secured. The law however, inflicts a penalty upon this mode of fishing, as it not only depopulates the rivers, but causes diseases among the people, who use river-water for every domestic purpose.

The sea on the Pacific shore is frequented by porpoises and blackfish, and the manati or sea-cow (*Trichechus manatus*, Linn.), one the herbivorous of the *Cetacea*, or whale-tribe, occurs on the coast of the Atlantic: it was well known to the Buccaneers, who in times of scarcity were compelled to subsist on it. The flesh is said to resemble beef in appearance, and to have the taste of pork: the skin of the back, says an old author, is two fingers thick, and when dried becomes as hard as whalebone and may serve to make walking-sticks.

Shells and Pearl Fishing

For centuries, pearl diving in the islands of the Pacific had been one of Panama's main economic activities, but gradually lost its importance until its final collapse in the 1920s. Seemann gives us the following account of the vast variety of shells to be found in the isthmus and provides some details of pearl fishing in the mid-19th Century:

Shells occur in great variety and beauty. . . . Species of *Arca,* and two kinds of oysters, are used as food; a purple dye is obtained from the *Caracolilla.* . . . Pearl-oysters are common on the whole coast of the Pacific, but more abundant in the Bay of Panama. Balboa, when he discovered the South Seas (1513), was the first European who heard of their existence, having been presented with some pearls by the Cacique Tamaco; shortly after the pearl-fishery commenced, and has continued ever since. It is now carried on by free labour, a diver receiving, besides his daily food, fifteen dollars a month: he is able, if successful, to bring up each time a dozen shells, four of which he puts between the fingers of the left hand and eight on the bend of the same arm, while his right arm remains free for separating the shells from the rocks. The divers complain of the *aguamalas,* or sea-nettles, species of *Medusa*, which cause a severe pain on touching the body; but they are most in fear of the sharks, which are frequently fatal to them. Scarcely a tenth of the shells are found to contain pearls, and even among these are many gray and bad-shaped ones, of little or no value. The pearls are sold by weight, and vary in price according to shape and colour. The largest and most perfect one perhaps ever found on the coast of the Isthmus was obtained at the Paridas Islands, and is now in the possession of Mr. James Agnew, at David; it is three-quarters of an inch in diameter, and perfectly round. These shells form a lucrative article of commerce, and are much inquired after by French vessels. The mollusks themselves are strung upon cords, dried in the air, and eaten. About thirty years ago a diving-bell was sent out by an English company, but it did not answer expectation: the expense at which it had to be fitted out and supported was too great, and the oysters did not lie in banks, as is generally the case, but were dispersed under rocks and on uneven ground; a peculiar ground-swell and motion under the water, together with a strong current, made it almost impossible to place the diving-bell in safety or to advantage.

The Geography and Population of Panama according to Berthold Seemann (1849)

Berthold Seemann's field notes provide a rich glimpse into subtle aspects of Panamanian society, for they pay great attention to small details missed by the average 19th Century traveler to the Isthmus. Seemann focused on plants and animals, but also on traits of the tropical landscape: the types of forests and savannas, the contour of the terrain, the location and conditions of the few existing cities and towns, the state of roads and ports, the ways of earning a livelihood, the political and administrative systems, as well as Panama's demographic and racial composition, particularly the prevalence of mestizos and of people of African ancestry.

According to Seemann, in 1849 the Isthmus of Panama, then part of New Granada, had 130,000 inhabitants. The capital and largest urban center, Panama City, had a population of only 5,000. Administratively, it was divided into two Provinces: Panama and Veraguas; and two territories: Darién and Bocas del Toro. The political head of each Province was the prefect. Provinces were subdivided into cantons, and these into parishes.

Ecclesiastically, Panama was a diocese, headed by a bishop; and judicially, it was one of the seven judicial districts of New Granada. The principal tribunal of justice was in Panama City, presided by two magistrates. Each canton had one to two judges. In the territories, the prefects administered the law.

The native democracy described by Seemann was very exclusive, rejecting the participation of most people. Only 114 electors, all property owners, selected the President, Vice-president, high officials, and representatives to the Granadian Congress.

Let us now follow his notes on the different regions of the Isthmus, starting with the isolated territory of Bocas del Toro on the westernmost Caribbean coast.

The Territory of Bocas del Toro

The territory of Bocas del Toro extends over the north-west corner of the Isthmus and the islands situated in the lagoon of Chiriqui, and contains about 721 square miles. . . . Originally its limits were more extended: a law of the 20th of November 1803, given by the King of Spain, placed the whole coast, as far as Cape Gracias a Dios, under the jurisdiction of the Viceroyalty of New Granada. As such boundaries were generally acknowledged when the Spanish Americans obtained their independence, the Government at Bogotá now claims the whole shore, and has, at least nominally, incorporated it with this territory. Bocas del Toro constituted part of Veraguas until 1843, when it was formed into a separate territory and, in order to induce people to settle, all who lived within its limits were till the 31st of August 1850, exempted from taxation, and Bocas del Toro up to the same date declared a free port. Having a rather unhealthy climate, it is but thinly peopled; indeed, the whole Christianized population amounted in 1843 to no more than 595. A prefect, who receives an annual salary of fifteen hundred dollars, governs it. The territory will probably soon be in a more flour-

A *bongo*, a medium size boat carved from a single tree, used for coastal trading during the 19th Century. According to Seemann, a *bongo* could weigh up to 12 tons.
Engraving from F. N. Otis: *Illustrated History of the Panama Railroad.* New York, 1862.

ishing condition. The old road connecting the town of David with the port of Bocas del Toro being so bad that only pedestrians can traverse it, a new one is about to be commenced by the Chiriqui Road Company, upon which the commerce of Western Veraguas and, what is of greater importance, a communication between the Atlantic and the Pacific will be conducted.

The Province of Veraguas

Next to Bocas del Toro lies Veraguas, having the Atlantic on the north, the territory of Bocas del Toro on the north-west, the Republic of Costa Rica on the west, the Pacific Ocean on the south, and the province of Panama on the east. Respecting the derivation of the name Veraguas various opinions prevail. Some contend that is composed of the words *ver*, to see, and *agua*, water, because between the town of David and the port of Bocas del Toro there is said to be a mountain from the top of which both oceans are visible. Others declare it to be a corruption of *verde* and *agua*, the waters of the river Veragua, they say, being at times a greenish hue; this having been observed by the discoverers, it was termed Verde–aguas, which name was afterwards changed into Veraguas, and extended over the whole district. A third party, derives it from "*ver agua*", because when Columbus discovered the northern coast he encountered much rain ("he saw water"), and from the constant dampness of the weather the clothes of the voyagers became "*averaguado*" (moldy): the verb *averaguar* being a provincialism used only in the Isthmus, this argument, it must be confessed, looks plausible, but, like the others, it is not in accordance with history. We find Ferdinand Columbus mentioning the name Veraguas long before his father had touched at that province. The name was very well known to the people of Careta, who accompanied Columbus as pilots, and the word Veraguas is therefore of Indian, not of Spanish, origin.

According to Seemann, Veraguas had in 1843 a surface of 7,416 square miles and 45,376 inhabitants. It was divided into two cantons: Santiago and Alanje. We will start with his description of the westernmost canton, Alanje.

The Canton of Alanje or Chiriquí

Alanje, or Chiriqui, numbers 15,111 inhabitants, and comprises the parishes of David, Alanje, Boquerón, Bugaba, Dolega, Gualaca, Remedios, San Félix, San Lorenzo, and San Pablo. The town of David is the principal place, or *cabecera* of the canton. This dignity however was conferred upon it only a few years ago; it was enjoyed formerly by Santiago de Alanje—or, as it is also called, Riochico—situated a few miles south-ward.

The Town of David

"David," recounts Seemann:

lies. . . .on the left bank of the river of the same name, in a beautiful plain, and is surrounded by the villages of Gualaca, Dolega, Boquerón, and Bugaba, and by mountains of considerable elevation. On the south-west rises the Volcano of Chiriquí, a peak 7,000 feet high; on the north the Galera de Chorcha, a flat table-mountain, which, as the first part of its name indicates, has some resemblance to a gallery or corridor; from the top a waterfall descends over huge blocks of granite several hundred feet in depth. During the wet season, when great quantities of water are discharged, it is very conspicuous, resembling from a distance a stream of silver, and serving navigators as a landmark, in making Boca Chica, the seaport of David.

Boca Chica was the westernmost port in Panama's Pacific coast, and the main port for the canton of Alanje or Chiriquí. Three rivers flow into the sea through a labyrinth of mangroves (Boca Chica, Boca de San Pedro, and Boca Brava) to form this port. Boca Chica was apparently useful only to small boats; it was neither mapped nor marked by buoys. East of Boca Brava stood the best natural anchorage in Veraguas, Bahía Honda, a deep cove resembling a volcanic crater; then further to the east stood Montijo Bay, the port for Santiago de Veraguas.

Retaking Seemann's narration, we read:

David has about six hundred houses, built of wood and clay, and generally one story high and, being all white-washed, they form sev-

mented by immigration. Several French, Italians, and North Americans have settled there, and it is principally owing to their exertions that David has risen within the last fifteen years from a paltry hamlet to a prosperous town. Though the Davidenians are mostly of a mixed race, the number of whites is considerable; their employment consists in breeding cattle, agriculture and commerce. The exports of the place are rice, coffee, sarsaparilla, pearls, hides, turtle-shells, dried meat, and some gold-dust. Several other natural products might be advantageously shipped. The Corpachi (*Croton*), the bark of which is highly valuable, grows plentifully in the for-

Panama City seen from Cerro Calidonia in 1837. Flamenco, the island on the extreme left, was the anchorage of the scientific expeditions of the HMS *Sulphur* and later, for the HMS *Herald*. From Edward Belcher: *Narrative of a Voyage Round the World*. London, 1843.

eral neat-looking streets. There is only one church, which stands in the center of the public square, where also the government offices are situated. The town contained in 1843, according to official statements, 4321 inhabitants; their number is however yearly aug-

est; the Quira is found in abundance in the neighborhood, and the Saumerio, producing an odoriferous balsam, is seen in extensive groves in the adjacent mountains. At present all the produce has to be carried to Panama, but when the road to Bocas del Toro is completed, and when a direct communication with Europe and North America has been established, many productions, which at present are not worth sending, will be exported with advantage. The climate of David if compared with that of other parts of the Isthmus is particularly healthy. Longevity is common; few of the cutaneous eruptions so frequent in other districts are experienced; the common fever is now becoming general, as there exists another Pueblo Nuevo on the Playa of Chiru, in the Bay of Panama which, by the way of distinction, is termed Pueblo Nuevo de San Carlos. Remedios is situated on the high road which connects David with Santiago de Veraguas, in a plain, at equal distances from the villages of Tolé and San Lorenzo. It consists of four hundred buildings, most of which are

Panama City, as seen from the Bay of Panama, in 1837.
For centuries navigators used Cerro Ancón or Ancón Hill as a landmark. Its vegetation attracted many naturalists in the late 19th and early 20th centuries.
From Edward Belcher: *Narrative of a Voyage Round the World*. London, 1843.

of the country being the predominant disease, and even this malady is only frequent during the change of season. The climate is annually improving: if we may believe the tradition of the country, the rainy season a hundred years ago was most violent, making it necessary to navigate from house to house in canoes.

The Village of Remedios

Among the largest villages of the Canton are San Lorenzo and Pueblo Nuevo de los Remedios. The name Remedios for the latter place slightly constructed of the bark and leaves of palms; only an inconsiderable number are built more substantially, and furnished with tile roofs and walls made of adobes. Remedios, being the head of the parish, has a church of considerable size, though smaller and inferior to the old building, of which the ruins are still visible. The number of its inhabitants was in 1843, according to the census then taken, 1,235; they are a mixture of the three races usually found in the hotter parts of Spanish America, the Caucasian, the African, and the American, mestizos and mulattoes being the predominant. Remedios was formerly a place of much more importance but, as in all places where a mixed population prevails, rather a decrease than an increase followed when immigration ceased. The exact time of its foundation is unknown; during the latter part of the 17th Century it was in prosperous circumstances so much so, that Buccaneers on the 23rd of May, 1680, thought it worth while to assault it. The inhabitants however made a gallant resistance on the riverside; the commander-in-chief of the pirates, Captain Sawkins, was slain, and Sharp, the second in command, disheartened by his losses, retreated. In another attempt on the 31st of June, 1685, the rovers were more successful: the village was taken, and shared the same fate as all the places which fell in to the hands of that terrible association.

The Canton of Santiago

The canton of Santiago, the eastern portion of Veraguas, contains 30,265 inhabitants, and consists of thirteen parishes. Santiago de Veraguas, the capital of the province, is situated in the canton of Santiago, in a plain on the southern side of the Cordillera, eight miles northward of the Port of Montijo, about thirteen miles south-east of the village of Mesa, and forty west of the town of Natá. The exact period of its foundation is doubtful, as most of the old chroniclers confound it with Natá: it is highly probable that, like most of the adjacent places, it was built shortly after the conquest. The houses, nine hundred in number, are chiefly composed of wood, and, with a single exception, are one story high. Except two churches and a hospital there are no public buildings of any importance. The principal streets run from north to south; a great part of their pavement is of petrified wood—the *chumicos petrificados* of the natives. . . . Santiago, as the capital is the residence of the governor and the chief judge of the province; the former, elected every four years, receives

annually eighteen hundred dollars. The number of inhabitants is about five thousand, a great part of whom are whites. Their principal occupation is breeding cattle, manufacturing hammocks, and plaiting the so-called Panama hats. Many of the wealthier people are engaged in mining speculations. . . .

The principal villages of the canton are Calobre, Cañajas, Mesa, Mineral, Montijo, Palmas, Rio Jesus, Soná and Tolé. Palmas was founded in 1774 by monks, Rio Jesus in 1755. In the neighborhood of the latter are the celebrated paradise-trees, which I have described in Hooker's "Journal of Botany". Mineral, about 22 leagues from Santiago, was formerly of importance on account of its gold mines, but has now sunk into insignificance. Calobre is famous for its hot springs. The town of Santafe, described by Herrera, was destroyed in 1805 by the Indians, and several of the other places mentioned by the same historian have disappeared without leaving a trace behind. Near Mesa, or "Mesita de Oro" as the village was called during the last century, on account of its prosperity, are the remains of a beautiful basaltic column. This column stood formerly on an eminence, which overlooks the adjacent country, but about seventy years ago it was thrown down by an earthquake, and broken into several pieces; it is 16 feet in diameter, and its height when entire must have been about a 150 feet. The natives call it Barca de Piedra—though it has not the slightest resemblance with a ship—and believe it to have been built by the Indians in order to serve them as a watch-tower, a belief to which its peculiar formation and former position may have given rise.

Seemann thought it not unlikely that this big basalt column had been originally called "Balcon de Piedra" (Balcony of Stone) and later became "Barco de Piedra" (Ship of Stone) because the Isthmians constantly confused the letters "l" and "r".

The Province of Panama

The province of Panama, the most important and populous district of the Isthmus, is situated to the east of Veraguas. The northern boundary is the Caribbean Sea, its western, the province of Veraguas, and its southern the Pacific Ocean and the territory of Darien. It extends over a surface of about 9,139 square miles, has a population of 10,494 inhabitants, and is composed of the cantons of Los Santos, Parita, Natá, Chorera, Portobelo and Panama.

The Cantons of Los Santos and Parita

The cantons of Los Santos and Parita occupy the little peninsula, of which Punta Mariato and Punta Mala form the southernmost points. Los Santos, having for its *cabecera* the village of the same name, is composed of the parishes of Pedasí, Pocrí, Las Tablas, and Los Santos, containing a population of 14,539. Parita is formed by the parishes of Macaracas, Minas, Ocú, Pesé, and Parita, and has 15,119 inhabitants; the *cabecera* is Parita. The people of both these cantons are considered the most industrious of the country.

The Canton of Natá

The canton of Natá is that part of the province which touches Eastern Veraguas. It contains 19,610 inhabitants, and comprises the parishes of Antón, Olá, Penonomé, Santamaría and Natá. The town of Natá, the principal place in the district, is interesting from being the oldest town of the American continent built by Europeans, having been founded as early as 1517 by the Licentiate Gaspar de Espinosa and several other gentlemen. Notwithstanding its age, it is but a small town. It is situated in a plain between the Rio Grande and Rio Chico de Natá, and has about eight hundred houses, two churches, irregular unpaved streets, and contains five thousand inhabitants. . . .The principal villages of this cantón are Santamaría and Antón. At the lat-

ter cocoanut palms are so numerous as from a distance to resemble a forest.

The Canton of Chorrera

The canton of Chorrera borders that of Natá, and contains 7,559 inhabitants; the parishes belonging to it are Arraiján, Capira, Chame, Chorrera, and San Carlos. Chorrera is the principal village of the cantón, and numbers 2,500 inhabitants. Having the advantage of a fine river for bathing, and a cool and salubrious climate during the summer, the place is much frequented by families from Panama, who repair thither for the restoration of their health and rural enjoyement. During the wet season Chorrera is very dirty, the mud and water in the streets being ankle-deep. Capira is a village of some extent, and produces coffee of superior quality. San Carlos or Pueblo Nuevo de San Carlos, is a pleasing little village, situated on the Playa of Chirú. Chame is but a short distance from San Carlos, and has 1,300 inhabitants. . . . Arraiján is a small village, situated at about equal distances from Cruces and Chorrera.

The Canton of Portobelo

The canton of Portobelo, the north-west corner of the province of Panama, comprises the four parishes of Chagres, Minas, Palenque, and Portobelo. The town of Portobelo is the cabecera of the district, it is situated. . . . close to the sea, at the foot of a high mountain that surrounds the whole port; it consists of a long street, circling round the bay, a few short ones branching off, and two squares, one in front of the treasury, the other before the church; the principal public buildings are the fortifications, the hospital, the treasury, and the church: but these, as well as the private houses, are in a very dilapidated state. Portobelo numbers about 1,300 inhabitants, chiefly Negroes and mulattoes; it has an excellent harbour, but, with this exception, there is nothing to recommend it. The climate is the most unhealthy in the whole country, and has proved fatal to many Europeans; there is seldom a fine day,—the place is almost always enveloped in vapour, arising from the rank vegetation of the neighborhood, or deluged with rain; the heat is so excessive, and the climate so noxious, that few white men have been able to live there for any time, and even some species of animals quickly degenerate. Formerly a paved causeway existed between Panama and Portobelo, but this is at present in very bad condition; it has been broken up by the violent rains, and, being for the most part overgrown by bushes and high trees, it is with difficulty traversed on foot.

. . . . Chagres contains about one thousand inhabitants, nearly all of whom are negroes or people of a mixed origin [mestizos]. From the number of steam and sailing vessels repairing thither, Chagres, during the last few years, has become important, but there is little hope of its becoming a large town, even if the present mode of communication between the Atlantic and the Pacific should be continued. The climate commits fearful ravages among new arrivals, especially the whites. The rainy season is prolonged to nine and even ten months, and this alone will be a barrier against permanent settlement of the caucasian race.

The mouth of the Chagres River, in the mid-19th Century, at the start of the California Gold Rush: the early days of steamboat navigation and the construction of Panama's Interoceanic Railroad. On the left, Ft. San Lorenzo; on the right, the settlement known as American Chagres. Illustration from J. H. Kemble: *The Panama Route, 1848-1869.* University of California Press, 1943.

The Town of Chagres

The town of Chagres is, like Portobelo, one of the most miserable and unhealthy in the country; it lies at the mouth of the river of the same name. . . .and is guarded by the castle of San Lorenzo, a dark looking fortification. . . .

The houses of Chagres are slightly built— mostly of the bark and leaves of palms.

The Canton of Panama

The canton of Panama adjoins that of Portobelo and Chorrera, and contains a population of 10,494 souls; it is divided into nine parishes, San Felipe, Santa Ana, Cruses, Chepo, Chimán, Gorgona, Pacora, San Juan, and Taboga. The city of Panama, the capital of the province, and also the *cabecera* of the canton, was built in 1673, two years after the destruction of the old town. Soon rising into importance trough its favorable situation, it continued prosperous till the abolition of the Galleon and Portobelo fair, when it became impoverished almost as suddenly as it had acquired its wealth: all the richer merchants left, most of the buildings fell into ruin. . . . The war of independence, and the great changes produced by it throughout Spanish America, were the causes of its revival: trade was opened, foreigners settled, representatives of different nations were appointed to reside at Panama, education began to spread, and thus the town gradually recovered. Nothing however has raised it more than the establishment of lines of steamers in the Pacific and the Atlantic Oceans. Since the first appearance of these vessels, and the subsequent discovery of Gold in California, the city has so much improved, and such great alterations have taken place, that one would hardly fancy it the same,—and the Isthmus, which was formerly merely a road subservient to the selfish politicy of Spain, became from that period the highway of nations.

The city of Panama lies. . . .at the foot of the Cerro of Ancon, on a little peninsula connected towards the west with the mainland. It is divided into two parishes: that within the walls, is called San Felipe; that without, the suburb, Santa Ana. Panama differs considerably from the other towns of Spanish America: its high buildings, tiled roofs, numerous churches, and massive walls, giving an air reminding one, at first sight, of a European town; on a closer inspection however the peculiarity of the old Spanish style becomes evident. San Felipe, the best and most regularly built part is surrounded by walls and watchtowers, which are at present rather dilapidated. . . . The city has four gates, two opening toward the sea, two toward the land; the traveler coming from Chagres enters by the western one, which was formerly strongly defended, and connected with the mainland by means of a draw-bridge. The principal streets run from west to east, and are crossed by others extending from north to south, from sea to sea, preserving a current of air, which greatly adds to the salubrity of the place. The streets are paved and regular, but rather narrow, seldom exceeding more than fifty feet in breadth; the pavements, for foot-passengers are covered by the balconies of the houses, and a person may walk almost all over the town during a shower of rain without getting wet. There are four public squares, three in San Felipe, and one in Santa Ana; the principal is the Plaza de la Catedral, situated nearly in the center or the city. . . . There are seven convents, six of which have partly fallen into decay. . . . The old Jesuits College is the finest ruin in the town; it was commenced in 1739, but was not completed until 1773 when the Society of Jesus was expelled from Spanish America. . . . Most of the private buildings of San Felipe are constructed of stone, those of Santa Ana of wood. They are two stories high, surrounded by balconies, and have tiled roofs, the violence of the rains not permitting the use of flat ones. All have large doorways, sufficiently spacious to admit a person on horseback. The halls are small. . . . In most houses the lower story is let to shop-keepers, spirit-sellers, and tradespeople; the first floor is inhabited by the servants and the upper the most salubrious, by the landlord and his family. All the apartments are large and airy, and the drawing-rooms are generally thirty feet long. . . . In all the rooms are hammocks, in which the Panamanians and the inhabitants of the Isthmus in general may be seen swinging themselves for hours in succession.

The Villages of Cruces and Gorgona

The principal villages belonging to the canton of Panama are San Juan [Pequeni], Che-

Panama City, circa early 1880s, as captured by French photographer De Sablá.
The view shows the *intramuros* or old walled colonial barrio of San Felipe.
Source: Panama Canal Commission.

po, Gorgona, Cruces and Taboga. The latter is situated on the island of the same name; Chepo on the river Bayano; while San Juan, Gorgona and Cruces are built on the left bank of the Chagres. Gorgona is of very recent date; Cruces however was known in the time of Herrera, who calls it La Venta. In 1671 the Buccaneers found it a considerable village; since that period it has suffered several times from inundations and conflagrations; in 1828 nearly the whole village was destroyed by fire. Had it not a rival in Gorgona, it would soon become a town. The two villages have each a church and several inns. The inhabitants are nearly all either owners of canoes and beasts of burden, or store-keepers, who take charge of goods, or are *bogas*, persons working the canoes.

Seemann reiterates Lloyd's words to the effect that few rivers in the world had a lovelier landscape than the upper Chagres, above Cruces; high, steep cliffs of calcareous rock with fantastically curious forms; sites where the savannas met the gallery forest at the riverbanks; spots filled with huge trees struggling among themselves for space like veritable vegetable giants; majestic fig trees whose branches spanned the breadth of the river, offering deep and refreshing shade.

The Territory of Darién

The territory of Darién is the fourth great political division of the Isthmus. It is bounded on the north by the Atlantic, on the south by the river San Juan, on the west by the Pacific and the province of Panama, and on the east by the Atrato. Including the Pearl Islands,

The landing at the village of Chepigana on the Tuira river, Darién, 1870. Photo by Timothy O'Sullivan. Source: Smithsonian Institution. National Anthropological Archives, Washington, D.C.

which belong to its jurisdiction, Darién covers a superficial area of about 16,941 square miles. It contains the parishes of Chepigana, Islas del Istmo, Molineca, Pinogana, Santamaría, Tucutí, and Yavisa. Yavisa, the *cabecera* of the district, contains 332 inhabitants, and is the residence of the Prefect, who receives an annual salary of a thousand dollars.

"Darién," says Seemann, "was primarily inhabited by an unknown number of indigenous peoples. The Christian population was 3,148, of whom 1,941 lived on the islands of the Las Perlas Archipelago."

Seemann was amazed at how little Darién's landscape had changed since it was first described by its discoverers: humid, dense forests reaching to the seashore, and a few isolated villages. It seemed to him that the the nature of the people had changed. When the Europeans came into contact with the inhabitants of Darién, they were warriors. Now they were the opposite: timid. They ran into the forest when they saw a ship. Seemann wrote that sometimes the residents abandoned their villages without explanation, as happened in Bahía Piñas. On December 14, 1847, upon their first visit to the bay, they found it densely populated; a year later there was no trace whatsoever of its inhabitants.

Among the positive traits of the locals Seemann stressed their hospitality, their courtesy to strangers and their generosity to the poor. In general, the Isthmians tended to prefer the French to other foreigners. Frequent contact with travelers from abroad had rendered the Panamanians more open to innovations than in other parts of Spanish America. Notwithstanding the large number of passengers crossing the Isthmus, crimes were few. Seemann found the country quite safe. "Highway robberies," he says, "are never heard of, murder is rarely committed, and great theft is unfrequent. . . . That the people have little fear of burglary, a glance at their dwellings will show: no iron bars guard the windows and doors as in most parts of Spanish America."

Seemann found remarkable that Panamanians had little regard toward time, distances, measures and weights; however, they were very fond of their extensive calendar of fiestas, including religious processions. Their main amusements were horse riding, cockfights, dances, music, singing, playing billiards and cards. "The worst feature in the character of the Isthmians," noted Seemann, "are want of moral principle and steadiness of purpose. . . . They are indolent, licentious, fond of gambling. . . ."

The common bread was the *tortilla de maíz*, made of yellow corn, unlike Mexico and Central America, where white corn is used. The locals ate large quantities of *tasajo*: meat cut into thin slices, salted and dried in the sun, and sold by the yard. The most demanded beverages among the men were the *aguardiente* from sugarcane and *chicha* elaborated from the fermented juice of corn, pineapples and palms. Smoking tobacco was widespread.

The Naturalist
Josef von Warscewicz in Panama
(1848-1851)

One of the most interesting and little known naturalists to study Panamanian flora and fauna during the 19th Century was Josef von Warscewicz, a Polish scholar born in 1812, who died in 1866. Between 1848 and 1851 he extensively explored the Isthmus of Panama, then part of the Republic of Nueva Granada.

Despite arduous efforts to obtain information on Warscewicz and his journeys, the results have been meager. His life continues to be a puzzle with key pieces missing. These uncertainties included even his name, for in some references he is called Josef, and in others, Julius. His last name is also spelled differently; here we have adopted one variant: Warscewicz.

Although Warscewicz was a pioneer in collecting orchids and hummingbirds—he discovered many of the most beautiful species in Central America and Panama—, and also collected reptiles, his contributions are hardly known. Paul Standley, in his 1924 article on the history of orchid collecting in Panama, dedicates barely three lines to him. Novencido Escobar is, perhaps, the only Panamanian author who mentions the polish scholar. In his book *El Desarrollo de las Ciencias Naturales y la Medicina en Panamá* (The evolution of natural science and medicine in Panama), he wrote:

> Many species of Panamanian plants and genera commemorate the name of Julio von Warscewicz. . . . He came to Panama in 1848 and explored the provinces of Panama and Veraguas. In 1851 he returned to the latter place. He specialized in living orchids and hummingbirds and he was for a long time an authority in these fields. To him goes the merit of having introduced into Europe orchids from Panama and other plants of economic value. His collection is to be found at the Botanical Garden in Berlin.

Josef Warscewicz came from a Polish family with a long military tradition. The Swedish King, Gustav Adolph, appointed one of his ancestors as a personal assistant, grant-

Josef von Warscewicz (1812-1866).
Polish naturalist, who explored Panama between 1848 and 1851.
Photo: Artura Grottgera, Jaguellonian University, Krakow, Poland.

ing him the noble title *von*. Josef's father headed the corps of engineers of the Polish army under the patriot, General Kosziusko, who fought in the United States Revolutionary War. Josef was born in 1812 in Vilna (Wilna), Poland, the city where the Russian czar Alexander had transferred Josef's father. Apparently, Josef studied some botany in the well-regarded Jaguellonian University in Krakow. After the Napoleonic wars, Krakow was annexed to the Austro-Hungarian Empire. In Krakow, home to the Polish

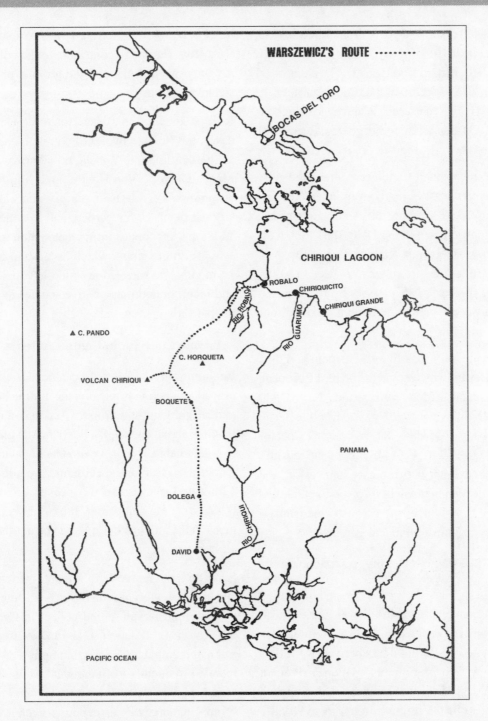

Warscewicz's route from David, on the Pacific, to the lagoon of Chiriquí, Bocas del Toro, on the Caribbean, in 1848.
Map from Jay Savage: *On the Trail of the Golden Frog: With Warscewicz and Gabb in Central America.* Proceedings of the California Academy of Sciences 38: 273-288.

intelligentsia, Warscewicz acquired his enthusiasm for botany from mentors like Judzill, Witzill, and Gorski. The latter hired him as inspector of botanical gardens in 1831. For five years Warscewicz directed the Garden at Insterburg, transforming it into a botanical jewel.

We have been unable to determine why Warscewicz emigrated from Poland to Germany, and later, to the American tropics. He participated in the 1830-1831 Polish insurrection against Russian rule, a revolt in which he was promoted to officer. The defeat of the Polish patriots by the Russian army could perhaps explain the exile of our naturalist.

His itinerary took him to Potsdam and then to Berlin, where some of the best European botanical gardens were found. From 1840 to 1844, Warscewicz worked in the Berlin Botanical Garden. The General Inspector of the Gardens, F. Otto, charged the recently arrived Pole with the care and restoration of the Neu Schoeneberg, a semi-abandoned area that Warscewicz transformed into a very beautiful botanical garden.

The Belgian Colony in Guatemala

In 1845 Warscewicz participated in a failed Belgian plan to establish an agricultural colony in Guatemala. He was sold the idea that he would find a prosperous city full of newly rich immigrants. Upon arrival, in February 1845, Warscewicz discovered that, instead of the promised city, there stood a poor village with a few thatched roofed houses. And instead of rich and active colonists, he found only sick immigrants who looked like resuscitated corpses. Of the 32 healthy people who arrived with Warscewicz from Europe to contribute to the colony, only our botanist and the group's physician survived.

In Guatemala he met Van Houtte de Gandawy, the Belgian owner of a great botanical garden in Santo Tomas, now known as Matías Gálvez. Van Houtte hired him for 30 pounds sterling to inventory and classify the plants of his garden, and to collect additional specimens from Guatemalan forests. With this grant, which lasted him for 14 months, he traveled around the country and incorporated many native species in to his patron's garden.

Private Collector in Central America

Beginning in 1846, Josef became self-employed, collecting tropical plants for the botanical gardens of Europe. Accompanied by the Belgian consul, Blondell, he traveled to Guatemala City. In 16 months he would gather 10,000 plant specimens, including 120 orchid species and 67 species of oaks (*Quercus*). He shipped 46 boxes of specimens to the gardens in England and another 12 boxes to Berlin.

Later he met George Ure Skinner, a friend and sponsor, who provided him with funds to continue to explore and collect in Central America. Skinner (1804-1867) was an English merchant, who, beginning in 1831, traveled frequently to Guatemala, where he established an extensive orchid collection. From Guatemala, Warscewicz traveled to El Salvador where, due to massive deforestation, he found few plants to collect. Then he proceeded to Nicaragua where he met Dr. Oersled, who provided him with information on the best areas for botanical exploration. Together, they traveled through the forests of Nueva Segovia, collecting 2,000 orchids. Warscewicz sent 15 boxes of plants to England and 5 to Berlin.

After that, Warscewicz changed course, setting out for Costa Rica, where he arrived in February 1848. In four months he gathered an excellent orchid collection: he sent 30 boxes of plants, including palm seeds, to Europe. In March 1848 he climbed Volcán Irazú in the Costa Rican Central Valley.

In Western Veraguas, 1848

We are unsure of the exact date in 1848 when Warscewicz arrived in Panama. We do know, however, that he entered the country along the western border of the Province of Veraguas, now Chiriquí. Warscewicz considered the Chiriquí highlands to be a paradise for orchid collectors. That year he crossed the Isthmus back and forth from David, on the Pacific side, over the continental divide, to the Lagoon of Chiriquí Grande in Bocas del Toro, then part of the Atlantic coast of Veraguas.

To travel from the Pacific to the Atlantic and back across the central cordillera, Warscewicz took the old trail that connected Chiriquí on the Pacific to the huge Caribbean Lagoon of Chiriquí Grande, in Bocas del Toro. The location of this route can be traced thanks to a map made by Moritz Wagner in 1863. From David the trail ascended gradually northward, crossing a landscape of savannas and gallery forests until reaching the village of Dolega and the valley of Boquete in the shadow of Volcán

Barú. This point marked the end of the savannas and the start of the cloud forests of the Central Cordillera. Edward Regel, a German, said in 1867 that Warscewicz had in effect reached the peak of Volcán Barú.

From Boquete, the path towards the dense wet forests of the Atlantic slope split into two. One trail snaked eastward around Volcán Barú, ending at the site of Ranchos de Robalo, at the mouth of the Robalo River, on the Chiriquí Grande lagoon. The other path went east of Cerro Horqueta, and emerged at the mouth of the Guarumo River, which flows into the Chiriquí Grande Lagoon.

Moritz Wagner, who in 1863 employed the same guides and porters contracted by Warscewicz during his crossing, thought that the Polish naturalist had first taken the road from Boquete to the Robalo River, mainly because a branch of this river led toward the summit of Volcán Barú (3,478 m), and that he had returned to Boquete by way of the trail along the Guarumo River, now in Bocas del Toro Province.

As a result of his work and collections in Chiriquí, Warscewicz sent 20 boxes of specimens to England and 20 to Berlin. After exploring western Panama, Warscewicz headed toward Ecuador. His explorations there were limited by the high costs of transportation; thus he collected a scanty amount of botanical material. From Ecuador he sent 10 boxes to England and one to Berlin. He sailed from Guayaquil towards San Juan de Nicaragua and afterward began to collect in Costa Rica. On March 10, 1850, he traveled to Europe, first to London and then to Berlin.

Return to the Tropics (1850 - 1853)

At age 38, destiny confronted Warscewicz with two choices. In Poland, he was offered the directorship of the Krakow Botanical Garden. Simultaneously, the English nobleman Lord Derby, an enthusiast of the tropics, begged him to continue collecting specimens, but of animals rather than plants, in which the Lord was keenly interested and willing to pay any price. Professor Czerwiakowsky made the arrangements that allow Warscewicz a three-year leave of absence while maintaining his position in the Krakow Botanical Garden until his return.

Warscewicz sailed for the Americas in November 1850. His plan for exploration and collection was published in 1852 by the journal of the Berlin Botanical Garden. He landed in Panama and headed towards his favorite exploration site, the western highlands of Veraguas. We don't know how long he stayed at Chiriquí. Most amphibians and reptiles collected by Warscewicz on the Isthmus were taken during this trip into western Panama. From these collections, made in early 1851, he would send two boxes of specimens to England and ten to Berlin.

By mid 1851, Warscewicz traveled to Guayaquil, Ecuador, and then to Peru. He found many new orchids in the valley of the Carabaya River, but he faced problems with the indigenous communities. Later, he proceeded down the Marañon River. He stayed six months in Bolivia, also gathering orchids and plants of economic importance. Then he headed towards Chile and Argentina.

His plans to continue exploring and collecting in the American tropics came to a sudden close when his sponsor, Lord Derby, died. Warscewicz traveled to the Republic of New Granada, where he explored the forests of Buena Ventura, Ocaña, the plateau of Cundinamarca, and finally the mountains of Antioquia. While travelling through Colombia, he was suprised by one of the many revolutionary wars taking place between conservatives and liberals. Embarking on the Magdalena River and navigating downstream, after two days Warscewicz's ship hit a submerged stump and sank in 15 minutes, with the loss of most of his collections.

These last expeditions cost Warscewicz's patron 2,230 pounds sterling, spent in paying for porters, renting mules and horses, and boat fares. Through his exhausting tropical journeys, Warscewicz always ate local food: rice, corn, *yuca,* and dried beef.

He returned to Europe on November 1, 1853, first to Germany and then to Krakow. There, he became Inspector of the Botanical Gardens. He died there on December 29, 1866, at 54 years of age. In 1880, the Jaguellonian University dedicated a statue of him at the Krakow Botanical Garden.

The herpetological material collected by Warscewicz in the Americas was deposited in Berlin, Vienna, and Krakow. Some specimens reached the Museum in Munich and the Botanical Museum in London. All the Central American reptiles were collected in Panama between 1848 and 1851. Most of the amphibians collected by Warscewicz were described and sketched in 1857 and 1858 by Oskar Schmidt.

The Explorations of Wilmot Brown, Jr. (1900-1904)

In 1905, Aurelio Moreno and Josefa Caballero, a peasant couple from Chiriquí, settled in the dense uninhabited forests of the Chiriquí Viejo River. They were my maternal grandparents. Affiliated with the Conservative faction, they had been forced to emigrate from the savannas of Alanje, ruined like thousands of other people from the isthmian countryside by the War of a Thousand Days (1898-1901), the bloodiest of the Colombian civil wars. They had to sell their lovely farmstead, Las Loras, now the site of the Carta Vieja Rum factory. Aurelio Moreno was from Dolega. Josefa was a Caballero, one of the families that founded Santiago de Alanje, a town established in 1598 at the western end of Panama's Pacific coast savanna. Later, their eldest son, Salvador Moreno, my uncle, married Serafina Brown Arauz, a teacher from Divalá, the nearest village. This tall, white woman, who had beautiful gray eyes and prominent cheekbones, inherited her artistic gifts from her father, Wilmot W. Brown, Jr., a North American naturalist who lived in Divalá at the beginning of the 20th Century.

Wilmot Wood Brown, Jr. was an indefatigable and methodical collector from Massachusetts who traveled around Panama between 1900 and 1904, a tumultuous period marked by the War of a Thousand Days, Panama's separation from Colombia and the beginning of the construction of the Panama Canal. When people saw him go off into the jungles to collect animals during the revolution of 1900 they would say *"El gringo Brown está loco"* ("Brown the gringo is crazy").

Along the Railroad, and the Las Perlas Islands

Brown arrived in Panama during the dry season of 1900. He came from Santa Marta, Colombia, where he had been collecting birds since 1897. His mission was to build up the most complete collection possible of birds and mammals of the Isthmus, a place in which the tropics of the two continental masses of the New World converge. Because in the tropics some birds are more abundant at some periods than others, according to the availability of fruits, flowers and insects, Brown was forced to remain for several seasons at each site in order to collect specimens. In March of 1900, the same month that the Liberal troops organized in Nicaragua by Belisario Porras disembarked from the steamer *Momotombo* on the beaches of Burica Point, Brown arrived in Colón. He settled in Loma de León or Lion Hill, a swampy jungle site on the banks of the Chagres River and the interoceanic rail line. There he collected many birds and a few mammals.

During the first three months of the rainy season of 1900, he explored San Miguel, the largest island of the Las Perlas Archipelago. There, he collected specimens of nearly all terrestrial mammals, and concluded that most were derived from mainland species. He even found a species of

Loma León, 1911, a station on the old Panama Railroad, now covered by the waters of Lake Gatún. Wilmot Brown and other naturalists studied the flora and fauna of the Chagres River from such stations. Along the 80 kilometers of track, crossing the narrowest and lowest part of the Americas, it was easy to observe the contrasts between the dry forests of the Pacific and the very humid forests of the Atlantic.
Photo by E. A. Goldman. Source: *Expeditions organized or participated in by the Smithsonian Institution in 1910 and 1911.* Smithsonian Institution Archives. Washington, D.C.

rat then thought to be unique to Trinidad. He also collected reptiles, amphibians, fish, birds, and species of trees and shrubs. He made observations on the geology of the island, about which very little information existed.

Chiriquí

Before the rainy season of 1900 ended, Brown moved to Chiriquí. Over the next two years, he collected birds and mammals from the Pacific coast to the Continental Divide. He started in the lowlands of Soná, working west until reaching Puerto Pedregal, the port of David. Then he settled in Divalá, an isolated hamlet in the forests of the Chiriquí Viejo watershed. These forests began at the Duablo River, the edge of the savannas of Alanje, and extended well beyond the border with Costa Rica. In Divalá, he fell in love with Leonor Arauz, with whom he had a daughter, Serafina. He explored the basin of the Chiriquí Viejo River and its main tributaries—Jacú, Gariché, Duablo and Divalá—and the area that today is known as the district of Bugaba.

In the dry season of 1901 Brown traveled into the highlands of the Volcán Barú and Boquete. During the rainy period, he covered the Atlantic or northern slope of the volcano. He confirmed that many bird species from the north side did not inhabit the southern slopes. He also discovered six species of birds new to science.

His house was always full of traps for capturing birds, although sometimes he hunted birds with a rifle. Upon capturing a bird, he would check the altitude and write it in a label, as well as the name of the species, the place and date. When he returned from his field trips he took time to sketch the animals, and since he was an excellent taxidermist, he would prepare them exquisitely before forwarding them to bird specialists in the United States.

From David to the Summit of Volcán Barú

Wilmot Brown kept a detailed field notebook. In 1901, traveling from David to the summit of Volcán Barú, he described the interface between the grasslands and forests in the lowlands and highlands and finally, the vegetation of the Chiriquí *páramo* in the following way:

Leaving the town of David on horseback one rides over a level savanna for about an hour before coming to the southern slope of the Cordillera de Chiriquí. The characteristic bird species of this savanna are the scissor-tailed flycatcher and the meadowlark. The scissor-tail is usually seen sitting on the ground, which is its normal habit on the plain. I often saw at one time as many as ten perched on the grass-covered plain about me. The meadowlark is very common and tame, and its song is very distinct from that of *Sturnella magna*. Turkey buzzards and king vultures are always to be seen overhead.

Upon reaching the foothills, which are covered by scrubby growth of trees, the trail gradually descends into a valley where the vegetation is much more luxuriant, and where one meets again the characteristic birds of the lowland forest,—toucans, jacamars, blue tanagers, red-rumped tanagers, and the like—as well as the big black and the red-bellied squirrels. After a gradual ascent one emerges onto another llano, or plain, like the first but higher. Here I saw the pigmy titlark. This attractive little fellow was a bird of the trail, running along in front of my horse twenty or thirty yards, then taking wing and alighting again, to repeat the performance as I came up.

After an hour over this llano the trail descends again to cross a shallow stream, which is wooded, and then begins gradually rising through a sparsely wooded region to the pueblo of Dolega, with its great plantations of cocoa, coffee, sugarcane, and bananas, at an elevation of about 700 feet. Many species of birds were to be seen about the plantations —parrots, hummingbirds, grass-quits, red-rumped and blue tanagers being the most conspicuous. Beyond Dolega, the trail crosses two rivers with wooded banks where king-fishers, doves, and blue herons were seen. Beyond the second river, another great llano, gradually ascending, opens out, with here and there a patch of scrubby timber and in other places covered with blackened rocks—said to be lava from the volcano. It affords good pasturage for cattle, but the ride of five hours across it is hot and monotonous.

On the further side of the llano at an altitude of 3,500 feet, the trail leaves the plain and passes through valleys and over hills, in a cool luxuriant forest with swiftly running streams and brooks rippling among fern-covered rocks. One begins to see an immense number of birds, all of different species from those of the lowlands–water ouzels dart about on the rocks in the foaming, rushing streams, small thrushes and solitaires are singing everywhere in the jungle, and the branches overhead are full of tanagers and warblers. This zone extends up to about 5,000 feet. Between 5,000 and 8,000 feet, another change in the bird life is noticed, but no so marked a one.

At 10,000 feet, the character of the forest changes decidedly, the trees become low and stunted, their trunks and branches are thickly covered with a cold, saturated moss. On some of the branches globular formations of moss give an odd appearance to the tree. The undergrowth is chiefly of berry-bearing shrubs and two species of cane, with ferns and flowering herbs. One shrub produces a berry about the size of a cherry, which has a rich flavor and of which doves and the big *Merula* are very fond. At 11,000 feet the forest ends, and at the timber line the characteristic species are the Junco, a big footed finch, the long-tailed ptilogonys and curious little wren with peculiar notes, that lives in the cane brakes [*Troglodites browni*]. The country is open, broken, barren and very rocky, but there is a growth of low huckleberry-like shrubs that average 10 inches in height and are literally black with berries. There are also low flowering plants, and some tiny ferns, different from any seen below.

Standing up high above this desolate region is the great rocky peak of Mt. Chiriqui, which I believe I am the only man to have climbed. The summit is a towering rock, its extreme point so sharp and narrow that I had to straddle it. Under one foot was a sheer fall of some nine hundred feet, under the other a sharp slope of six or seven hundred. I found no signs of any previous ascent, but left two records of my own visit. From the top I looked down on the waters of the Caribbean Sea and of the Pacific Ocean, seeing distinctly the indentations of both coasts. To the west I could see the Costa Rican mountains, and to the east stretched an ocean of small peaks. My aneroid registered 11,500 ft.

According to my family's oral tradition, Brown left two messages in glass flasks on the summit of Volcán Barú. During his time in Chiriquí, Brown received important support from Captain Hughes, skipper of the Chiriquí steamboat, who collected birds in his free time and generously gave them to Brown. In addition, Henry Watson, owner of large coffee and cocoa plantations in Boquete, also helped him greatly.

Divalá, a peasant village at the western end of the Pacific savannas of Panama, where
Wilmot W. Brown, Jr. set up camp to collect birds and mammals in the forests of the Chiriquí
Viejo River, between 1900 and 1902.
Photo by Forbes-Lindsay, from *Panama and the Canal to day*.
L. C. Page Co., Boston, 1910.

Thayer's Expedition to Las Perlas
(1904)

Brown returned to Las Perlas in 1904, sponsored by the expedition of John Thayer, because during his 1900 field trip he had only collected specimens in San Miguel. During February, March, and April he worked on the islands of San Miguel, Saboga, and Pacheca. He discovered that the fauna of San Miguel was the richest in the archipelago, and that many of its species did not exist in the smaller islands. He collected 92 specimens of birds, of which 33 were migrants from North America; the rest were resident in the islands. He did not have sufficient time to study the behavior of the birds.

Wilmot Brown's last explorations of Panama took place in the rainy season of 1904. He collected birds from the outskirts of Panama City, then the West Indian *barrio* of Calidonia, across the natural savannas that bordered the Pacific coast and extended eastward toward the town of Pacora.

Wilmot W. Brown's contribution to the knowledge of Panama's wildlife is not widely known. But, as Edward Goldman stated in 1922 in a report for the Smithsonian Institute:

It was not until the year 1900 that mammal collecting by modern methods began in earnest. In March of that year, Mr. Wilmot W. Brown, Jr., who was employed by Edward A. and Outram Bangs, began to work in Panama . . . . The results of his extensive scientific work, which also included birds, covering a section with an altitudinal range from sea level to over 11,000 feet, were published by Outram Bangs (1902), and constitute one of the most important contributions made to our zoological knowledge of a single area in Middle America.

Outram Bangs and the Harvard Museum

The funds to finance Brown's expeditions came from Outram Bangs, a wealthy patron of the sciences. Bangs, an avid bird hunter, became a dedicated collector and scholar of birds, and later Chief of Ornithology at the Museum of Comparative Zoology at Harvard University. His dream was to have the most complete collection in existence of birds from Mexico, Central America and the Caribbean. To that end, he hired experienced naturalists and taxidermists. One of the most important contributions to the prestige of Harvard's Museum collections of birds and mammals, were thousands of specimens that the "crazy gringo from Divalá" collected at the turn of the century in the Panamanian forests.

The Smithsonian Institution and the Biological Survey of Panama (1910-1912)

The Panama Canal and Tropical Biology

The contributions made by the Panama Canal to the development of international trade and commerce are very well known. Less known is the stimulus it gave to scientific research in the tropics. As Novencido Escobar succinctly stated "in no other part of the world was so much done for the natural sciences in such a short time as took place here [Panama]."

The canal facilitated transport to Panama and promoted a revolution in public health that, in turn, made scientific work far easier. With vision, canal and Panamanian officials supported a critical mass of scientists who began to converge on the Isthmus at the beginning of the 20th Century.

Since the start of the French efforts to build the canal in the 1880s, naturalists around the world had stressed the need to make exhaustive studies of Panama's flora and fauna. Such pleas were in vain. However, this changed fast after the new century began. In April 1910, at the end of the dry season, the waters of Gatún Lake began to rise behind the huge earthen dam across the Chagres River, creating the largest artificial reservoir known until then. Suddenly, faced with the immediate flooding of 60 villages and over 500 square kilometers of lowland Caribbean forest, the biological evaluation of the area affected by the huge canal works became a top scientific priority.

In the ensuing saga of the quest for knowledge that unfolded in this section of the Isthmus, the Smithsonian Institution, with its headquarters in Washington, D.C., would play a prominent role. Between 1910 and 1912, it carried out the first great biological study ever made of Panama. For the Smithsonian, as well as for the North American scientific community, the Canal marks a milestone in the study of the New World tropics.

The huge work camp at Culebra, headquarters of the Isthmian Canal Commission and field base for the Smithsonian Biological Survey of Panama (1910-1912).
Photo ICC, 1907.

Justification for a Biological Survey

Unlike the Suez Canal, built between 1857 and 1864, through desert sands which did not generate great concerns among naturalists, the linking of the Atlantic and Pacific oceans at Panama presented a major scientific challenge. The tropical nature of this sliver of land, the narrowest and lowest link between North and South America, posed a complex set of scientific concerns. The few studies and collections undertaken, albeit on a small scale and limited primarily to the historical transport route across the Isthmus, suggested that this physically small, narrow territory had an extremely rich flora and fauna. Nonetheless, little was known of the magnitude of this diversity.

Scientists stressed the importance of establishing the precise geographic distribution of the organisms inhabiting the Isthmus, a land bridge that had facilitated the migration of animals and plants between North and South America.

Central to their concerns of the canal's impact upon nature was the formation of Lake Gatún. It was feared that its waters, by inundating the forests of the lower Chagres River, would drown plants and force animals to flee, wiping out many unknown species. Similarly, although it was known that plants and animals living in the Caribbean rivers differed from their Pacific counterparts, the scale of such differences remained uncharted. Another key question revolved around the changes that would result from the mixing of the waters and organisms from both continental slopes. Since the Canal would operate by locks, waters from the Chagres, a Caribbean river, would begin flowing southward past the huge Gaillard cut into the Pedro Miguel and Miraflores locks, and finally, into the Pacific ocean. The mixing of these waters, it was feared, would erase natural differences existing in the distribution of the flora and fauna.

Finally, there was a practical reason for undertaking an extensive biological survey of this magnitude: to augment the Panamanian collections of flora and fauna housed in the natural science museums of the United States. For example, the National Museum in Washington, under the auspices of the Smithsonian Institution, lacked a collection of Panama mammals. The bird collection was minimal, composed primarily of species collected along the Panama Railway and the western highlands of Chiriquí. The collection of freshwater fishes was also poor. At the same time, there existed great interest in comparing isthmian species with South American ones. The museum also lacked samples of terrestrial and fresh water mollusks. With respect to plants, U.S. herbaria lacked sufficient material to be able to compile a general flora of Panama, a work considered to be essential.

Organization and Funding of the Study

Given the magnitude and pace of the canal works, the complexity of tropical ecosystems, and the limited time available, required the rapid and urgent assembly of an inter-institutional, interdisciplinary team of experts. The U.S. government assigned this task to the Smithsonian Institution. A research proposal was prepared and approved by President Taft. He authorized the Smithsonian to obtain assistance from other government agencies, whose support would be vital to the undertaking.

The cost of the study was $11,000. To obtain the money, the Smithsonian Institution resorted to its tradition of appealing to the private sector to underwrite its great explorations and expeditions. Over half of the funds for the biological survey in Panama came from donations made by citizens interested in promoting scientific advances.

Expedition Members

On December 28, 1910, the first group of naturalists disembarked in Cristobal, in the province of Colón. It consisted of two botanists: Francois Pittier, from the Bureau of Industrial Plants, charged with plant collections, and William R. Maxon, curator of the plant collections at the National Museum; two fish specialists, Seth E. Meek and Samuel F. Hildebrand, from the Bureau of Fisheries; two entomologists from the Department of Agriculture, E. A. Schwartz and August Busk, who was to study mosquitoes; and Edward A. Goldman, a zoologist from the U.S. Biological Survey.

Besides the initial group, many other specialists participated, some for short periods, others for longer ones, such as the ornithologist Edward W. Nelson, Dr. Malloch, and Dwight Marsh. Marsh came to Panama for four weeks in the dry season of 1912 to collect samples of fresh water plankton in rivers and lakes. Because there were no large

Excavations on the Panama Canal, circa 1911 or 1912. View of the town of Paraiso at the edge of the Gaillard or Culebra Cut, where a huge channel was built to funnel water from the Chagres, a Caribbean river, to the Pacific. Photo: Panama Canal Commission.

natural lakes, he studied the great reservoirs constructed by the French and the Americans at Cocolí, Río Grande, Camacho, Carabalí, Aguas Claras, and Brazos Brooks.

The expedition headquarters were at Culebra (or Summit), on the continental divide. There, the scientists established a great friendship with Colonels George Goethals and David D. Gaillard, both engineers supervising the canal construction, who greatly facilitated the naturalists' tasks. Goethals, chief of the Isthmian Canal Commission, offered them access to ICC lodging, commissaries, hospitals, restaurants, free train transport, and steamboats. He requested that members of the expedition carry out experiments with native plants that could help to fix the soil and prevent landslides from obstructing the waterway.

The original plan called for a one-year study, limited to the vicinity of the canal excavations. Nevertheless, the scientists soon realized that it was imperative to modify the survey's initial plan and timetable. The natural ranges of the flora and fauna did not coincide with the project's administrative boundaries. It would be imperative to study areas beyond those encompassed by the canal works. In his first field report to the Secretary of the Smithsonian, written on December 1910, Pittier recommended extending the survey beyond the Canal Zone, since the vegetation along the old Panama railroad and the canal was mostly secondary and adventitious. According to him, the truly characteristic and interesting samples of Panamanian flora were to be found in the more remote districts. He was already planning trips to Chepo, Yavisa, Nombre de Dios, and Chiriquí.

The Panamanian government backed up the idea and, with the support of Federico Boyd, then Minister of Foreign Affairs, the biological survey was extended to the entire country. "If it should happen,"wrote Boyd on December 28, 1910, to the American Charge d'Affaires in Panama, Campbell, "that the members of the Smithsonian Institution wish to visit any other Province of this Republic, I request that you will be pleased to so advise me in order that I may ask the proper authorities to lend aid in their inspections."

Individually, or in small groups, the expedition covered nearly all of Panama, from the provinces of Chiriquí and Bocas del Toro on the boundary with Costa Rica, to San Blas (now the Indian Comarca of Kuna Yala) and Darién, on the Colombian border.

Entomologist August Busk, who participated in the Smithsonian Biological Survey of Panama. Photo: Smithsonian Institution Archives, Washington, D.C.
Illustration on pages 86-87:
The rising waters of flooded Gatún Lake and the dying jungle on the lower valley of the Chagres River, 1912.
Photo: Panama Canal Commission.

THE WHITE HOUSE

WASHINGTON

October 27, 1910.

My dear Mr. Walcott:

I have yours of October 27th, in which you seek the
cooperation of the War Department, the Bureau of Fisheries
of the Department of Commerce and Labor, the Department of
Agriculture, and the Isthmian Canal Commission, so far as
may be practicable, in securing a biological survey of the
Panama Canal Zone.   I fully approve your suggestions,
and transmit this letter in order that you may visit these
Departments, confer with their heads, and secure the cooperation necessary.   This I believe, according to your letter,
will include transportation of men and equipment on the
same terms as the Commission's employees on the steamers
between New York and Panama and return, and the transportation of collections; the privileges of purchasing supplies
and medical stores from the Commission on the same terms
as for the Commission's employees; also the use of such tents,
boats, and rooms in houses, etc., as may be available, on
reasonable terms.

I understand that the experts whom you will send will
not exceed ten in number, probably.

Sincerely yours,

W H Taft

Hon. Charles D. Walcott,
     Secretary, Smithsonian Institution,
        Washington, D. C.

Letter from U.S. President William H. Taft to Charles Walcott, Secretary of the Smithsonian
Institution, approving the biological survey of the Panama Canal Zone.
Source: Smithsonian Institution Archives, Washington, D.C.

Results of the Survey

The work performed by members of the biological expedition in Panama from 1910 to 1912 was extremely important to the development of tropical biology. The extraordinary increase in knowledge that resulted was immediately reflected in the number of scientific publications that came out, describing new findings about the country's wildlife and vegetation. In 1912, the Smithsonian Institution published ten articles about discoveries made in Panama. Three by Edward Nelson concerned new bird species, including a hummingbird. William Maxon presented studies of two new species of ferns and mosses, and August Busk announced new species of microlepidopterans (tiny moths). Edward Goldman, who first focused his research in the area of Gatún Lake, announced new findings about the flora and fauna, including twelve new mammal species. Goldman, "the most productive zoologist of the Canal construction era," as John Dwyer described him, would leave us his monumental work *Mammals of Panama*, based on his extensive and detailed studies of eastern Panama and published in 1920 by the Smithsonian Institution. Ichthyologists Meek and Hildebrand published a host of articles on the fishes. Their opus magnum *The Marine Fishes of Panama* was published, beginning in 1923, by the Field Museum of Chicago in three volumes.

Henri Pittier collected 3,600 plant specimens, the majority of them now in the National Herbarium of the United States in Washington. "As an indication of the biological value of the survey," stated an enthusiastic Secretary of the Smithsonian in 1912, "I may mention that only among the grasses about 150 species were collected, four to five times as many as were previously known from that region. In the collections of birds and mammals there are likewise many forms new to science."

The natural history collections belonging to museums in the United States received enormous valuable materials comprising isthmian mammals, birds, fish, reptiles, amphibians, terrestrial and freshwater mollusks, flowering plants, ferns, and microscopic plants.

A surprising number of these specimens were new to science. The original intention was to publish the results of the Smithsonian Biological Survey of Panama in several volumes, as a summary of the flora and fauna of the Isthmus, but this became untenable. Most of the information was therefore published as independently authored articles in different scientific journals, resulting in a loss of the common spirit of joint enterprise that had been generated during the massive field survey. Perhaps this was due to the lack of funds as the First World War erupted in 1914. Maybe it was the inter-institutional composition of the expedition, whose members had to return to their respective academies, each with its own priorities or perhaps it was the psychology of the naturalists themselves, their tenacious pursuit of the objective of each of their own respective studies, their marked individualism, and their reticence to work as a team.

Henri Pittier:
Botanical Studies in Panama
(1897-1916)

Henri Francois Pittier, who conducted several surveys in Panama between 1897 and 1916, was one of the great naturalists from the Panama Canal construction days. He was chief botanist of the Smithsonian Biological Survey of Panama, from 1910 to 1912. In 1911 alone he visited Chiriquí three times and spent 200 days in the field, an enormous achievement given the lack of roads, the intense rain, and his desperate and constant need to dry the plant samples he collected.

Between 1914 and 1915, at the request of Panama's President Belisario Porras, Pittier organized the first exhibit of native timber trees, and contributed to the creation of the country's first agricultural research and extension system.

By the time he died in Venezuela in 1950 at age 93, Henri Pittier had published more than 300 books and articles not only on botany, geography, and agriculture, but also ethnography, for he was passionate about the customs of the indigenous peoples of the American tropics.

A Man from the Alps
with a Taste for the Tropics

Henri was born in Bex, a little Swiss village on the Italian border, the son of Alpine farmers. He was a tall, robust man, who always maintained a formal European demeanor. He was tenacious, driven as he was by a thirst to know all about nature. Son of a carpenter, he obtained one of the best public educations in the world thanks to state scholarships. He received a degree in civil engineering from Lucerne, and a doctorate in natural sciences from Jena, Germany. Between 1882 and 1887, Pittier taught natural history and geography at the University of Lucerne in Switzerland.

In 1887, Pittier accepted an offer from president Ricardo Jiménez to lead a Swiss mission that would establish the foundations of Costa Rica's modern educational system.

Henri Francois Pittier (1857-1950).
Swiss naturalist, botanist, and climatologist, with a passion for the indigenous cultures of the
Americas. Responsible for the botanical studies of the Smithsonian Biological Survey of
Panama, 1910 to 1912.
Photo: Smithsonian Institution Archives, Washington, D.C.

He would learn Spanish and reside in Costa Rica for several years. During his stay, Pittier held a number of posts, including Director of the Physical Geographical Institute. While exploring the Costa Rican flora, he became possessed by the "spirit of the forest," becoming a tropical botanist. He collected plants in Panama for the first time in 1897, at Cañas Gordas in Chiriquí, then in Punta Peña, Bocas del Toro, in 1903.

From 1905 to 1919, Pittier worked as "Special Agent of Botanical Investigations in Tropical Agriculture" for the Bureau of Industrial Plants of the Department of Agriculture of the United States. As a botanist who identified tropical plants with possible industrial potential he conducted many expeditions across Central America, Colombia, and Venezuela.

Culebra, or Summit

On December 2, 1910, the U.S. Department of Agriculture notified Pittier of his assignment as head of botanical collections on the Smithsonian's Biological Survey of Panama. He boarded the steamship *Colón* on December 22, arriving at Colón on December 28.

Pittier settled in Culebra, an enormous encampment at the edge of the canal works and the interoceanic railroad, with access to the very wet Caribbean forests and the dry forests on the Pacific side of the Isthmus. "In compliance with your instructions," he reported to the Secretary of the Smithsonian, "I beg to report my arrival at Colon on December 28 past."

After mature consideration of the conditions, I asked and obtained to be located permanently at Culebra. Besides affording easy communication with the offices that may help in my work, this town, situated on the divide, is the healthiest of the Zone. Its climate is relatively dry, what will lessen the work of drying specimens. Any point on the railroad between Colon and Panama can be easily visited in the day, leaving here in the morning and returning the same day.

All my requests as to quarters, free transportation, etc. have been met with the greatest courtesy by Col. Goethals, and every person I have come in contact with, either in official or private capacity, has shown me much kindness for which I am grateful, and eager desire to help in the fulfillment of my mission.

George Goethals, Chief, of the Isthmian Canal Commission, and David Gaillard, engineer, responsible for digging the Culebra Cut, generously supported the expedition. Pittier lodged in two rooms at the Commission's Hotel. The Zone would offer many facilities to researchers. Pittier's only complaint was the misspelling of his name. In a grumpy complaint he said: "I wish to observe that my name is not H. A. Pittier, but simply H. (Henry) Pittier."

Facing Biodiversity Alone

This is Pittier's description of his first encounter with the awesome diversity of isthmian plants:

My installation was completed Friday night, and yesterday, Dec. 31st 1910, I commenced

Photo on opposite page:
The hydrographic gage station above the village of Alhajuela on the Chagres River, 1911. Photo by A. Busk. Source: *Explorations and Field-Work of the Smithsonian Institution in 1912*. Washington, D.C., 1913.

collecting. At the very start, I had to convince myself of the impossibility of coping single handed with the profusion of plants flowering during the first months of the "verano" or dry season. Having walked about one mile to Rio Grande, I stopped at the first plant that interested me, and there, without moving my press and within a radius of less than fifty meters, I collected eighty-four species in full blossom. And many more were in sight.

He requested that William Maxon, a botanist from the New York Botanical Gardens, be sent to aid him in collecting ferns, mosses, cacti, orchids, and bromeliads. He also hired E. D. Christopherson, a natural history teacher at Gatun High School, as his field assistant to prepare plant specimens. He tried to get his old friend Adolfo Tanduz to work as an assistant, but the latter had left Costa Rica for Guatemala. On January 9, 1911, Pittier sent his first shipment of plants from Panama to the Smithsonian in Washington.

The Zone, the Railway, the Canal, and the Chagres River

Pittier concentrated on the forests of the Canal Zone, along the Canal excavations and the railway. Aware of the value of these surveys, Panamanian authorities requested U.S. officials to allow the naturalists of the Biological Survey to explore other areas of the Isthmus. On January 19, 1911, Pittier received a letter from the Smithsonian, asking him to extend his studies to the rest of Panama. It was a great decision, but it was, as always, limited by the scarcity of funds.

Henri's first expedition outside the Zone was up the Chagres River, as far as the hamlet of Alhajuela. Later, he traveled to Portobelo, on the Caribbean side. He considered these trips to "have been quite rich in botanical results. A good number of my plants, although not new, are additions to the list of species hitherto known from Panama."

Pages 94-95: The rise of Gatún Lake, 1912.
In the background the Panama Railway,
soon to disappear under the waters of the
lake, together with 50 villages and train
stations along the Chagres valley.
Photo by E. Goldman.
Source: *Expeditions organized or participated
in by the Smithsonian Institution in 1910-1911.*

By March 1911, Pittier was out in the highlands of Chiriquí, visiting Boquete, Volcán, Caldera and Cerro Horqueta. He also explored the open grasslands around the towns of David and Remedios. Maxon stayed behind to cross the Central cordillera to the Atlantic side.

In April, Pittier explored sites on the Atlantic side of the Canal: Gamboa, Las Cascadas, Matachín, the Río Indio (a tributary of Gatún Lake), Mamei, the Masambí River, Frijoles, and Bohío. On June 22, he returned from a short trip to Costa Rica, together with a geologist from the Isthmian Canal Commission, D. McDonald, to study Tertiary and Quaternary formations near Puerto Limón.

Trinidad and Cirí Rivers

In July, Pittier ascended the Trinidad and Cirí Rivers, the main western tributaries of the Chagres River, both now flowing into the new Gatún Lake. "We went up for about 30 miles," he wrote in his report, "10 of which in the newly formed swamps above Gatun, and 10 more between high banks and flat forests where the most abundant tree is *Prioria copaifera*, one of the surest indicators of bad lands in this region. Farther up we found gravel beaches, bordering on better soils, with rubber trees (*Castilla*)."

He was highly pleased with the adventure. He wrote to the Secretary:

I accomplished my projected trips up to the Trinidad River and its main affluent the Cirí, with results which, although not so brilliant as I had hoped, give me some satisfaction because of the relative high percentage of new things collected. But I did not collect as many species as I did around Nombre de Dios, and the expense was much higher than in that former expedition. Mr. Saville, of the Canal Commission, kindly offered to make all the necessary arrangements, and I was more or less bound to accept his aid, as he has a better knowledge of conditions on the river. I found however, that we could have managed with a single canoe and two men, instead of the two canoes and four men, and other details could have been simplified so as to reduce the expense. As a general rule, I have found that I can manage better all by myself, only there are cases where it is convenient to accept suggestions and help.

On the Atlantic Coast

On August 18, Pittier returned from a three-week exploration of Nombre de Dios, a forest-covered Caribbean landscape of coastal plains and small hills. "The country visited lately was found exceedingly interesting," he wrote, "the number of species collected is not very large, it is true, but most species are new to my collection." He gathered samples of 50 timber tree species and forwarded them to dendrologist C. D. Mell at the U.S. Forest Service. This shipment consisted of samples of woods, flowers, leaves, and fruits from each tree. The idea was for the Smithsonian Institution to publish an article by Pittier and Mell on Panamanian commercial timber species.

Pittier returned to Nombre de Dios on August 21, 1911, to explore the coast eastward towards San Blas as far as Puerto Obaldía and Cabo Tiburón. On September 13 he was back in Culebra. He considered the trip to be, botanically, quite successful; above all, because he found the forests around Puerto Obaldía to be quite different from those at Nombre de Dios.

Savannas and Forests of the Pacific

During the month of October, Pittier again collected along the Panama railway. He also undertook his first trip to the natural savannas east of Panama City. From Chepo, a town at the edge of both the savannas and forests of Eastern Panama, he prepared his entry into the dense forests of the Bayano River, an area historically controlled by the Kuna people. He returned from Chepo on November 3, 1911.

By November we find him on the savannas and highlands of Western Chiriquí: San Felix, the Dupí River, Hato Jobo, and Remedios. At the end of December he visited the *llanos* or plains of Coclé: Penonomé, Natá, Aguadulce, Olá, and Pocrí. On New Year's Eve 1912, he is in the *llanos* of Remedios, in Chiriquí. Afterwards he traveled east, to Darién, visiting Garachiné, the Sambú River, Punta Patiño, Pavarandó, and Cerro Garagará.

Although Pittier collected many orchids, mainly in the highlands of Chiriquí, as well as all kinds of plants, he paid special attention to the herbaceous species of the Pacific savannas. He collected and classified 300 species of grasses. Pittier concluded his Pa-

nama botanical field studies for the Smithsonian Institution in March 1912.

When Pittier began his explorations, some 1,115 plant species had been catalogued from a limited number of sites in Panama, 80% of them having been obtained from near the railway, the Chagres River, and around Panama City. Pittier collected and classified 1,750 plant species from 154 sites throughout the country. Herrera and Los Santos were the only provinces where he did not do any botanical work.

The final Report:
Latin vs. English

After returning to Washington, Henri and his young and capable assistant, Paul C. Standley, embarked upon the gigantic task of analyzing and publishing the scientific information obtained about the vast collection of Panama plants, many new to science. These publications were meant to be published under the seal of the U.S. National Herbarium and the Smithsonian Institution.

"On account of the large proportion of new or critical species in the collection," Pittier wrote to the Secretary on January 12, 1914, "its complete study by one man would have been almost a life-long undertaking, and the publication of the results would have been delayed indefinitely." It was vital to obtain the inputs of other botanists to "insure effective help in making the Panama Biological Survey a piece of work worthy of the patronage it has enjoyed from the Smithsonian Institution."

Among the European botanists who contributed to Pittier's efforts were Casimir de Candolle, from Geneva; Drs. Radlkofer, from Munich; Lindau, Krause, and Schlechter, from Berlin; and Fritsch, from Vienna. For these Old World naturalists Latin was the scientific language of botanical discoveries.

On August 1913, Dr. Radlkofer sent Pittier his first contribution describing, in Latin, some new Panamanian plants. The Smithsonian Editorial Board returned the manuscript to Pittier, requesting him to translate it from Latin to English. Pittier angrily responded that:

> All botanists feel the impossibility of having typical diagnoses published indiscriminately in any language, particularly in such languages as Russian, Japanese or Chinese, which would, however, have just as much claim to be used as any of the current European languages. In the same way, very few would fail to agree that Latin is, and will remain, the more adequate instrument for the taxonomic description of new types of plants.

> Latin is supposed [he added ironically] to be the most precise technical vocabulary, having been used in botanical work and constantly improved upon for several centuries, it has been selected as the classical language of botany and is to-day used as such by nine-tenths of systematic botanists.

Suddenly, the analysis and publications on the vast collections of isthmian plants rekindled an acrid quarrel within the botanical community on which should be the proper language for scientific discoveries: Latin, the classic language of the sciences until the beginning of the 20th Century; or English, the idiom of the new scientific and technological revolution.

In Solomonic fashion, the Secretary of the Smithsonian decided to publish the manu-

scripts partly in English and partly in Latin. The quarrel regarding the proper language of science delayed the publication of the Panama material, straining relationships between European and North American naturalists. These difficulties faded in 1914, with the beginning of the First World War, which severed communications among the international scientific community.

On January 12, 1914, Pittier drafted a note to the Secretary of the Smithsonian, summarizing his work in Panama, including these lines: "I returned to Washington in March 1912 with over 4000 specimens, to which smaller collections made by various other persons have been added, and since my return I have been working steadily. . . . upon the final classification of these plants, which have proved to be an unusually valuable addition to the National Herbarium."

The Canal Exhibition

Upon completion of Pittier's work for the Smithsonian, Panama petitioned the U.S. Department of Agriculture to have him prepare a collection of timber trees from isthmian forests to be shown at the opening of the Panama Canal Exhibition. Henri turned his attention to forestry, and invested his efforts to "exploring the marvelous forests of Darien on both sides of the Cordillera." Both slopes were botanically almost unknown. On one of these trips he suffered a serious accident. His life was saved by the heroic actions of his Choco Indian companions, who took him to the coast and, unable to find any coastal steamers, paddled him in a fragile dugout canoe to Panama City. Based on these trips to Eastern Panama,

ALL CORRESPONDENCE
SHOULD BE ADDRESSED
TO THE SECRETARY

SMITHSONIAN INSTITUTION.
Washington, U.S.A.

UNITED STATES NATIONAL MUSEUM
INTERNATIONAL EXCHANGES
BUREAU OF AMERICAN ETHNOLOGY
NATIONAL ZOOLOGICAL PARK
ASTROPHYSICAL OBSERVATORY
INTERNATIONAL CATALOGUE OF
SCIENTIFIC LITERATURE

Culebra C. Z., Jan. 9th 1911.

To the Secretary, Smithsonian Institution
Washington D.C.

Sir:

On second thought, I find it advisable to send my plants as soon as they are dry, instead of storing them here until I have enough to fill a box. I have just mailed my first instalment, consisting of two packages. In Washington, they can be easily sheltered from insects and humidity. I beg to suggest that these plants are kept together until I can attend to their preparation for the mounting. They do not even need to be unpacked unless you so desire, as they are thoroughly dry.

I have begun to extend my survey to some distance from the canal works and am going to-morrow to Alajuela, up the Chagres and outside the Zone.

Respectfully

H. Pittier.

One of many letters and field reports sent by Henri Pittier from Culebra to the Secretary of the Smithsonian Institution, Charles D. Walcott.
Source: Smithsonian Institution Archives, Washington, D.C.

Pittier would publish *A Century of Trees of Panama*, co-edited with C. D. Mell. Perhaps it is during this period that he and María Luisa de Meléndez translated into Spanish Berthold Seemann's *Introduction to the Flora of Panama*, a work that would not be published until 1928.

Pioneer of Panamanian Agricultural Research and Extension

Around 1913, Panama's President Belisario Porras asked the United States to send Pittier once more, to help establish the foundations of modern agricultural research in Panama. Pittier arrived in the dry season of 1914. He undertook an evaluation of the appallingly backward condition of the agricultural sector, stressing the "lack of interest of intelligent men for work in the countryside, the abandonment of rural life, the congestion of people in the main urban centers." He felt that Panama, astride a great transit route, should promote agriculture based upon scientific investigation of its own physical and cultural reality. He recommended that the new Republic become a pioneer in the new science of tropical agriculture and refuse imitating the agricultural methods of temperate countries.

Pittier was a key player behind President Porras' decision to create the Agricultural Service within the Secretaría de Fomento (Secretary of Development), at the time under the direction of Ramón Acevedo, with the goal of "promoting the interests of national agriculture." This established the foundation for Panama's agricultural research and extension system. Eventually, the Agricultural Service became Panama's present Ministry of Agricultural Development.

Pittier was entrusted with establishing a center for agricultural research. The government of Panama had no lands available near Panama City, the largest internal market, since they had mostly been appropriatded by the Canal Zone, so that Pittier had to seek a landed patron. He explained his dreams to Mrs. Genarina de la Guardia, who, convinced of the importance of Pittier's ideas, donated 20 hectares of land along the Matías Hernández River, on the road to Juan Díaz. Thus arose the Matías Hernández Experimental Station, Panama's first agricultural research center, with Pittier as its first director from 1915 to 1916.

In one of his last writings on Panama, in 1916, Pittier described land uses in this manner: six tenths at least of the territory of Panama was covered with forests, including all of the Atlantic coast and the Darién. Natural savannas and dry forests on the Pacific occupied another 25%. Only 5% of the land had been cleared for human subsistence; these cleared areas were usually located near the few and scattered settlements. Pittier also classified Panamanian plants as belonging to four life zones: the highlands and lowlands of the Atlantic, and the highlands and lowlands of the Pacific. This classification would be used later on by other naturalists.

Henri Pittier:

Botanical and Ethnographic Studies on the Coasts of Colón, San Blas, and Puerto Obaldía (1911)

In the rainy season of 1911, Pittier explored the forests of the humid Atlantic coast three times . He traveled 280 miles eastward from Colón to Cabo Tiburón, on the Colombian border. First, he visited Portobelo, then Nombre de Dios and Puerto Escribano, the furthest coastal black community to the east, and right on "the border of the Territory of the San Blas Indians," as he jots down in his reports. Finally, he entered the lands of the Kunas, traveling along the Mandinga Peninsula and the entire coast of San Blas until reaching Puerto Obaldía. Here he stayed 13 days, collecting 151 species of trees and shrubs, mostly new to the Panamanian flora and many new to science. He also gathered land shells, zoological specimens, and collected many Kuna words for plants and trees.

Nombre de Dios

Pittier used as his operational bases the large work camps established by the Isthmian Canal Commission at the historic ports of Portobelo and Nombre de Dios. For years, hundreds of Spaniards and West Indians had labored here, extracting stones and sand for the Gatún locks and dam. Nombre de Dios had been established by the Spaniards in 1510, and Portobelo in 1584. According to Pittier, "the present Nombre de Dios is about one mile east of the site of the old Spanish town, destroyed about 1590. The native name of the former is 'Fató,' a word that might be of African origin. The old town site shows only small mounds, remains of houses. Excavations made through a few of them by a former resident physician of the ICC have brought to light a few interesting objects, and the place would be worth searching thoroughly."

Pittier registered the following account of why sand for the huge Gatún locks and dam could not be procured from the San Blas Kunas but had to be extracted from the black coastal community of Nombre de Dios: "I am told that when Col. Sibert visited the coast of San Blas, in quest of good sand for the building for the Gatun dam, he first fixed his choice on the deposit at the mouth of a river in the Calidonia Bay. He tried to buy the right of exploitation from the Indian chiefs. But one of them, very old, told him: 'We cannot sell you sand. He who made it, made it for the past generations, for the present ones, and for the ones to come. How could we sell you that in which we have only a life interest?' So Col. Sibert had to fix his choice on the Fató's sand."

Origins of the *costeño* or Black Coastal Communities

To the east and the west of the Caribbean entrance of the Panama Canal lie stretches of white coralline beaches, dotted by coconut groves, here and there small villages of black people, known in Spanish as *costeños*. They are the descendants of the old *cimarrones* or runaway slaves, who fought vehemently against Spanish domination. The eastern sector of the coast is known as *costa arriba* or upper coast; to the west lies the *costa abajo* or lower coast. Pittier provides us with a unique insight into the life of the *costeño* communities of the upper coast of Colón at the time of the building of the canal.

"As the tradition has it," writes Pittier in his notes:

the forefathers of the present negro population were slaves escaped from Porto Bello.

Portobelo in 1911, where thousands of Spanish and Jamaican workers quarried rock for the Isthmian Canal Commission to use in the construction of the gigantic Gatún Dam. Photo by Henri Pittier. Source: Field Museum Archives, Chicago.

They founded a large village in the upper valley of the Santa Isabela, in the middle of hostile Indians [Pittier is referring to the Kuna], who later drove them to the coast, along which they gradually extended westward. They sustained perpetual warfare with the Indians, but seem to have been very little hostilized by the Spaniards, who had enough to do protecting Porto Bello and the road to Panama City. Little by little, these negroes drove away the Indians from the cocoplantations along the coast as far as the Sta. Catalina River, east of Pto. Escribanos. And they are still encroaching today. But the Indians object being thus dispossessed and up to about 1885 there were frequent fights between the invaders and the legitimate occupants of the land. The former would go along the coast, scare away the families of the latter and steal their coconuts and their canoes. Then the Indians would reach the negro villages from inland, marching along the foot of the hills, and sack and burn them. At Fató, the people place the last attack at 1884 or 1885.

The Economy of *Costeño* Society

Pittier, a man of many talents and interests, not only tirelessly collected and classified plants unknown to science, but also recorded anthropological and economic information on *costeño* society: "The coast belt, from Nombre de Dios to Puerto Escribanos," he jotted down:

is an almost continuous Coconut Palm plantation, interrupted only at a few places by large estuaries and mangrove patches. Coconut are, with the ivory nut and the balata gum, the principal export products of the country.

The villages, rather numerous, are scattered along the coast, their thatch and cane huts regularly disposed in long parallel rows facing the beach. Some of these villages, as Viento Frio and Culebra, owe their existence to former manganese mines, today abandon-

ded. The whole zone is a negro country, settled originally by slaves escaped from Porto Bello. But as a general rule, these negroes are clean, laborious and rather prosperous. Each family owns its house on the beach, and somewhere inland, in the bush, its rice field, banana plantation and patches of cassava and yuca. These give them their food. The other necessities of life are obtained from the sale of coconuts, (selling today at $34 per thousand), ivory nuts and balata. Life is so simple among them, and the requisites for food, clothing, pleasures, etc., so few, that the necessity for money scarcely exists. So, even though labor is plenty, no large enterprise would be likely to succeed in this region, at least for the present.

The Tagua Palm and the Cascuá Tree

During the 19th Century, one of the most important exports from the Isthmus, and a principal cash source for the *costeño* communities, had been the extraction of *tagua*, or the vegetable ivory nut. Pittier left us the following account on the distribution of this valuable palm:

In my first visit to Nombre de Dios, I made an excursion up the Fató Valley, interesting on account of its very extensive groves of Ivory-Nut Palms. I repeated the trip, extending it to about 12 miles into the interior, up to the foot of the high hills, without however reaching the upper limit if the Ivory Palm belt. That palm grows only in the river bottoms with rich clayey sands, and under the shade of many species of high trees, among which I recognized a Iloanea, a Mimusops, a Coccobola, and several others as the Iguanero, Almendro, etc, not yet botanically identified. In these same forests I was lucky enough to find again the *Cascuá* or *Namaguá,* incomplete specimens of which were collected for the first time by B. Seemann in 1846. . . . This tree is of a great economic importance among the Indians, who use the fiber to "manufacture sails for their canoes, garments and mats to sleep upon". So says Seemann, but to-day the sails are made of common canvas, and the garments from fabrics sold by the traders.

Níspero Rubber

During the second half of the 19th Century, several tropical trees had found a market for their rubbery sap, one of them being the Níspero. This is Pittier's account of it:

The gum of the Níspero tree, a Mimusops, is now exported from this country in very large and increasing quantities. The identity of that gum with the balata of British Guayana, extensively used for the insulation of electrical wires was discovered about 6 years ago by a Mr. Wilcox, a trader of the San Blas coast. Since then, the exportation of that new product from Panama has been on a rapid increase. I have studied the way the milk is collected and prepared. West of Mandinga Bay, the trees are bled in the same way the Castilla trees are, but I am told that the Indians fell the trees and tap them on the ground, a process that will bring quick destruction of that useful tree.

La Gloria Hill and the Río Indio de Fató

On the back of Nombre the Dios, or rather Fató, there is a heavily timber hill called "Loma de la Gloria". From the American settlement, distant about one mile, I located with my glasses about a dozen trees in bloom, which I would then hunt with the help of my guides and fell. Two or three of them are absolutely new to me and I cannot even place them in their families; other appear to be co-types of species known only from Panama, and all are used in one way or another in the native industry. So I collected not only botanical specimens, but also samples of wood. . .

On the 23rd, I made a complementary excursion along the ridge that leads inland from the "Loma de la Gloria", a really "glorious"

locality from the point of view of botany, raising just back of Fató, between the Nombre de Dios and Fató Rivers. On the 24th, I went by sea to the "Rio Indio de Fató", which empties in a spacious bay of the coast of Nombre de Dios. There I observed very remarkable features of the mangrove formation, and also met for the first time in Panama with three palms, the investigation of which has been especially recommended by Mr. O. F. Cook, our authority on the group.

On his return from Río Indio de Fató, Pittier was threatened by a storm out at sea, and according to him, his dugout canoe was prevented from sinking, thanks only to the "strength and audacity of my native helpers." Thoughtfully he wrote: "how frequently these narrow escapes occur in the life of an explorer."

Santa Isabel

On August 25, 1911, while in Nombre de Dios, Pittier boarded a small gasoline powered boat, the *Union* (formerly the *Elsmere*, an old Boston-built yacht). Every two weeks, the launch, under captain Calvert, carried passengers and mail along Panama's eastern Caribbean coast. On board, he met E. D. Christopherson, a schoolteacher from Gatún High School, who had repeatedly begged Pittier to employ him as his field assistant. Pittier hired him for $20 a month, plus travel expenses. The *Union* set off, arriving at sunset at Santa Isabel, which Pittier described as:

. . . .the last "civilized" settlement along that coast. It is a negro village, and the only evident signs of civilization are in fact the presence of a Panamanian Police Inspector, and schools for boys and girls that are elementary in all respects, and a "commissary" where bad alcoholic liquors constitute the principle article of commerce, being mostly bartered for coconuts, ivory nuts and balata.

We left Sta. Isabela again at about 1 am on 26th, entering a region not yet visited by me and, in fact, "terra incognita" as far as its natural productions are concerned. We followed first the northern shore of the Peninsula of Mandinga, the interior of which has never been investigated by any white man and is full of wonders according to the natives. There is a very extensive lake emptying partly in the deep bay of Escribanos, partly through a branch of Rio Sta. Isabela. This lake, a paradise for alligators and mosquitoes, is hidden among precious hills, densely covered with forest, and in which there are deep caves.

Political Divisions in San Blas: Robinson and Inapaquiña

Pittier arrives at the Archipelago of San Blas, inhabited by the Kuna people, at a time of great political and cultural stress. Some villages wanted to be part of the new Republic of Panama; others considered they should remain within Colombia. The 20th Century struck the Isthmus like a hurricane. The Kunas, like other ethnic groups in Panama, had to decide how to deal with what seemed an endless sequence of social and cultural innovations imposed upon them by the outside world. For the white elites of Panama, "modernization" meant that all ethnic minorities, like the Kunas, had to blend with the mestizo, Spanish speaking majority, as well as dress and dance in a western fashion.

Lets us now return to the narrative of our naturalist:

After reaching the Punta de San Blas, we entered the very dangerous Archipelago of the Mandingas or of San Blas, where hundreds of shoals and islands, these mostly diminu-

tive ones, are scattered, to the great inconvenience of navigation. We never would have gone through, it being nighttime, without the help of several experimented San Blas Indians, who were on board as passengers. Among them was Charles Robinson, the supreme authority on this coast and as representating the Panamanian Government. As a boy about 6 years old, Robinson was taken to the States by a trader, receiving there a good education. He came back when about 20 years old, to live in his native village, Nárgana. The Republic of Panama invested him with the authority of a chief, but there seemed to be another supreme "cacique", whose title is hereditary, and who lives, it is said, at Aligandi. For every village there seems to be two factions, the one supporting Robinson, the other Inapaquiña, the hereditary chieftain, the former well inclined toward strangers, the other quite adverse to them. And this is what makes it so difficult for a foreigner to penetrate among them. On account of the factional spirit, the Indians west of Aligandi acknowledge the Panamanian flag, while those farther down the coast, including Aligandi, hoist the Colombian flag as soon as any large vessel approaches their shore.

Nárgana

We reached Nárgana at dawn, and did not stop there long enough to go ashore. My first intention had been to stay there, but Charles Robinson could not be made to give his approval to the plan, not because he was personally unwilling as I could well see, but because he felt uncertain about the feelings of his people. For botanical purposes, I realized that Port Obaldía would do just as well, if not better, so when we arrived at Nárgana I had already made up my mind to go on to the end of the yacht's run.

Nárgana is a large village on two small islands about 300m apart and fronting the mouth of the Diablo River or Tíguala. The big houses are closely packed together and cover the whole surface of both islands. Each house is about 50m long by 10m broad, with a gable roof 10 to 12m high at the middle ridge. That roof covered with palm thatch, is suspended by posts that divide the interior in many square spaces, each of which is occupied, as it seems, by one family. These squares are disposed in two lateral rows, separated by a common passage just under the highest part of the roof. The side walls, made of split palm trunks, bamboo, and other canes or sticks, and not over 2m. high. The doors are at both ends, just under the gable, and are very low for an American or European of average size, as the San Blas Indians themselves are seldom over 5 feet.

Pittier considered that every house lodged between 14 and 20 families, each family with an average of 5 individuals.

The Nárgana Indians own most of the innumerable coconut palm-covered islands around their village, and their cornfields, rice fields, and other plantations are on the mainland along the Tíguala River. Their village is the only one where priests, of the Roman Catholic Church, are allowed, and one of them, Father Gazó, has resided there for many years, but I was told with few practical results. Father Gazó seems to be quite familiar with Tule or Kuna languages, and it would be worth the while for the Bureau of Ethnology to investigate about the possibility of obtaining from him the necessary elements for a thorough study of that language, the place of which has never been clearly settled. I have been myself one of the advocates of the theory that there is a close relationship between the Indians of the Central American Coast of the Atlantic, including Panama, and the Chibcha stock, but I am sorry to confess that the personal observation that I have been able to make on this trip go strongly against an idea that rested mainly on [Alphonse Pinart's] very unreliable vocabulary.

The Coast from Nárgana to Pinos Island

At about 7am. we sailed from Nárgana, continuing our route eastward in close proximity of the coast. The day was a glorious one, cloudless and full of wonderful tropical light. And the country in sight, made more clear and beautiful by the former could only awake the explorer's desire to be given the opportunity to see it at shorter range. At times, the forest-covered hills reached to the shore, at others the country is flat and open where large rivers descend from the mountains. The divide between the Pacific and the Atlantic, however, is always close to this coast, so that there is really no space for the development of any considerable water system. The numerous gaps that appear on the main ridge indicate so many facilities of transit from the Atlantic to the extense drainage basins of the Bayano and Chucunaque rivers. The highest, dome shaped mountains, hardly reach 1300m. of altitude and many of the passes must be below 300m.

Faulty Maps

One of the most daunting challenges for naturalists and explorers of the Isthmus had been the lack of good maps. Those available until quite late in the 20th Century had major errors on the contour of the coastlines or the exact course of streams and mountains. It was easy to get lost in the forest. Pittier paid great attention to the general limitation of the existing charts:

Every time we had the opportunity to compare our maps with the details of the coast, we can convince ourselves of the imperfection of the former. The coast-line is mostly wrong and the nomenclature needs a thorough revision. Topographic mistakes cannot very well be indicated in writing, so I will cite only one case, and not the most important. Pinos Island is drawn as an elongated body of land, about twice as long as it is broad. In fact, it is almost perfectly circular, so as to appear from every side the same size, with the characteristic aspect to which it owes its Indian name "Tubapaki", i.e. Whale Island. The name Pinos Island is in no way due to the presence of pines there. "Pin", in the language of the coast Indians, means the "Espavé" (*Anacardium Rhinocarpus*), a well known tree of Tropical America, which forms the main element of the primeval forest of the island.

The Kuna Language and Place Names

As to the nomenclature of the several places along the coast, every indigenous name has its signification and the mode of their formation is very uniform, two circumstances that makes it easy to discover any misspelling. Most of those names end in "gandi" and not a small number in "gana". This last word means "many", and is the plural suffix, or postfix, in the Kuna language. Thus "Pino-gana" means "(a place of) many Anacardii"; "narr" is a species of palm, Nárgana is the place where this certain palm is abundant, etc. "Di" means water or river and "gandi" is a contraction of "gana-di". "Ali" or "Agali" means mangrove, Aligandi is the river of the many mangroves. But many of those names cannot be translated as they are written in the map; thus we should have: Pingandi = river of many Anacardii, instead of Pitgandi. Putugandi = river of many partridges, and not Portogandi. Napagandi = river of many calabashes, and not Navagandi. Cuibgandi = river of many Cavannillesia trees and not Cuigandi. Further, we should have Azachu-cum = bay of the dog's nose and not Ana-chucuna; Shia-tinaca = mouth of the Cacao River, and not Chotinaca; Chachardi = river of an unknown tree, and not Sasardi.

On August 26, after traveling all day, the *Union* reached Caledonia Bay at dusk, and arrived in Puerto Obaldía, near the border with Colombia, at midnight.

Puerto Obaldía

Port Obaldía is a recently established frontier post of the Panamanian Government, situated more or less where the village of Armila, near Cape Tiburón, stands on the map of the War Department. It is approximately 160 nautical miles to the southeast of Colon, and the ground on which it stands has been taken from the Armila Indians, notwithstanding their protest. But for the barracks, the schoolhouse, and the residence of the officer in charge, it is a conglomeration of some 25 miserable shacks and huts, inhabited mostly by Colombian negroes and a few Panamanians deported there for being inveterate drunkards. The armed force of 20 men is composed of 18 Colombians, 1 Spaniard, and 1 American: it is to be born in mind that this is a Panamanian garrison, on the border of Colombia! As these sons of Mars are quite inactive, they all suffer with malaria or some other disease, and the remainder of the people, when in the village, spend their time in drinking bouts, balls and the celebration of their religious feasts, which occur 3 to 4 times a week.

Mr. Navas, the founder of Port Obaldía and its chief, received us with every courtesy, and did everything in his power to be of use to me during the 13 days I spent there or near by. The school-house was put at my disposal, and as it was relatively sheltered from the nocturnal rains, it was really a boon to have it, even if I did spend most of my nights fighting the ants!

Tropical Forests and the Extraction of Níspero Latex

I lost no time in starting the exploration of the surrounding forest, the composition of which is remarkably distinct from that around Sta Isabela or Nombre de Dios. The Mimusops or Balata tree is still the dominating tree, but contains orders, as the Moraceae and Lecythidaceae, acquire here an unexpected importance. Among the first, I discovered a new

Castilla, which however does not yield rubber and I was given the opportunity to get acquainted with the *Galacto Dendrón* or Cow-milk tree, as well as with several other species, some of which will certainly prove new to science. Of the Lecythidaceae, represented in the Canal Zone by one or two species only, I observed and collected six species, a few of which have fine and valuable wood. I obtained the fruit of two Monkey-pot trees, and was surprised to learn that the natives ignore absolutely the nutritive value of the nuts, similar to the Brazil nut. Many other highly interesting trees were collected, among them a Sapotacea which must be undescribed, and a new Sapium, the Cerillo, economically important. Referring again to the níspero or Balata tree, I have to modify one of my anterior statements: the San Blas Indians do occupy themselves with the extraction of the balata gum. The Fató and Portobelo people simply bleed the standing trees, but the Palenque and Sta. Isabela negroes fell the same, killing them outright. At Port Obaldía, the balata trade is carried only by a few Sta. Lucia negroes, and the forests still hide large fortunes in that line.

Gathering *Tagua* Nuts

The ivory nut-palm is also an important product of this district. A remarkable feature is that, while around Fató that palm assumes universally a creeping habit, it rises from one to seven meters in the forest of Armila and Port Obaldía. I am not familiar enough with the Palms to decide whether we have to do with distinct species, or if the difference in habitats is simply the result of distinct conditions of environment. . . . The Phytelephas-groves [*tagua* trees] are here limited in extension, and they people the ground under the high forest trees to the almost complete exclusion of other underbrush. Indians and negroes spent part of their lives in those forests, collecting the nuts from the ground. The ones on the trees are generally too soft to be of any commercial value.

Kuna Men:
Physical Aspect and Clothing

Almost daily I had opportunities to converse and get acquainted with Armila, Pito and Shiatiwaka Indians, who were busy fishing along the coast. I found them a lot very superior to the so-called civilized negroes, who live shamelessly of what they can extract from the legitimate owners of the soil. All these Indians are healthy looking, of low stature but strongly built. Their hair is cut short and they are beardless. They dress like all the natives, i.e. with a cotton shirt, usually blue, and pants of the same color, but of stronger materials. When they have a hat, the form is much smaller than the head of the owner, on the top of which it is awkwardly perched.

Kuna Women:
Appearance, Ornaments, and Clothing

At Armila the first Indian village west of Port Obaldía, I had for the first time the occasion to examine well a few woman....First of all, these women cannot be said to be ugly as a rule and many of them could even be called pretty, but for their cropped hair and the gold nose ring that is universally worn by them, being inserted at a very tender age. At Nárgana, I saw about 50 little girls congregated in the shed used as a church. It was pretty dark and while the intelligent little faces were only dimly distinguishable, the gold rings hanging from their tiny noses formed long bright lines in the semi-darkness. The rings have all the same shape and weight and are made in the villages by native goldsmiths, with gold collected in the alluvium of the rivers or bought outside. Those rings are also in the trade. In their ears, the married women often wear large gold discs hung in the same way the earrings of our white ladies are, and their throat is adorned with a few rows of cheap beads or red coral. These, however, seem to be an exception, the neck being in most cases quite free.

A *tagua* collector in the forests near Portobelo, 1911.
Until the dawn of the 20th Century, before the invention of plastics, one of Panama's major exports was non timber forest products such as the nuts from the *tagua* palm.
Photo: E. A. Goldman, *Mammals of Panama*. Smithsonian Institution, Washington, D.C, 1920.

I had no time nor opportunity to investigate thoroughly their physical characters but my impression is that both men and women differ in many details of their bodies from the Santa Marta and Costa Rican Indians, both of whom I am very well acquainted with. So, if the Kuna Indians belong to the Chibchan stock, the Guaymies, Bribri, and other affiliated tribes of Costa Rica, Nicaragua and Honduras do not. And if these latter are really the farthest remnants of a Chibchan migration or expansion, the links showing the route of said migration should be sought for in southern Darien or elsewhere.

These San Blas Indians are all small, and the body is unusually developed in comparison with the limbs, being long and broad. The nose is very long and often aquiline. The head

A *tagua* collector with his harvest of nuts on the *costa arriba* or Eastern Colón province.
Photo from E. A. Goldman: *Mammals of Panama*. Smithsonian Institution, 1920.

is mostly round and large. The color is between 3 and 5, or between dark reddish-brown and copper in the men, but commonly much lighter in women.

At Armila, I had also the opportunity to observe the wife of the chieftain, who is evidently the villages' belle. Besides wearing the usual nosering and ear disc, her legs were encased in three bands, about 3 cm. broad and made of beads of several colors. These ornaments must have been put on when the calves were still small, as these were now divided into two separate and bulging parts. . . . The chieftain's wife had on her gala garments of appliqué work [mola], both skirt and waist. . . . No woman was seen with painted face, and all had beautiful, well kept white teeth.

At Puerto Obaldía, some of the boys of Shiatinaca we saw had a thin strait blue line, traced with jagua sap or dye, along the ridge of their nose, and a "lele", or medicine man of the same village had evidently rouge (achote dye) on his prominent checks, but these were the only instances of face paintings.

Kuna men commonly wore hats as well as cotton shirts and trousers, preferably blue. Photo by E. D. Christopherson, 1912. STRI Archives, Washington, D.C.

The use of a golden nose ring was a common practice among Kuna women. The ring, in addition to being decorative, was used in barter. Photo: H. Pittier, 1912, possibly in Nárgana or Armila. STRI Archives, Washington, D.C.

In other women I had occasion to notice, the garments were of simpler materials. The innermost visible piece is a short skirt, red or blue, extending from the hips to the knee. The upper part of the body is covered with a loose blouse, the sleeves of which do not reach the elbow. Over these two pieces there is a second skirt, reaching from the waist to the ankles. Both skirts consist of a piece of calico, each being 6 to 8 yards long. . . . Larger boys seen elsewhere wore in their ears the same discs often seen in women, but they were never worn by male adults.

At Armila and Pito, the houses were smaller than those seen at Nárgana, and sheltered only one or two families each. There seem to be numerous local variations, not only in the way of building the houses, but also in customs, clothing and language.

The language is the same, with slight variations, all along the coast. Besides collecting on my trip several hundred words, I have brought back a young boy-servant, with whom I am continuing the study of the language.

I wish to state one mere fact about funerals. . . . A big square ditch, about 3x3x2m. is dug, and solid stakes are planted at about 1.50m. from the bottom at two diagonally opposed angles. On these stakes the hammock of the deceased, containing his extended body, is hung, and provisions are laid by the side, on the bottom of the hole. Then the grave is covered by a horizontal roof, the upper surface of which, on a level with the surrounding surface, is covered with a thick layer of earth.

It has often been said that it is impossible to travel from one coast to the other in the region inhabited by the Indians. From what information I have been able to gather, there is a wild tribe, hostile to both Coast Indians and non-Indians, occupying the headwaters of the Bayano and Chuqunaque Rivers, and the corresponding part of the northern watershed. But the transit is free between Sta. Isabela and the Mamoní River to the west, and from Pito to the Membrillo River to the east. Travelers passing in one day from the San Blas coast to the southern watershed.

Pittier started his return trip from Puerto Obaldía on September 9, making a quick visit to Nárgana, where, according to him, he had the opportunity to take the first photographs ever made of San Blas women. The permission from the husband cost $1.25. On the 13th, he arrived at Culebra on the banks of the Canal, his operational headquarters. Jubilantly, he concluded that he had done it with "all my collections in good shape and satisfied to have succeeded relatively well in this first trip of a naturalist along the San Blas Coast!"

The historic village of Gatún on the Chagres, before the construction on the huge dam and locks for the Canal. Photo taken during the 1890's by an unknown photographer. Source: Smithsonian Institution, National Anthropological Archives, Washington, D.C.

Henri Pittier:
Chiriquí in the Dry Season of 1911

The Topography of the Isthmus and the Survey Strategy

In 1911, Henri Pittier explored the province of Chiriquí three times. Intrigued by the topography of the S-shaped Isthmus–high on both ends, narrow and flat in the center–, he concentrated his fieldwork in the higher, less explored mountainous peaks at the western and eastern borders of Panama. He also aspired to clarify the relationships between Panama's flora and fauna and that of the highlands of nearby North and South America. "Panama," he said in his report, "is hardly a country for mountaineering, most of its area being below the 3,000-foot contour line." And:

> The highest elevations are in the western part, which is an extension of the Costa Rican system. There, the Chiriqui Peak, or Volcán de Chiriqui, as it is more commonly called, attains 11,000 feet and is worth ascending. Farther eastward and on the main divide, several bold peaks can be seen from both coasts; they very likely reach the 10,000-foot line, but they have never been ascended, and their exact altitude, names, and even their true geographic position are still to be recorded.

> The same can be said of the eastern-most group of high ranges, on the Colombian border, an undeciphered mass of domes and peaks, which have never been explored, and whose real relation to the western Cordillera of Colombia has never been ascertained. It is almost certain, however, that they form an independent system, and that the old notion of the South American Andes forming also the backbone of the Central American Isthmus should no longer appear, as it often does, in modern writings.

According to Pittier,

> from the naturalist's standpoint, these highest mountains at both ends of the Panamanian territories are of special interest. As few or no collectors have ever visited them, they are likely to be the abode of many unknown forms of both vegetable and animal life. They are also the most advance[d] outposts of the fauna and flora of neighboring countries. Besides, they are attractive even to the ordinary tourist, on account of their beautiful scenery, and

of the marvelous changes observed within a few hours as one rises from the lower to the upper regions, experiencing at the same time a corresponding variation in climatic conditions. This is best seen in the ascent of the Chiriquí Volcano, the summit of which can be reached on three days from David by way of El Boquete.

Preparations for the Expedition

Aware of the botanical richness of Panama, Pittier asked the Smithsonian for an assistant. On January 19, 1911, he was notified that William R. Maxon, plant curator of the New York Botanical Garden, would accompany him in his expeditions to the Chiriquí highlands, to study and collect ferns, mosses, orchids, and cacti.

Pittier wanted to begin his work in Chiriquí by the end of January, but the New Year began badly. Returning from Portobelo, in an Isthmian Canal Commission tugboat, he fell in the dark, breaking several bones in his hand. Then he lost a trunk with photographic equipment, which his friend Colonel Goethals managed to find before Pittier departed for Chiriquí.

While convalescing, Goethals asked Pittier to determine if the unexpected mass of floating aquatic vegetation found in the newly formed Lake Gatún could interfere with canal navigation in the future. Later, Colonel C. Mason, superintendent of Ancón Hospital (today, Gorgas Hospital), begged him to study and identify the numerous trees found at the site of this medical center, some dating to the French era. Mason wanted to create an arboretum of Panamanian flora at Ancón.

Maxon arrived in Panama on February 3. Pittier had everything ready to sail to David on the 10th. Immediately, he was faced with a disconcerting pattern, constant in isthmian life: the high price, low quality, and unreliable public transportation. He had paid $80 for three round trip tickets, Panama City-David, for himself, Maxon, and a porter. He carried an additional $80 to pay for guides and porters in Chiriquí, plus $60 for lodgings in Boquete. Arriving at the dock, they found that they had lost their berths, which had been unexpectedly taken up by the large entourage of the Minister of Government and Justice. Pittier finally departed on February 23.

Geology and Topography of the Plains around David

Setting off from Pedregal, the port of David, they took the horse trail that, meandering across the dry savannas of the Pacific, ascended to Boquete, a small coffee-growing and resort town at the foot of the Central Cordillera. From here, they wanted to explore the areas surrounding the Volcán Barú (or Volcán de Chiriquí), the highest point on Panama's continental divide. They also hoped to reach its summit. For Pittier, the savannas around David, with their subsoil formed by deep horizontal layers of marine sands, seemed to have emerged quite recently from the sea. The banks of rivers and streams along the path seemed to him like a book on the geological past of Chiriquí.

Pittier's narrative resumes as the group gradually ascended northward:

David stands at about 12 miles from the seashore, in an open, slightly undulating coun-

Members of the Smithsonian expedition on the peak of the Barú Volcano, Panama's highest point. To establish the relationship between the flora of Panama and that of North and South America, Pittier concentrated his field-work on the higher mountain zones at both ends of the Isthmus, Chiriquí on the west and Darién to the east.
Photo by Henri Pittier. Source: "*National Geographic*" magazine, Vol. 23, 1912.

try. It is one of the most rapidly improving towns of Panama, on account of the varied and abundant resources offered by the surrounding country and the affluence of foreign European and American settlers. . . .

The deep ravines, cut through these terraces by the many streams descending from the mountains, allow an insight into the recent geological history of the district. Thick layers of a fine sand, almost horizontal and apparently devoid of organic remains, show that the whole plain is an ancient sea-bottom, uplifted at a not very remote time, either by some sudden cataclysm, or insensibly by the slow process that governs the emergence and subsidence of coastal lands all over the globe. In former explorations, in the adjoining parts of Costa Rica, I have noticed the same indication of a general upheaval, the neck of the Osa Peninsula still showing unmistakable evidences of a recent, broad sea-channel, and bluffs, bearing the peculiar relief due to the action of the waves, lifted to nearly 300 feet above sea-level.

According to Pittier, many years ago the Chiriquí Viejo River flowed into Golfo Dulce on the Costa Rican side of the border, but as the seacoast rose, its mouth moved east of Punta Burica to the Panamanian side.

Vegetation of the Savannas

Most of the flat country about David is utilized as grazing land, and during the dry season it is constantly swept by the strong trade wind, reaching over the mountains through the deepest depressions of the Cordillera. Only in sheltered places along the rivers, behind the knolls that rise here and there, and around the houses, is there any show of arborous vegetation, among the most conspicuous representative of which may be cited the algarrobo and the corotú. The tamarind and mango, two East Indian trees now naturalized all over the tropics, and the native wine and plum palms, are the trees most generally seen around the houses. Extensive forests, displaying the luxuriant and generous proportions of real tropical vegetation, are found only at some distance to the west, on the lands adjoining the Chiriquí Viejo River, or to the east, between Gualaca and Horconcitos.

Wind Marks on the Rocky Savannas towards Boquete

Going north in the direction of the Chiriquí Peak, one is soon struck by the peculiar range of low hills running, as it seems, between the plains and the mountains, and parallel to the sea-coast. The road winds between these and, mostly following the Dolega River, ascends gradually toward El Boquete. The general incline is so insensible that one travels nearly 25 miles before reaching the foot of the volcano, at an altitude of about 3,000 feet. The ride is mainly across savannas, or through what ecologists call a park-like landscape.

During the dry season, the long stretches bare of arborous vegetation are constantly swept by the north trade wind, which attains its major intensity between 9 o'clock a.m. and 3 o'clock p.m., and is often of such violence that even the horses find it difficult to stand and to proceed on their way. Every detail of the surrounding landscape bears the impress of the wind. In the most exposed places, the surface of the soil is submitted to active aerial erosion, the minute particles of ground being whisked away the moment they become loose.

The meager sod is characteristic in appearance, consisting not of a continuous carpet of grasses as in most savannas, but of isolated tufts of sedges and small plants (mainly *Leguminosae* and *Rubiaceae*), distinguished by the unusual development of their root system.

Many an acre is absolutely bare, and at places long stretches of stones running from north to south, are explained by the natives as being remnants of former eruptions of the volcano. They are really what is left of low ridges demolished by the wind.

In hollow places, as along the dry bed of creeks that flow only during the wet season, the trees show some attempts at congregating in small groves; but they have a stunted appearance, their trunks are twisted and knotty, their limbs few, and all strikingly growing in a southerly direction.

The few head of cattle browsing through these thinned savannas are shaggy, and even the people and their dwellings, the former with their large hats tied upon the head, and the latter with roofs half gone, or mended temporarily with leaves of the native royal palm, show the permanent action of the wind.

Not to impress the reader too deeply with the dreary barrenness of the country, it should be added that to the south-side exposures of the hills and deeper valleys offer sheltered nooks, with prosperous villages surrounded by patches of grassy pastures and of forests.

Through this rather desolate region several rivers have cut deep, narrow canyons, in which subtropical vegetation is mixed in a curious way. Oak are seen growing next to palms, giant elms mingling their branches with those of the towering ficus, and, among herbaceous plants, clematis and nettles side by side with showy bignonias and fragrant epiphytic orchids. Bathed in the perpetual but never excessive dampness of the foaming river, sheltered from wind and strong nightly radiation by the high surrounding walls, and with an atmosphere incessantly renewed, the hidden recesses of these gorges assume, indeed, a singularly beautiful appearance. They are, however, difficult of access, and not only teem with insect life, but offer favorite refuge for snakes, which are attracted by the latter and, by the many small mammals.

Boquete: Coffee and Tourism

Near El Boquete, the road leaves the savannas to penetrate into the upper Caldera Valley. This is the favorite summer resort of the Panamanians and of many Canal Zone Americans, and also the only coffee-growing section of the whole Republic. On account of prohibitive tariff, the latter is one of the best paying products of native agriculture, and several foreigners have established here prosperous plantations. But El Boquete, half in the windy semi-arid zone and half in that of continued rains, has a very limited producing capacity, and cannot by far supply the rapidly increasing coffee consumption of the larger centers. It is not equipped, either, for a summer resort, as the "Hotel de Lino" is simply a farmhouse, where abundant meals and a kindly hospitality are the welcome, but sometimes inadequate compensations for the lack of worldly comfort.

At the Lino Hotel, Pittier paid $4 a day, which included food and lodging for three people. From this coffee-growing town nested in a valley and crossed by the Caldera River he would explore the nearby highlands.

The Magnificent Highland Forests of Boquete

"We located at El Boquete," Pittier told the Secretary of the Smithsonian, C. D. Walcott, in a report dated from Culebra for April 6, 1911:

and found the middle and upper valley of the Caldera River very interesting floristically. It is in close proximity to the interoceanic divide, so that at short distances types of both the xerophilous and hygrophilous vegetation can be found. The district is wonderfully rich in orchids, some of which are beautiful, and as Mr. Maxon has made a good collection of them, we hope to have soon in Washington the living specimens of many of the specific types of the Warzcewicz collection, made in the sixties (1863?) in the same region.

The forests of El Boquete are simply magnificent, and I wish I could find English words to give you even a short description. They are especially rich in Lauraceae, Cedrelaceae and Euphorbiaceae, all of portly dimensions; also, one of the dominating species is a giant elm, which I never met in other parts of Central America. Of course, it is very difficult to get botanical samples of these trees, but I have been rather successful in that line and hope to be able to fill many gaps in the U.S. Nat. Herbarium.

"To the lover of nature, however," he would later remember in an article for the *National Geographic* magazine of 1912,

the surrounding forests are forever a source of healthy enjoyment, among which, orchid hunting is not the least exciting. Several of the most highly prized species hide on the moss-grown trees, and often their exquisite perfume is the only indication of their near presence. Now and then the eye is attracted by white or pink patches of Trichopilias, or by the curiously shaped, although less conspicuous, flowers of the Catacetum.

The Chiriquí Volcano

According to Pittier, the climb to the top of the Barú or Chiriquí Volcano could not be made within a day:

There is a first camp in a picturesque gorge about half way up from El Boquete, and then another at the bottom of the large northern crater, in one of the nooks formed by the narrow gorges leading to the highest summit. Here, temperature goes every night near or

The small coffee growing town of Boquete in the dry season of 1911.
Pittier described the forests of this highland region as "magnificent".
Photo by H. Pittier, from: "*National Geographic*" magazine, Vol. 23(7), 1912.

below the freezing point, and the cold is very intense to people accustomed to the heat of the lower plains.

The visit to the Chiriquí Volcano is usually made from here (El Boquete). It is an 8,000-feet ascent to the top, and is scarcely to be recommended to ladies. Not that it offers any danger, or even chances of dramatic situations, but it is a straight and exhausting climb, rendered difficult at times by the unsteadiness of the loose soil, the intricate thickets, and, even in the upper belt, by high tangled grass-fields. Rocks, all of volcanic origin, are seen only in deep gorges, or near the top. Snow and ice are out of the question, and though still called a volcano, the Chiriquí Peak is a dead one. . . .

The trail leads first through savannas and beautiful oak forests, mixed with sweet cedars and other subtropical trees, and as it goes higher and higher, always straight toward the top without any superfluous windings, the attention of the traveler is distracted from his toilsome physical exertion by the successive appearance, in the middle of a strange vegetation, of many familiar-looking plants, like trailing bramble-vines loaded with luscious blackberries, less welcomed nettles, just like those seen around old farm-houses in northern climates, alders, and the like. A formal investigation of the flora of the upper mountain belt would show, in fact, that it is a mixture of a reduced endemic element with representative of the flora of our northern countries, and of the South American Andes.

As a keen economic botanist, Pittier mentions that between two and three hundred meters of altitude, in these highland forests, there existed a tree related to the avocado. He recommended that it be taken to California for acclimatization, and to be used for grafting, or as a budding stock.

We camped at the bottom of an old crater north of the peak. March 12th, at 7 am. The temperature was about 31.5 F (-1.2 C); every drop of water was congealed and the ground covered with a fine white frost.

In clear weather the panorama from the summit is splendid: to the south, the vast expanse of the Pacific and the beautiful lowlands of Chiriquí, all interlaced forests and savannas; to the north, a labyrinth of unexplored valleys, covered totally by virgin forests running down to the Caribbean sea; westward, the Costa Rican mountains familiar to the writer; and to the east, many a lofty peak of no despicable prominence and virgin yet of any white man's footprints. From the top, we had only a momentary vision of a faraway silvery ribbon, the Río Chiriquí Viejo, several thousand feet below us to the west.

We had intended to spend a few days at our upper camp and to explore the upper part of the mountain as thoroughly as possible. But on returning to the camp, we were greeted with the news that there was not a drop of water left, and a careful search of the neighboring gorges had failed in revealing a new supply of it. Under such circumstances, the only thing to do was to go home. That night we went to bed without dinner, and our imagination helping, we felt awful thirsty. Early in the morning, we started without breakfast, and were glad when we found the first wild pine-apples (epiphytic Bromeliads), in the folial axils of which there is almost always a small supply of water. Our return looked as a rout (*déroute*) and I seriously think of having my *revanche* in June, as this would be, botanically speaking, a more favorable time for collecting, and there will be then plenty of water.

Cerro de la Horqueta

We ascended the Chiriquí Volcano, and the Cerro de la Horqueta, which I found to be respectively 3,374 and 2,268m (data subject to revision) high. The former is entirely located in the semi-arid region of the Pacific. At about 1,800m, the oaks have become the dominating element of the forest, and they remain so up to about 3,000m, although mixed still in the lower belt with a gregarious *Persea,* very close related to the common alligator-pear [avocado]. On the side we ascended, the upper limit of the oak forest is marked by the cratered ridge that surrounds the main peak on its n.eastern flank. The inside of the ridge, and the slopes of the highest peaks up to about 3,150m are clad in a forest in which *Mirtaceae* and *Ericaceae* seem to predominate.

March 17-19 we went to Cerro de la Horqueta, which is as wet as the volcano is dry, although not 10 miles distant on the opposite side (N) of the Caldera Valley. Here the forest is very dense and the *Lauraceae* dominate up to about 2,000m, intermingled with a few oaks. The upper part of the peak is buried under a low, scrubby forest, very much mixed as to families, and fierce when it comes to cut a trail trough the tangle of distorted trunks, vines and bamboo, all uniformly clad in a thick, dripping mantle of mosses and allied plants. This was a paradise for Mr. Maxon, who collected no end of rare ferns. I think we were the first people to ascend that peak, as no traces of an old trail could be discovered in the upper part of the peak.

Pittier comments that he collected about 600 species of plants from Boquete and the Caldera River valley.

The Return to David

Pittier departed from Boquete towards David on March 21, passing through Caldera, a village known to ethnologists, such as the Frenchman Alphonse Pinart, on account of its petroglyphs. He returned by foot, taking a closer look at the savanna vegetation. He also had plans to travel to Remedios, where Berthold Seemann had collected plants in 1848. But, fearing to loose the steamboat back to Panama, he contented himself with a few excursions to the *llanos* around David.

He found Chiriquí fascinating, and made up his mind to return to study its unexplored caves, its countless Indian burials waiting to be excavated, and the indigenous peoples of eastern Chiriquí, the Guaymies, about whom little was known at the time.

Henri Pittier:
The Guaymies of Chiriqui (1911–1912)

We believe that Pittier, the naturalist with an anthropological eye, obtained the bulk of the data for his notes on Guaymí culture during his trip to eastern Chiriquí between December 15, 1911, and January 4, 1912. The following text is extracted from a more extensive article published by the *National Geographic* magazine in July 1912, a time in which interest on Panama was at an all-time peak.

The article carries a very interesting map, shown on the following page, on the distribution of the indigenous people of the Isthmus at the turn of the 20th Century.

This map has acquired great relevance today, given Panama's current debate over how to define the boundaries of the *comarca* or reserve of the Ngobe-Buglé, as the Guaymí people are now known. In the 1910s, the Guaymí lands in Chiriquí and Veraguas corresponded to those they presently occupy. However, in Bocas del Toro,

their territory was smaller than today. According to Pittier's map, there were few or no Ngobe communities in regions such as the Valiente Peninsula, the Chiriquí Lagoon, and the Gulf of Mosquitos. The Guaymies would occupy these areas later in the 20th Century.

At the time Pittier prepared his map, by far the largest Indian territory in Panama was that of the Kuna. On the Caribbean side, the Kuna extended from Puerto Escribanos to Puerto Obaldía on the Colombian border, and from the coast to the continental divide.

On the Pacific side, the Kuna encompassed the broad valleys of the two largest rivers of eastern Panama, the Bayano and the Tuira-Chucunaque. The Chocoes, or today's Emberá, were then mostly limited to the valley of the Sambú River. Let us now follow Pittier during his travels in eastern Chiriquí and into the land of the Guaymí.

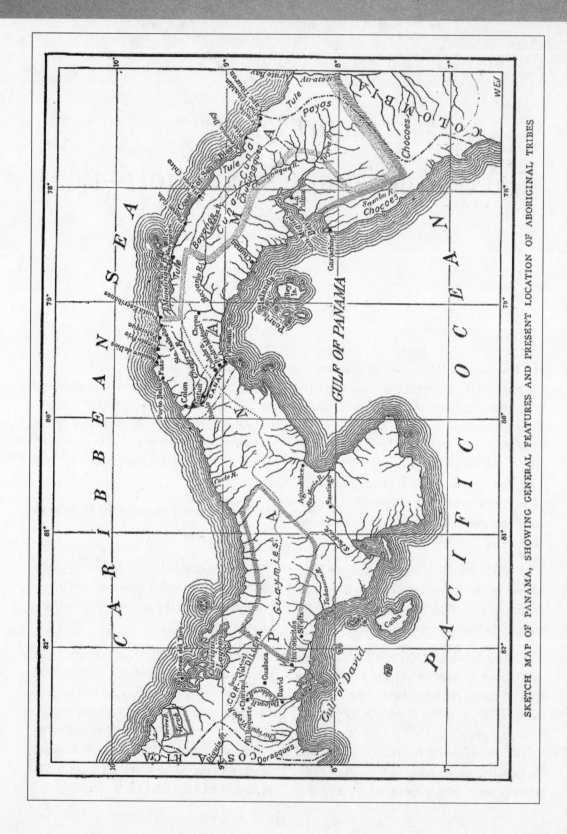

SKETCH MAP OF PANAMA, SHOWING GENERAL FEATURES AND PRESENT LOCATION OF ABORIGINAL TRIBES

Indigenous Peoples of Panama

In the years 1501 to 1503, when Rodrigo de Bastidas and Christopher Columbus visited the northern coast of the Isthmus, they found it densely populated. About ten years later, Balboa met with identical conditions along the southern coast, and all subsequent reports of early explorers give evidences of the fact that the whole country was in possession of numerous clans, the names of many of which have been preserved.

The two principal nations were the Guaymies, extending from the Chiriquí Volcano, eastward to what is today the Canal Zone, and the Cuna-Cuna, on the opposite side of the Isthmus. West of the volcano, in the valleys of the Chiriquí Viejo, Chánguena and Diquis rivers, and possibly a little farther east along the Pacific Ocean, were the Dorasques, a warlike and more civilized race, to whom the beautiful pottery and gold ornaments found in the ancient graves of Chiriquí are often attributed. As can be deduced from these relics, the Dorasques had trade relations with the Niquirans and Chorotegans, of Costa Rica, and through them felt in some degree the influence of the Nahuatl, in far-away Mexico. Today, they have completely disappeared as a tribal entity.

On the southeastern border of the present Republic of Panama dwelt the Chocoes, who are still numerous, and extend from the Pacific coast northward to, and even beyond, the Atrato River. They formed a kind of buffer state between the Central and South American nations.

In the course of my work I had the opportunity of spending many weeks among representatives of the three groups still in existence–that is to say, the Guaymies, the Cuna-Cuna, and the Chocoes.

The Guaymí

Up in the forbidding mountains and valleys that form a background to the landscape for the traveler on the steamers plying between Panama and David, dwell the mass of the present Guaymies, about 5,000 in number, in their homes scattered through savannas and forests. From the time of the conquest to the beginning of the past century, they have been more or less under the influence of Catholic missionaries, but since been left to go back to most of their ancient customs and ways of living.

Dress

Among the few vestiges left of that transitory, semi-civilized condition under religious discipline, perhaps the most conspicuous is the flowing gown of the women, tight at the neck, and reaching down to the feet. In every aboriginal tribe commited to their guardianship, the first care of the pious fathers seems to have been to create among those simple creatures, not the sense of modesty, which is innate among them, but a feeling of shame of their physical beauty.

This is why in countries with a constantly warm climate, where the ragged topography, the predominance of brush and bush, and the multiplicity of rivers make it necessary only the scantiest clothing, we often see the poor females moving awkwardly in their cumbrose imposed garments, under which, however, they still wear the primitive and more practical bark shirt. It is true that, when there is no stranger near, the gown is mostly discarded, and if a rain shower surprises a caravan on the trail, the women quickly strip, wrap their togs in a large Calathea or Heliconia leaf, place the parcel in their load, and then continue on their way.

The men do likewise and, besides when they go on a hunting expedition they invariably abandon their trousers before starting on a run after some wild animal. This practice has been adopted by the other more civilized native in some parts, and sometimes one discovers a whole collection of blue trousers hanging on the lower branches of some tree at the opening of a forest path. In this case, the shirt that forms the only other part of the male wearing apparel is taken off and tied around the loins.

Physical Appearance

The Guaymies are usually not of a very prepossessing appearance. Their stature is rather variable, and their bearing has not the stateliness that is often noticed among other Indians. Among the men the face is seldom attractive. The lips are usually thick, the nose is flat and broad, and the coarse, black hair worn short.

Among the woman a few were met who were positively pretty and is it necessary to say? knew it. But beauty is not at a premium among Guaymí females. A woman ought first to be strong, healthy, a good beast of burden, and day-worker. The children, especially the little girls, also have frequently lovely faces, with a warm brown, velvety skin, and beautiful eyes. When they reach the age of puberty, their hair is cropped short, and not allowed to grow it again until the first baby is born. Maidenhood, however, is a short stage of life of Guaymí women, who not infrequently become mothers before having reached their twelfth year.

Facial Decorations

Face painting is a common practice, restricted apparently neither by age nor by sex, although the women adorn themselves thus only on great occasions. Black, red, and white are the favorite colors, the latter being obtained, as I

Facial decoration of a Guaymí man in Chiriquí, showing an inverted V shape design. Right: Guaymí woman from Chiriquí. Note the women's diverse necklaces, ornamental style still in use today. According to Pittier, face painting was traditionally more common among men than women.
Photos (2) by H. Pittier. Source: "*National Geographic*" magazine, Vol. 23, 1912.
Photo on opposite page: Guaymí girls from Chiriquí. The Guaymí girls had, according to Pittier, "adorable faces and lovely eyes."   Photo by H. Pittier. S.I. Archives, Washington, D.C.

have been told, by the use of an ordinary oil-paint, which the Guaymí obtain at Bocas del Toro. Little girls keep their faces clean, but boys under twelve were seen with broad black blotches, without definite outline, around their eyes.

In men the decoration is always more elaborate, and certain peculiarities in the patterns, as well as the exact repetition of these by distinct people, lead to the belief that they had formerly, and may still have a significance as a totemic or tribal emblem. The groundwork almost always consists of two black lines, starting obliquely downward from between the eyes so as to form on the face a broadly open ^ [inverted V], the apex of which is on the nose ridge. These black lines are variously supplemented by white or red parallels,

terminal appendages in pink colors, by means of an tatto, of the outline of the lips, which then appear much thicker than they naturally are.

A Woman's Economic Role

In certain communities, the wealth of the people is estimated by the number of their cattle. Among the Guaymí, the number of wives is the standard. The role of these in the domestic economy is not, however, merely that of a toy, as among certain Oriental nations. They constitute the working capital of the family, and their way of courting the preference of their master is not through love, but toil. Even thus, and though they are little more than mere beasts of burden, they seem to be quite satisfied with their lot, and it will be a

Traditional Guaymí house, Chiriquí, 1912. Note its round shape, the absence of windows, and a conical roof made of straw. Subsistence crops and then the surrounding forests.
Photo by H. Pittier. Source: *"National Geographic"* magazine, Vol. 23, 1912.

long time before they feel the need of joining in the throng of modern aspirants for sex equality.

Dwellings

The typical Guaymí dwelling is a round house, about eight meters in diameter, with a conical, thatch roof. The bare ground constitutes the floor, and the fireplace is either in the middle, or at the side. These houses are not always walled. When they are, they have no windows, but two doors placed at the opposite ends of a secant to the circumference of the structure. The walls are made of erect sticks, brought close together, and tied with vines. On the north side plaster made of cow dung and clay is sometimes applied so as to afford protection against the wind. . . . Benches along the walls are used as beds, although at high altitudes, where the temperature is often very low at night, the resting place is on a light floor just under the roof. Large nets, hanging from the beams, are used in lieu of wardrobes and closets, and the tilling, fishing, and hunting implements, all of a primitive type except the guns, complete the house furnishings. Nowadays, the kitchen crockery is mostly imported ware, the only exception being the large earthen jars used to keep the *chicha*, or corn-beer, and the calabashes, of universal use in the tropics.

Their dwellings are located either in the midst of the forests of the lower belt, in solitary clearings far apart, or in the high savannas. In the first instance, they are always at some distance from the sea, as the Guaymies, forced back into the mountains by the Spanish invaders, have long since lost the art of navigation.

These forest dwellers are of a quieter and more submissive disposition, though their daily contact with the stealthy and hidden animal life of the woods has made them more cunning and distrustful than their brothers of the savannas. These, living amidst rugged hills, in a relatively cold climate, and enjoying day after day the magnificent panorama of the surrounding mountains and the plains, always framed in gray clouds and blue skies, are more energetic, open and proud of their undisputed independence.

The Chepo Savannas and the Bayano Forests according to Henri Pittier (1911)

At the end of 1911, after exploring the Atlantic coast east of Colón and the San Blas Islands, Pittier proceeded to study the flora of the eastern half of the Province of Panama. From early October until mid-November he collected plant specimens, wood samples, and tried, unsuccessfully, to record ethnographic data on the Kuna of the Bayano River.

First he focused on the natural savannas that extended east of Panama City up to Chepo, where the Bayano forests, in Kuna territory, began. On horseback, he visited the different *llanos* or grassy plains making up the savannas of Pacora, Juan Corso, Dormisolo, Jaquinto, and Camino Boticario. Three times he visited the Portala lagoon. He also passed through Chararé and La Capitana. Thereafter, he ascended by dugout canoe up the densely forested Bayano River.

Violent and prolonged thunderstorms hindered his fieldwork. The Bayano overflowed its banks and Pittier's plant samples rotted because he was unable to dry them. "My photographic work was a decided failure," he confessed to Secretary Walcott on November 29, 1911, "so far it refers to the use of films. Of 18 exposures taken up the Bayano River, I saved 3, the others being ruined by mildew. Plates are decidedly better, and I brought back a few very good natural-size pictures." We don't know if Pittier managed to publish the few photos of the Bayano which he had saved from the dampness.

Chepo

His first notes recording his explorations around Chepo, dated October 20, were written from Culebra, his headquarters on the shores of the Canal, soon after returning from the savannas of Eastern Panama to prepare his next expedition up the Bayano River. In his report to the Secretary Walcott he stressed the harshness of conducting botanical fieldwork during the tropical rainy season and the appalling state of transportation in Panama:

In order to get provisions, and to complete my outfit for the extension of my work in the Upper Bayano Valley, I came back from Chepo after about ten days of fruitful preliminary excursions in the neighborhood of that town, arriving here Sunday 15th. As the regular gasoline launch was scheduled to make the trip from Panama on the 17th, and it was the only available safe conveyance for the transportation my equipment, I had to come from Chepo in a 'bongo' or sail-dugout, and only reached Panama after having spent three nights and two days to travel the 30 (or 28) miles between the mouth of the Chepo River and Panama! To make things worse, when I arrived on the beach Tuesday morning, after having spent the night at the Tivoli Hotel, and having incurred in useless extraordinary expenses, I found that, notwithstanding the notice published in all newspapers, there would be no gasoline launch of the regular service until the 24th inst [instant]! There was nothing left for me but to come back to Culebra and wait in comparative inaction, for most of my working outfit is in Chepo. But last night I was informed that one of the launches of the Bayano Lumber Co. would probably be leaving for their place Saturday morning.

So I went to Panama to-day, and now all is settled and I shall leave to-morrow, probably reaching Chepo in one day, and thus gaining three days of the seven I was expected to wait until the 24th. I am exceedingly sorry for the loss of time, but could hardly have helped it.

Pittier took advantage of his return to Culebra to review his field notes and catch up on his correspondence. Among the letters is one from a Smithsonian museum requesting that on his forthcoming trip to the Bayano he bring back large samples of all the timber tree species that he would come across, to mount an exhibit of Panamanian hardwoods in Washington. Angrily, Pittier responded: "I fear it is out of question to bring such specimens from all the trees collected in the Bayano Valley. It would mean tons and tons, the transportation of which would cost beyond the means at my disposal. I will try, however, to bring large samples of the most interesting and well identified timbers."

He returned from his mission to the forests of the valley of the Bayano River in November 1911. And on the 15th he reported to Secretary Charles Walcott:

On the whole, and notwithstanding the heavy rains of the last two weeks, the results of the expedition are satisfactory. My 4 days trip to the Upper Mamoní, however, was practically useless as to collecting, as I had to throw away almost every specimen and in my three days navigation up the Bayano River, I had more rain than I have seen in the remainder of my sojourn in the Isthmus. We reached the Rio Diablo del Sur, and ascended it up to the limit of canoe navigation, where we found an Indian house, empty, a near-by plantation of plantains and bananas, and the beginning of the trail leading to Nárgana on the coast of San Blas. But here, again, my plants were found rotten in the blotters, the navigation on the Bayano was impossible because the depth of the flooded river did not permit poling, and the current too swift for paddling. We were within one-day distance of the first Indian

Pages 130-31:
The Peaks of Olá in 1911. Note the contrast between the savanna vegetation and the gallery forests along rivers and streams, a formation typical of the dry Pacific slope. Photo by Henri Pittier. Source: *Expeditions organized or participated in by the Smithsonian Institution in 1910 and 1911.*

The elegant Tivoli Hotel at Ancón Hill.
Photo probably taken by Alexander Wetmore in the 1950s.
Source: Alexander Wetmore Papers. Smithsonian Institution Archives, Washington, D.C.

settlement. But on account of the above-mentioned difficulties, and also of the impossibility of collecting plants, I reluctantly gave up my plan to visit these Indians. The botanical result may not have corresponded to the expense, and notwithstanding my ethnological ambitions, I did not feel justified in going farther.

Chepo itself is in the middle of a savanna district, and I had a very good opportunity to study the vegetation in detail. They belong to a type quite different of those of Chiriquí, being more "parklike", with a more fertile soil, and apparently less wind during the dry season. The cordillera itself is less conspicuous, hardly reaching 1000m. in altitude, with gaps 300m. above sea level at the bottom. A very interesting fact with relation to plant migration may be mentioned in connection with those low cuts in the divide: wherever two valleys, one in the northern slope and the other on the opposite side, are in close communication by means of a low depression, the *Phytelephas* Palm or Ivory-nut palm, has penetrated from north to south, although never going very far towards the coast. So that palm is found in one valley, and not in the next one, and its absence in a valley is a sure indication that said valley does not penetrate to the core of the mountains, or does not meet any of the valleys on the opposite side.

On account of the very heavy rains and the flooding of the Bayano, Pittier was forced to remain a week in the town of Chepo. He took advantage of this period to study "the technical process in the preparation by the natives of several kinds of palm oil, and also that of the cultivation of rice, and of the several varieties of that cereal. I have [collected] about 10 of these, in original, and in natural-size photos, and think this is the first attempt in this direction, at least in Central America and Panama."

At the beginning of 1912, Pittier's contract to explore Panama expired. The uncertain future worried him. He wanted to explore the botanically unknown peninsula of Azuero as well as Bocas del Toro. In his note of November 29, 1911, he reiterated to the Secretary of the Smithsonian:

I had been seriously considering a proposal to stay here in the employment of the Panamanian Government, with the hope to be in position to continue the work that is so well on its way presently and which I deeply regret to abandon so soon.

Since then, I have come to the conclusion that it would not be safe to accept such a position as the one mentioned above, and that I would be better placed in Washington to aid in the continuation of my work, either by effective participation, or indirectly. It is also becoming urgent to coordinate the large amount of materials already collected, so as to make it possible to extend the future researches on every group in the same proportion. In your note of Oct. 30th, you kindly express your willingness to help me in obtaining an extension of my detail for another year. I believe that the good conduct of the botanical survey requires at about this time a thorough examination of what has been collected so far.

From 1913 on, Pittier began to take his leave from Panama. He busied himself more intensively with a study of the flora of Venezuela, where he would settle in 1919 and where, in the words of Yolanda Texera Arnal from the Universidad Central de Venezuela, "he would become the man who was to dominate the natural sciences." He tried to impose scientific standards on a society that was just taking shape at the beginning of the 20th Century, and where the dictatorial regime of Juan Vicente Gomez considered science to be at the service of the *caudillo* or political leader.

In Venezuela, Pittier was entrusted with the Museo Comercial sobre Productos Naturales (Commercial Museum of Natural Products). In 1933, he became director of the National Observatory and, in 1936, of the Botanical Service, where he established the National Herbarium. His concerns for conservation led to the creation in 1937 of the first Venezuelan National Park along the coastal range, originally called Parque Rancho Grande but now bearing his name.

The Zoological Explorations of Edward A. Goldman (1910-1912)

In the language of the Cueva people, who inhabited the Isthmus at the time of the arrival of the Spaniards, the word Panama meant "abundance of fishes." But it could just as well mean the abundance and diversity of mammals, birds, and plants. Edward A. Goldman was a naturalist who made a major contribution to our understanding of the biological wealth of the Isthmus.

In John Dwyer's words, Goldman, author of 206 scientific articles, was "the most productive zoologist from the

Edward A. Goldman (1873-1946), circa 1938.
Zoologist and member of the Smithsonian Institution's Biological Survey of Panama (1910-1912), Goldman authored the first book about mammals in the Isthmus. Photo from W. Taylor: "Edward A. Goldman" in: *Journal of Mammalogy*, 1947, Vol. 28(2).

Panama Canal construction era." More than 50 species of mammals, reptiles, and plants bear his name. In 1920, the Smithsonian Institution in Washington published his greatest work *The Mammals of Panama*. Edward A. Goldman died in 1946.

A Graduate from the School of Life

Son of Franco-German immigrants, Edward Alphonso Goldman was born in Mount Carroll, Illinois, in 1873. Initially, the Goldman family settled in Pennsylvania, but later they moved to Nebraska, and to California in 1888. Edward acquired his love of nature from his father, a farmer. In 1891, at the age of 18, he became field assistant to Edward William Nelson, a great naturalist of the time, who later became director of the United States Biological Survey Bureau, today's Fish and Wildlife Service. For 40 years, Goldman worked closely with Nelson.

Edward only finished high school. What he achieved during half a century of zoological research, he learned as a field naturalist, a graduate of the school of life. He read avidly and took many short self-improvement courses. He was an excellent hunter and field collector with the observational skills of an Indian forest trekker. He was blessed with a great sense of humor and got along well with people, rarely becoming irritated. He was among the first naturalists to document his field explorations with a photographic camera.

Prior to coming to Panama, he had studied and collected the fauna of Mexico for over 14 years, getting to know practically all of the Mexican states and territories. He spoke fluent Spanish. During the First World War

he served in the U.S. Army with the rank of major on the Western Front.

As a member of the great Smithsonian Biological Survey of Panama, Goldman made two extensive field expeditions before completion of the canal works, mostly to collect and study in great detail birds and mammals, although he also included reptiles and amphibians. It was feared that the immense canal works would alter and complicate problems regarding the geographical distribution of plants and animals in the Isthmus. This region was of increasing biological concern, given its configuration, topography, and key geographical location, as well as for its role as a corridor for the migrations of animals of the Americas.

His field studies in Panama coincided with efforts to demarcate the boundaries of the Canal Zone. In accordance with the Canal treaty of 1903, Panama had agreed to transfer to the U.S. control over a strip of land 5 miles wide on either side of the canal. The delimitation, which had moved slowly since its initiation in 1904, gathered speed when Abel Bravo, an engineer, took charge of the task for the Panamanian government. The demarcation caused deep fears and uncertainty among the people living within the new zone, in the old villages along the Chagres River or the Panama Railroad, "the Line" as it was called. People would see the survey teams measuring the land and placing banners and stakes. Then came the *aviso* or warning from the local Mayor or *alcalde*, telling the residents that they had to abandon their farms and households. Many resisted the eviction orders. It was a dramatic time for peasants occupying lands along the

The expedition of Edward A. Goldman in the dry season of 1911, crossing the savannas of Chepo, on the way to Cerro Azul, at the continental division of the waters.
Photo by E. A. Goldman. Source: *Mammals of Panama.* Smithsonian Institution, 1920.

huge waterway and the new Canal Zone. They were the first Panamanians in the 20th Century to pay a steep price for progress.

FIRST EXPEDITIONS: 1910–1911

Lake Gatún

Goldman's first field expedition lasted seven months, from December 1910 to June 1911. He arrived in Panama on December 28, 1910, on board the SS *Colon*, together with H. Pittier, S. E. Meek, and S. F. Hildebrand. Initially, he set up headquarters at Culebra, at facilities provided by the Isth-

Goldman and his *bayanero* porters, climbing through the steep forest of the Mamoní River, eastern Panama province, in March 1911. Photo by E. A. Goldman. Source: *Mammals of Panama*. Smithsonian Institution, 1920.

mian Canal Commission. On December 29, he met Colonel Goethals, chief engineer and director of all canal operations. In his field diary, transcribed by Storrs Olson in 1990, Goldman jotted: "I was able to secure an assignment to Gatún, which will enable me to work in the vicinity of Lion Hill."

By December 30, he installed himself at the big Gatún encampment and started collecting and setting up traps on January 1, 1911.

From January 4–9, he was in San José, Costa Rica, to secure the services of Adán Lizano, an experienced taxidermist from the National Museum of Costa Rica who became his field assistant.

Back in Culebra, Goldman collected mammals and birds around the new Lake Gatún, just before its waters began to flood some 164 square miles of tropical forests, first near old towns such as Gatún and Lion Hill. On January 24, he went off in a canoe trip up Río Gatún as far as Monte Lirio. By January 26, he had explored Río Trinidad, several miles above the Agua Clara. During February he made forays down the Chagres and up the Indio River in a dugout canoe. On March 13, he and Dr. Meek took a launch from Colón to Bahía de Las Minas, landing near a small hut, and then walked back to Majagual. There, in a canoe, they crossed back to Colón. Goldman noted that to the east of Colón the "country is heavily forested." While studying the rising lake, he traveled around in a *cayuco* or dugout canoe, that extraordinary cultural artifact of the forest people from the Caribbean side of the Isthmus.

The Savannas of Chepo
and the Highland Forests of Cerro Azul

In March 1911, we find Goldman on the Pacific side of the Isthmus. In a launch belonging to the Bayano Lumber Company, he headed east of Panama City towards Chepo in quest of the headwaters of the Chagres River. His field journal for March 17 states:

> Left Gatun by the early morning train for Panama, where Lizano, my hunter Juan Martis and I, in company with Meek and Hildebrand boarded the small launch of Mr. Bowdry. Leaving Panama at 10 A.M., we arrived at Hato Bayano at the mouth of the Mamoní river about 4 P.M. [A]fter considerable delay during which I was the guest of Mr. and Mrs.

Johnson at Hato Bayano, a large canoe was secured in which my outfit was taken up the Mamoní to La Capitana where I arrived after dark. Leaving my outfit in charge of a native at the landing I walked with Juan to Chepo.

Chepo was an old town at the eastern edge of the savanna belt that extended along Panama's Pacific coast some 450 kilometers west, as far as Chiriquí on the border of Costa Rica.

On March 18, he transferred his equipment from La Capitana to Chepo. On the mouth of the Mamoní, he noticed the extensive mangrove and flooded forests, and the spectacle of hundreds of alligators sun basking along the sandbars. Hato Bayano was located at the point at which the Mamoní flows into the Bayano.

From Chepo, Goldman could see his target: Cerro Azul, a sharp peak 3,000 feet high, on the continental divide that lies a few miles from the Pacific. There, he spent two days hiring *bayaneros* or local porters and guides, who were the descendants of the fierce *cimarrones*, runaway slaves who, under their leader Bayano, had fought the Spaniards throughout the 16th Century. Among these, he hired Santos Maldonado. He also rented horses. Goldman departed on March 20, at 5:45 a.m., traveling 18 miles northeastward over the hot savanna. After crossing the Pacora River, the expedition veered north, toward the southern base of Cerro Azul. Here, they met again the majestic forest that then formed a dense, uninterrupted green carpet extending along the whole of the Isthmus, from the foothills of the central cordillera on the Pacific to the Caribbean beaches on the North coast.

Goldman was astonished by the sharp demarcation that existed between savanna and forest. In one step he went from the burning plains to the cool darkness of the jungle. Here, at the point where the savannas meet the forests, he camped by a small stream near the upper end of a savanna known as "Llano de la Mesa." The equipment was unpacked and the horses were sent back to Chepo. He proceeded on foot, with three *bayanero* porters and two guides, Juan Martis and Lizano. On January 21, he commented that the supplies and equipment were being carried by porters for three miles through rough, rocky country, up the winding stream courses, to a place called Cabobré, a branch of the Río Pacora at 800 feet altitude. A palm leaf shelter was erected and preparations made to ascend Cerro Azul on the next day. Sandflies and mosquitoes would be their permanent visitors.

On March 22, with two machete men cutting a trail and a hunter to procure wild meat, Goldman reached the peak of Cerro Azul on the continental divide, separating the waters of the Pacora River, a Pacific stream, from the Chagres, a Caribbean river. They climbed using the native technique of following river and streambeds.

His entry for this date reads as follows:

> Made an ascent of the mountain today, and returned to camp at Cabobre. I took Juan Martis and two porters and reached the top about 11:30 A.M., working upward rather slowly cutting a new way along the old trail and shooting a few birds. The climb is not very steep except in a few places. The most difficult part is at the lower end, working up stream beds strewn with large smooth boulders more

or less dangerous to climb over, owing to their waterworn condition: they are often quite slippery, especially when wet. The forest is much smaller toward the top of the mountain, but is more dense, the undergrowth becoming much thicker, the forest shows evidences of a much more humid climate above 2,000 feet elevation and the humidity evidently increases rapidly toward the top. The summit and north slopes down for perhaps 500 feet are covered with a dense growth of low trees, loaded with moss, orchids, and bromeliads and the ground also is well covered with these plants.

From March 23 to March 26, Goldman and his men made several trips from base camp to the summit, setting traps and securing birds. The traps were checked daily.

From the top of Cerro Azul, Goldman could see both oceans. His field journal for March 26 says: "Made another trip to summit today and brought down traps. A few more birds were secured. From the summit, a part of which was cleared of timber by the engineers about two years ago, fairly good views were had of the Pacific coast, from near the mouth of the Bayano River, to Panama. Ancon Hill and the point beyond were clearly seen. The Atlantic coast toward the northeast, and some of the San Blas Islands were seen also."

As it was the middle of the dry season, the Pacific savannas resembled a vast and irregular chessboard: brownish areas of dry grasses separated by thin greenish belts of gallery forests delineating the river courses. Numerous fire lines, driven by strong northerly winds and leaving a blackened earth behind, advanced uncontrolled and enhanced the checker board-like appearance of the landscape.

On March 27, Goldman came down from his camp to the edge of the savanna, sending Santos Maldonado to Chepo to fetch the packhorses. Santos returned at mid-day on the following day. They reached Chepo late that evening. The next day, Goldman took a launch to Panama City, boarding the 5:30 p.m. train to Gatún.

During April and May 1911, he continued explorations along the Canal, collecting around Gatún, Tabernilla, and Lion Hill. On April 9, he went up Caño Quebrado as far as the *cayuco* would go. The remainder of April found him making forays into the forests around Lion Hill, Tabernilla, Gatún, and Bohío Soldado. On May 1, he and his West Indian helper, Herbert Butler, were at Lion Hill. "The water is rising in the Lake but rather slowly, no very heavy showers apparently having occurred up river," he scribbled in his diary. The following day, he traveled to the hills west of the huge earthen dam at Gatún. Then he was off to Colón, where he found Dr. Meek, who had just returned from "Porto Bello" (Portobelo) after being hospitalized with malaria.

From May 3 to May 21, Goldman set traps in the forests around the train stations and at the work camps of Bas Obispo, Matachín, Gamboa, Frijoles, and Miraflores. From May 14 to May 21, he stayed at Gatún, since his Costa Rican assistant, Lizano, became severely ill. From May 22 to June 2, Goldman explored the area around the historic town of Portobelo.

On the Upper Coast of Colón

On May 22, Goldman crossed over to the very rainy Caribbean coast of Colón. Taking an ICC tugboat in Colón, he arrived at Portobelo, where hundreds of laborers were quarrying rocks to build the huge Gatún locks. The government of Panama had transferred the quarries, owned by the Rodriguez family, to the ICC. The camp, made up mostly of Spanish workers and dubbed *El Otro Lado* or "The Other Side," was a lawless, boisterous place, where fights and disputes were common. Goldman settled there, hiring some robust Jamaican workers as porters.

From May 22 to June 2, he explored the forests around Portobelo. From June 3 to June 9, he ascended 18 miles up the Cascajal River, from the mouth to its headwaters in Cerro Brujo, at 3,000 feet. Leaving Portobelo, he and his men first followed the old Spanish mule trail that crosses the Isthmus, up to a point on the Cascajal River known as Cascajal, where several houses made up the last settlement on the stream. From this point on, most of the way was up the bed of the river, with thick forest on both sides. "The first night out,"reported Goldman, "camp was made at an old tumbled down shack, the shelter of which was supplemented by one of our tent flies. The next day we were in river the entire day, wading in water of all depths up to about waist deep. In the late afternoon it began to rain very hard and we arrived at a point which I calculated to be about abreast of the high Cerro Brujo. A permanent camp was made on the left bank of the stream, and from this point work on the mountain was carried out for nearly a week."

For a week it rained non-stop. Making and keeping a fire lit to cook and dry clothes became a serious problem. Matches didn't work. More effective was a local native technique: a flint piece was struck against a piece of metal to produce a spark that was then projected into a roll of dry cotton fabric. Only the core of some woods, known exclusively to the natives, could burn. "My specimens," says his narration, "were beginning to mold however and I have become very foot sore–My feet constantly wet had softened and in climbing the epidermis has began to be chafed off over large patches. Rain fell during most of the time; everything gradually became wet and nothing dried. It was necessary to put on wet clothing every morning. On the 9th I decided to return, hoping to be able to return later to this interesting region. A long hard day's march took us back to Porto Bello where I arrived with my feet in very painful condition."

At Portobelo, he photographed the main economic activity of the black communities of the upper and lower coast of Colón: the extraction of *tagua* nuts, also known as vegatble ivory, a valuable product of a wild palm exported to the U.S. and Europe. So important was the *tagua* palm to the coastal communities that the government had declared the forests on the Atlantic side "inalienable," that is, not be appropriated by private individuals.

On June 14, he returned to base camp at Gatún. Thereafter, he made additional trips to Corozal and San Lorenzo Fort, on the mouth of the Chagres River. He spent June 22-23 packing to depart for the United States. His final journal entry for 1911, dated 24-30 June, is brief: "Sailed from Colon on the steamer 'Colon'–the same ship

that took me to Panama–and arrived in New York June 30, just in time to catch a fast train to Washington (D.C.) where I arrived about 4:30 P.M."

Thus ended the first stage of Edward Goldman's field studies in Panama.

SECOND EXPEDITION: 1912

The Railroad Line and Lake Gatún

Goldman's second field expedition to Panama took place between January and July 1912. He returned to the Isthmus in the SS *Panama*, arriving in Colón on January 15, and reaching Culebra the same day. The ship also brought Dr. C. D. Marsh, to study plankton, and ichthyologists S. Meek and S. F. Hildebrand. Colonel Goethals renewed all the privileges granted to Goldman. This time, his headquarters would be the ICC's camp at Emperador, located halfway across the Isthmus.

On January 20, he worked in the vicinity of the ruins of Old Panama. On the 23d, with Dr. Marsh, he visited the forest reserves at Mount Hope and Gatún to study the abundant animals living there. The caretaker at Mt. Hope, Frederick Stevens, gave him a tapir skull.

Goldman would now study the forests along the Panama Railroad, in sections about to disappear under the ascending waters of Lake Gatún. Gradually, the old towns along the Chagres and the stations on "The Line", were being abandoned, as Canal Zone authorities relocated their inhabitants. Goldman explored these new ghost towns. The abandoned houses, soon to disappear under the rising waters of Lake Gatún, fascinated

Goldman, who found in them many rare species of bats. Thanks to the support and information of sanitary inspectors Verner and Campbell, he visited one of these towns, Bas Obispo, collecting bats in a tunnel made by the French long before to divert a stream.

Up the Chagres River

On January 29, 1912, departing from the "lost towns" of The Line, Goldman headed up the Chagres River as far as the hamlet of Alhajuela:

Left Matachín for Alhajuela at 8:15 A.M. and arrived there about 3:30 P.M. Had a pleasant trip up river in a large cayuca with two men poling in the bow and one at the stern. The river is now much lower than usual even in the dry season. Near the zone line the Indian town of Las Cruces was passed, standing close to the right bank, the houses of the common, thatched Panama type.

30 Jan. Left Alhajuela with Dr. Marsh and two guides to visit the bat caves at 7:30 A.M. Returned to Alhajuela about dark. The caves we visited are near the Chilibrillo River a few miles south of Alhajuela. They were reached by following a recently made trail southward to the Chilibrillo and then wading downstream for perhaps two miles. The caves are located about 400 yards up a small stream entering the Chilibrillo from the north. . . . There is water flowing through the caves, which are mainly large rifts in the limestone-like formation. There are several fair-sized lateral chambers however. The main one being circular 30 or 40 ft. in diameter and about 25 ft. from floor to roof. In this chamber I found the principal colony of large fruit eating bats in the same place there are several tons of bat guano and abundant evidence that the cave has been in use by these bats for a long period. Dr. Marsh made collections of copepods.

31 January. Alhajuela: Made a trip, with Simon Boliver as guide, from Alhajuela to the natural bridge about 10 miles away, on the Río del Puente which enters the Chagres above El Vigía. The start was made at 12:30 P.M. The trail led through the forest and across several small savannas to near El Vigía where it turned off to Casa Larga, a group of scattered Indian huts on an open rolling savanna several hundred acres in extent. From this point we turned eastward to the Río del Puente which was then descended by wading for about a mile in the water. The bridge has a vaulted roof about 30 ft. in height and the river passes under it for a distance of about 100 ft., turning sharply to the left so that from one entrance the other can scarcely be seen and the river seems to be flowing into a cave.

1 Feb. Empire. Left Alhajuela at 9:20 A.M. and reached Matachín about 1 P.M., where I had to remain until the evening train passed through, the time meanwhile, was used in getting specimens cleaned up to date. The banks of the Chagres are of alluvial deposits and about 10 ft. in height along most of section from Matachín to Alhajuela and are flooded at times by the river. On these banks small banana plantations periodically flooded and fertilized by the river seem to thrive. Yuca is another crop commonly grown, and sugarcane might be mentioned. Corn is usually planted on the slopes of the hills. The valley of the river from Matachín upward is quite narrow and bordered by hills which are more or less rocky. Below & near Alhajuela the river passes through a rocky formation. . . . The hills usually bound the stream within ¼ or ½ a mile on either side. The river banks are usually 10-15 ft. high the alluvial deposits most recently placed are overgrown with coarse grass and later by caña blanca, a cane-like plant used for making the sides of native houses, bamboo, guarumo, Ficus and Erythrina trees. . . . From near Alhajuela savannas are said to extend interruptedly across to the Pacific coast, the hills being rather low in the

View of the historic town of Cruces in 1912. For centuries thousands of passengers and countless treasures crossing the Isthmus passed through this village on the banks of the Chagres River. Its ruins now lie covered by the jungle near Gamboa on the Panama Canal.
Photo: Isthmian Canal Commission.

direction of the headwaters of the Juan Diaz River.

On February 4, Goldman went into Panama Bay accompanied by Marsh, Meek, a Mr. Osgood, and Malcolm Anderson. Meek used dynamite to secure fish. They worked near Naos Island and the San José Rock. They found a colony of pelicans and cormorants among the cliffs, and large iguanas.

On February 6, Goldman traveled to Lion Hill to secure more birds and the following day to the ruins of Old Panama to capture bats. He frequently went into the forest at night to catch bats. On February 10, he was

back at Portobelo, from where he went up the Cascajal River with J. W. Irwin, who operated the wireless station there.

Satisfied that he had gathered the most complete collection possible of the most accessible mammals and birds from the central part of the Isthmus, Goldman broadened the scope of his studies to include Darién, hoping to establish relationships between the fauna of eastern Panama and South America. His idea was to set a camp in the Serranía del Pirre, a mountainous chain rising along the border between Colombia and Panama. In Darién, the Pirre Mountains

Boca de Cupe, the last *darienita* village in the upper reaches of the Tuira River, June 1912. Photo by E. A. Goldman. Source: *Smithsonian Miscellaneous Collections*, Vol. 60(30), 1913.

separate the valley of the Tuira, Panama's largest river, from the Balsas, one of its tributaries. Goldman was attracted by the old belief that it was from the heights of Cerro Pirre where Vasco Núñez de Balboa had seen the Pacific Ocean for the first time, in 1513. His interest was also sparked by the fact that, unlike the rest of the Americas where most of the main rivers flow into the Atlantic, Panama's largest streams, such as the Tuira-Chucunaque and the Bayano, flow into the Pacific.

Darién: To Boca de Cupe
by Steamer and Piragua

In the company of Seth Meek and Samuel Hildebrand, both experts on fishes, Goldman traveled to Darién on February 21, 1912, on the small steamer *Cana*, owned by the Darien Gold Mining Company. At sunrise of the 22nd, they reached the Gulf of San Miguel, and then went up the Tuira River. They made brief stops at La Palma and Chepigana, communities of thatched-roof houses inhabited by *darienitas,* black people who had lived in Darién since colonial times. The merchants of these towns were Chinese. Large mangrove forests and stands of cativo trees covered the lower Tuira valley. At sunset, they anchored at the mouth of the Chucunaque, awaiting the tide that would allow the *Cana* to steam ahead to Marragantí, the uppermost navigable site on the Tuira. Here, the Darien Gold Mining Company had a station.

His entry for February 22, reads as follows: "Arrived in Marragantí about 9:30 P.M. A few minutes later the manager for the company there, Dr. Pedro Campagnani came aboard and took us ashore with him in a large dugout canoe, here called a 'piragua.' I had brought a letter from Mr. Pinel to Mr. Campagnani and he furnished comfortable quarters."

Campagnani, who would be of great help to Goldman, welcomed them warmly. Marragantí is half a mile up from the legendary town of El Real de Santa María, whose fortress was built in 1665 to protect the gold mines of Darién from pirates. Goldman's diary reads:

> 23 February. (Friday). Left Boca de Cupe with our outfits Meek, Hildebrand, Scott and I, in two large piraguas manned each by two natives, who poled us up the Tuyra 30 miles to Boca de Cupe. It was a rather tedious trip, very few birds being seen and the country along the banks changed comparatively little in character. Very large numerous Cuipo trees were perhaps the most striking features of the vegetation. We arrived after nightfall and the piragua was half dragged over the shoals by the men who were in places obliged to get out into the water and hold the bow and stern of the very long piragua in their hands. The river is very low owing to the prolonged dry

season. . . .Arrived at Boca de Cupe later in the evening.

Goldman was impressed by the native *piragua*, a craft carved out from a single tree trunk, with elegant lines, a flat bottom and a shallow draft, very stable on torrential rivers, and propelled by men using long poles. Those tall *cuipo* trees, which attracted his attention, are of South American origin. They have a spongy wood and short roots that barely allow the tree to grasp the soil. Many of them fall down in the storms of the rainy season.

The Cana Gold Mines

Boca de Cupe was the last important black village in the upper Tuira. Further up, it was Kuna territory, their main hamlets here being Paya and Púcuro. The Kuna were extremely wary of outsiders, black or white. From Boca de Cupe there began a narrow tramline, which ended 30 miles south, at the Cana gold mines. Getting there was an adventure. These are Goldman's notes:

> February 24. Cana (Sat.). Left Boca de Cupe by the tramroad which connects this point with Cana, 30 miles away. A gasoline engine hauled the short train to Mt. Kitchener which is about 12 miles from Boca de Cupe. From this point on the track is in bad shape and the journey for another 12 miles–as far as Paca–was continued on a push car. At Paca, Scott and I were met by a mule drawn car which took us the remaining distance, about six miles to Cana. The road is pretty steadily uphill all the way, the altitude at Cana being about 1950 feet. As far as Paca there is comparatively little change in the character of the vegetation, but beyond that point the country is more mountainous the road rising into the foothills of the Mt. Pirri region. The ascent is mainly along the cañon of a small stream un-

The steamer *Cana,* owned by the Darien Gold Mining Company, which in 1912 took the expedition of the Smithsonian Institution from Panama City to the Tuira River. Photo by E. A. Goldman. *Smithsonian Miscellaneous Collections,* Vol. 60(30), 1913.

til a few miles below Cana we came out on the Cana Plateau, or valley. Here is a stretch of comparatively level land several miles across. Much of the valley was formerly planted to sugarcane. The Cana and Setigantí rivers enter the valley and along their courses near the upper end are marshy areas.

Since its discovery in 1502, Darién had been very famous for its gold. According to Gonzalo Fernández de Oviedo, the Spanish king ordered it to be named Castilla del Oro or Golden Castille. Around 1665, one of the richest gold mines in America was discovered: Espíritu Santo de Cana (the Holy Ghost of Cana). In 1680 alone, some 20,000 pounds of gold came out from its legendary "royal vein." In barely 15 years, Cana became the biggest town in Darién. Thousands of miners and workers arrived here, mostly black, zambo, and mulattos (the latter being the offspring of blacks and Indians, and blacks and whites, respectively). The wealth of the place was a magnet for English and French pirates, who captured Cana in 1684, 1702, 1712, and 1724. Af-

terwards, the fierce Kunas revolted. Finally, the galleries collapsed, a disaster probably caused by a quake. Cana was abandoned and the jungle devoured it.

A century and a half would pass before new attempts were made to reopen Cana. In 1840, a Frenchman, Emile Breton, began some explorations, but later abandoned them and departed for California. Around 1881, an American spiritualist, O. M. Wozencraft, received a message from the hereafter, telling him to go seek the treasure of Cana. After many adventures and misadventures he failed to find it, and another spiritualist and friend of his, Newcombe, took over. Newcombe set up a new company which, after many accidents and troubles, went bankrupt. When Goldman visited the mines, the concession was held by the Frenchmen Masse, Michel, and Degoutin. They would help the naturalists with transport, lodging, and other supports.

When Goldman asked about the old stone trail that in Spanish times connected Cana to El Real de Santamaría on the Tuira, no one knew where it had been. A dense forest covered everything.

The Valley of Cana
and Serranía del Pirre

Goldman described Cana as a slightly inclined plain, at an altitude of 1,800 feet, up against the Setetule Hill. Several streams converged on this beautiful valley: the Cana, Setegantí, the Escucha Ruido, Limón, which in turn formed the Río Grande, a local name for an upper tributary of the Tuira. Cana was ideal for zoological studies: steep mountains covered by very dense vegeta-

tion, criss-crossed by many streams and rivers. Close to the mine there were many areas that had been cleared and were now covered by shrubs and secondary growth, all providing a diversity of environmental conditions.

Between February 24 and April 11, he worked intensively around the mines at an altitude from 1,800 to 3,000 feet. On the 25th, he traveled to the Seteganti River to shoot birds. From February 26 to March 2nd, he collected birds on the forest around Cana. Meek and Hildebrand finally arrived from Boca de Cupe, and together they trekked nine miles east of Cana to the Río Grande. "Meek," Goldman commented, "obtained some interesting fishes and I shot some good birds."

From March 5-6, he explored Cerro Pirre, looking for a future campsite from which to explore the higher slopes. Although the crest of Pirre stood barely six miles from the mining camp, it was almost unknown save to the Choco Indians, who had an old trail that led across the top. March 7-27 was spent in intensive forays around Cana. On March 28, Goldman left Cana to go back to the Tuira River.

Left Cana about 6 PM and descended the mountains by the narrow gauge railroad to Boca de Cupe. After leaving the Cana plateau the road descends steeply to a point called Quebrada Chonta, the cars used running by gravity along nearly all the way. Starting from Cana a run by gravity was made to San José, where the mules were attached to the car and we were drawn to the edge of the Cana plateau near the head of the Paca River. The car then was allowed to run by gravity as far as Paca, the company's first station. Here the

Cana, Darién, the most famous gold mine in the Spanish Main in the 17th Century.
View of the camp and the narrow railway that connected the mine with the town of Boca de Cupe in the Tuira River, 1912.
Photo by E. A. Goldman. Source: *Mammals of Panama*, Smithsonian Institution, 1920.

mules were again attached for a short time until the top of a hill was reached, beyond which the car ran by gravity to Mt. Kitchener. At Mt. Kitchener a stop was made for dinner at the camp of Mr. Vagedda who is in charge of the railroad. In the afternoon, I continued on the train from this point to Boca de Cupe. The train is drawn by a small kerosene burning locomotive. A pleasant evening was spent at Boca de Cupe with the company's engineer MacMillan, the surveyor Grist, and station keeper Villar.

On the 29th, Goldman went down the Tuira in a *piragua* to Marragantí. Here, Campagnani provided him with a room. Goldman waited for a steamer until April 7. When none arrived, he headed back to Cana to complete his field work in the highland forests of Pirre before the rainy season set in. Mr. Vagedda provided him with a push car to make it back to Cana.

"10-11 April. Remained at Cana preparing for mountain trip. Weather still dry, but air very thick and hazy. One or two slight showers accompanied by thunder have occurred, but not regular rainy season showers. It clears off at night, and at daybreak in the morning is thick and hazy again. This hazy condition of the air is said to increase as the rainy season approaches."

On April 12, helped by several miners, Goldman established camp at 5,100 feet high on Cerro Pirre, 200 feet below the crest, on the banks of a tributary of the Limón River. He sent the miners down, but kept two as camp helpers. Although it was still the dry season, the forest above 4,500 feet was covered by clouds and dripping humidity, contrasting with the dry conditions at the Valley of Cana a few miles below.

Goldman was constantly being surprised. The noise from grasshoppers and crickets made it difficult to listen to the sound of other animals he wanted to trap. One day, a cloud of locusts fell on a patch of scrub near his camp. In a few hours, the voracious insects covered 25 hectares of forest, devouring all the leaves and even the thinner branches. Such was their massed weight that they would break the stems of bushes less than an inch wide. They disappeared as abruptly as they came, flying above the forest, leaving the area as if a bush fire had scorched it.

The first heavy thundershowers fell on April 23 and the air became misty, which was said to indicate the start of the rainy season. By the first week of May, it began to pour. Goldman descended to the mine camp on May 4. For two days, he remained preparing specimens for shipment. On May 9, he left Cana, arriving in Boca de Cupe late in the evening. He made a side trip to a rubber plantation at Aruza, managed by Juan Maniba.

When it cleared up, fog covered the Darién mountains, revealing a majestic spectacle: the peaks, such as Tarcarcuna, and Pirre, where legend had it Balboa had seen the Pacific in 1513, resembled forest islands arising from a misty and frozen white sea.

As the rainy season gathered force, frogs and toads became ever more numerous, their calls breaking the silence of the summit. At sunset their voices seemed to come from the treetops, and even from the bottom of the earth. Goldman caught many. He continued his studies above 4,000 feet until May 6, when he went down to Cana with his

The Pirre Mountains, as seen from the Cana Valley at an elevation of 1,800 feet.
Photo by E. A. Goldman. Source: *Explorations and FieldWork of the Smithsonian Institution
in 1912*. Washington, D.C., 1913.

priceless collection of specimens, samples that he had kept dry by having a fire lit in camp at all times. After packing them up, he went back to Panama and sent the specimens to the Smithsonian Institution in Washington, D.C. He got more supplies and went back to Darién on May 17 aboard the steamer *Cana*. The following day, he went up the Tuira on a *piragua*, until reaching Boca de Cupe. A *cuipo* tree that had fallen over the railway delayed the train ride from Boca de Cupe to Cana.

Darién's fauna, especially the birds (to which Goldman paid great attention), seemed inexhaustible. Every day he made many important additions to his collection. These specimens indicated to him that the Darién fauna was more similar to that of South America than to the fauna from Western Panama, which shared more traits with the fauna of Central America.

He stayed at Marragantí during May 10 and 11, loading up his specimens and baggage on the *Cana*. His entry for Sunday, May 12, reads as follows:

On board 'Cana'. Early in morning we stopped at Sumacato, a timber camp about 1.5 miles above Chepigana, with a leaking boiler tube which took until 2 PM to fix. I was ashore there for a short time and found a large pile

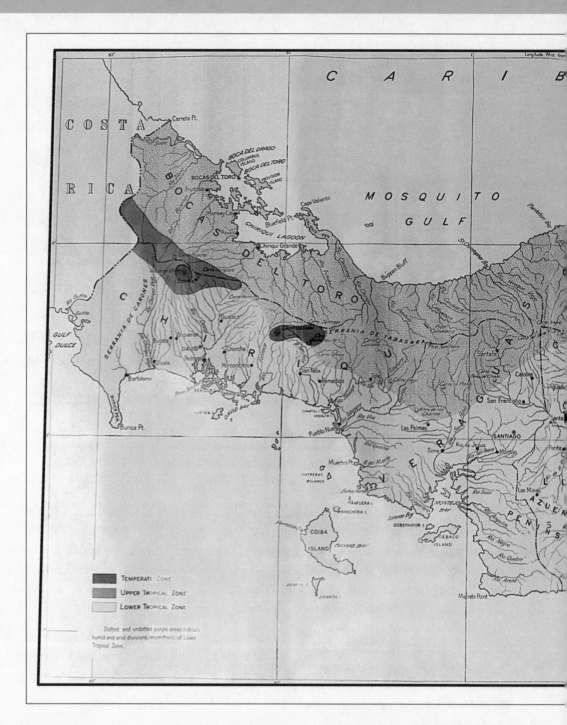

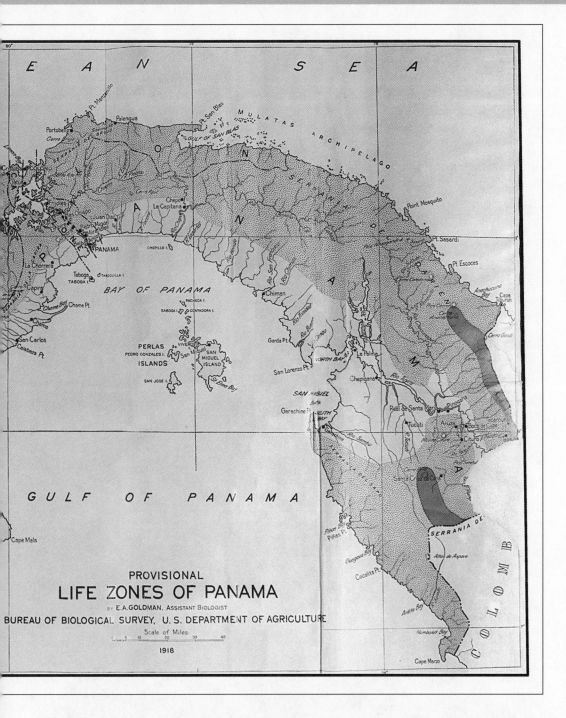

The first provisional map of Life Zones in Panama, prepared by Edward A. Goldman, and
published in 1918 by the Bureau of Biological Survey of the U.S. Department of Agriculture,
Washington, D.C. Source: *Mammals of Panama*, Smithsonian Institution, 1920.

Palms and tree ferns, the vegetation at the summit of Cerro Pirre, Darién, at 5,200 feet elevation. Photo by E. A. Goldman.
Source: *Explorations and Field-Work of the Smithsonian Institution in 1912.*
Smithsonian Institution, Washington, D.C., 1913.

of irregular-sized pieces of coco-bolo wood which are being gotten by a chinese company. Cocobolo is very hard and sinks at once when placed in water. The wood is said to be used in the manufacture of knife handles. The cocobolo grows abundantly on the low lying land in this vicinity."

They then passed through the Pearl Islands, enjoying a fine view of the fabled archipelago. On May 13, the *Cana* anchored at Panama City. Goldman reached Emperador by train on March 14, and began to prepare a final trip to Darién. He boarded the *Cana* again on the 15th, arrived at Marragantí the 16th, and at Boca de Cupe the 18th. On the 19th he comments laconically in his journal: "Returned by the tram road to Cana."

From May 20 to June 12, he worked the highlands around Cana, particularly the slopes from an altitude between 3,000 to 3,500 feet. On June 13, he left Cana for Boca de Cupe. During June 15-16 he is in Aruza, a rubber plantation on the banks of the Tuira, where he did some additional collecting.

From the 17th to the 20th he was back at Boca de Cupe, and on the 20th at Marragantí, boarding the *Cana* on the 22nd and landing in Panama City on the 23rd. That same day he was back at his quarters in Emperador. From June 24 to June 26, he prepared for his return to Washington, D.C. On June 27, he left from Cristobal on board the steamship *Allianca*, arriving in New York on July 3, 1911.

Seth E. Meek and Samuel F. Hildebrand: The Fishes of Panama (1910-1944)

Seth E. Meek.

On December 28, 1910, at the height of the canal construction, the steamer *Colon*, sailing out of New York, arrived at Cristobal. On board were four naturalists from the Smithsonian Institution's Panama Biological Survey. One of them was Seth E. Meek, a well-known and respected specialist on fishes. He was 51 years old and worked for the Chicago Field Museum of Natural History. He brought along as a field assistant a promising 27-year-old student, Samuel

Seth E. Meek (1859-1914).
Great ichthyologist of the Field Museum, Chicago.
Meek led the study of freshwater and marine fishes of the Isthmus during the Smithsonian Biological Survey of Panama (1910-1912).
Source: Ella Tourner Meek, *Seth Eugene Meek.* Curtis Johnson Printing Co., Chicago 1915.

F. Hildebrand, whose work would eventually surpass that of his mentor.

Between 1910 and 1912, Meek and Hildebrand would make two extensive exploratory trips to Panama. Their thorough fieldwork and exhaustive literature surveys allowed them to publish works that would set the foundation for contemporary ichthyology in Panama.

Studies of Panama's Fishes

At the beginning of the 20th Century, the fishes of Panama were almost unknown; the limited number of available studies had focused on the Gulf of Panama. There was hardly any information on fishes from the Atlantic. It was not known how many species existed in the Isthmus, where they originated, their geographical distribution, and what differences existed between the species of each coast.

In 1860, John M. Dow, captain of a steamer of the Panama Railroad Steamship Company, collected fishes in the Gulf of Panama. He was followed by Franz Steindachner, who, besides doing fieldwork, contracted locals to gather curious specimens. In 1881 and 1883, Charles Gilbert carried out several investigations, but a fire that swept Panama City destroyed his notes and samples.

The first research vessel to obtain fishes at great depths in the Gulf of Panama was the *Albatross*, during its trip between 1888-1891 from Panama to the Galapagos Islands. The vessel returned in 1904 and 1905, in the course of its expedition from California to Peru. In 1896, Gilbert gathered 283 marine species, 43 of them new to the Isthmus. His

article "The fishes of Panama Bay" included the most complete and updated bibliography on the marine fishes at the time. We owe the first study of fresh-water fishes to G. A. Boulanger, who in 1899 completed the first survey of the fishes in the Tuira River, Darién.

First Expedition to Panama

Meek and Hildebrand tackled their first field season in Panama in the dry season of 1910. First, they occupied themselves with the newly formed Lake Gatún, for it was feared at the time that fish species from the Chagres, the Caribbean stream recently dammed to supply water to the Panama Canal locks, would enter the Pacific when the Canal began operations. Later, they explored the rivers near the Pacific entrance to the Canal: Río Grande and Río Chorrera, and to the east the Mamoní and the Bayano.

They concluded their first survey in May 1911, when the rainy season surprised them on the Atlantic slope, near Portobelo. Meek suffered a serious bout of malaria and returned to the United States. Hildebrand, after shipping eight barrels of specimens to the Smithsonian, went home in August 1911, to marry Claudia Chaillaux, his fiancée since 1907.

Second Panama Expedition

On January 15, 1912, Meek and Hildebrand disembarked again in Cristobal, setting up headquarters at Culebra, a camp on the banks of the Canal, near the continental divide. They spent the first months of the dry season collecting marine fishes in the Bay of Panama, at the entrance to the Canal, in

Balboa, and at Punta Chame. Then they moved on to the Caribbean, collecting at Cristobal, Colón, Toro Point (today Fort Sherman), and Portobelo. They also returned to the rivers near the Pacific side of the Canal.

mountains at Cana, a distance of about 30 miles. This was followed and some of the small streams en route were fished. At Cana the small Rio Cana and the somewhat larger Rio Seteganti were visited and rather extensive collections made in each. An overland trip of about 10 miles was made from Cana to

On February 21, 1912, they traveled to the Darién in the small steamer *Cana*, to explore the Tuira River and its tributaries, the Cupe, the Setegantí, and the Cana.

"From Boca de Cupe," wrote Meek,

the Darien Gold Mining Company has constructed a small tramway to its mines in the

the Río Grande another one of the upper tributaries of the Río Tuyra. These small mountain streams are all very rocky and collecting is difficult. Most of the streams were clear and cool at the time of our visit, but the Rio Cana was very turbid with reddish sediment on its bed. However, a number of very interesting forms not seen elsewhere were secured from the latter.

The Trinidad River, a house threatened by the rising waters of the new Gatún Lake,
circa 1911-1912. Page 158: Cana, Darién.
Photos (2): Seth Meek or Samuel Hildebrand. Source: Field Museum Photo Archives, Chicago.

Darién, 1912.
The tram line between
Boca de Cupe, a town
at the Tuira River and
the gold mines at Cana.
Lantern slide by
Seth Meek.
Source: Field Museum
Photo Archives,
Chicago.

Pages 160-161:
The Trinidad River, a
tributary of the Chagres,
1911. Seth Meek is in
the stern of the canoe.
Source: Field Museum
Photo Archives,
Chicago.

Some of the upper tributaries of the Río Tuyra and those of the Atrato of the Atlantic slope of Colombia come very close together and the water shed between the two basins is very low. We were informed by the employees of the Darien Gold Mining Co. that the Indians of this region, during the rainy season when the streams are high, often drag their canoes from the headwaters of one basin to those of another, and inasmuch as the fishes of the two streams are much alike it seems very probable that within a comparatively recent times a gap remained somewhere along this water shed.

In May, Meek became ill again and had to return to Panama and then to the United States. Samuel Hildebrand arrived home just in time for the birth of his daughter, Louise, on June 12, 1912.

The Isthmian Coasts and Collecting Methods

In their work, Meek and Hildebrand contrasted the major differences that exist be-

An Emberá Indian family on the Tuira or Chucunaque rivers, Darién, 1912.
The tall man in the back could be the young Samuel Hildebrand.
Lantern slide by S. Meek. Source: Field Museum Photo Archives, Chicago.

Dramatic scene of a peasant hut on fire near the canal works. Women and children stand
outside while men try to save scanty household items.
Lantern slide by Meek or Hildebrand. Source: Field Museum Photo Archives, Chicago.

tween the two coasts of the Isthmus: the Atlantic, rainy, low and swampy, with large lagoons, mangrove forests, and extensive coral reefs; the Pacific coast, drier and with a higher coastline, dotted by many rocky promontories and offshore islands. In the rivers of the Pacific coast, strong tides allowed marine fishes to swim quite far upstream. In contrast, on the Atlantic side,

tides were far weaker and had little effect on the rivers.

The physical differences between the two coasts obliged the scientists to use different fishing methods: dragnets, line fishing, wooden traps and dynamite for turbid waters. They collected specimens from tide pools on the Pacific coast and placed nets at the mouths of rivers. Often they visited the markets in Panama City and Colón, to buy rare specimens. But the most unusual collection method was discovered at Punta Chame, the peninsula west of Panama City that extends 30 kms into the Pacific.

Robert Tweedlie and the Dredge at Punta Chame

Robert Tweedlie was the engineer in charge of a great ocean dredge that the Isthmian Canal Commission had at Punta Chame to suction off sand, day and night, for the construction of the Canal. Tweedlie was an amateur naturalist who collected the rare species extracted by the dredge from the sea bottom along with the sand. Tweedlie gave his extremely valuable collection of species to Meek and Hildebrand, many of them new records for Panama, and others completely unknown to science.

Meek and Hildebrand's Publications about Panama

In mid-1912, Meek traveled from Chicago to Washington to begin with Hildebrand the analysis the 16 barrels of fish from Panama. That year they published the article "Descriptions of new fishes from Panama," in which they revealed the existence of novel species from Panamanian rivers. Their work "New Species of Fishes from Panama," describing fishes from the Tuira River, was published in 1913.

Suddenly, in April, Meek fell ill again; returning home to Chicago, he died of a heart attack on July 6, 1914. Hildebrand, his student and assistant, assumed the responsibility of analyzing and drafting the final reports on the fishes of Panama. Hildebrand

could only dedicate himself part time to this task because he was named director of the Biological Station in Beaufort, North Carolina.

Meek and Hildebrand's book about the fresh-water fish of Panama came out in 1916. Their splendid work on the marine fish fauna was published in three volumes in 1923, 1925, and 1928.

The Isthmus as a Barrier to Marine Fish

In their work on marine fishes, Meek and Hildebrand noted that fishes from the Pacific Coast were more diverse and larger than those from the Atlantic Coast. The majority of Pacific coastal fishes belonged to the North American fauna. They identified 403 species from the Gulf of Panama and 283 species from Caribbean coastal waters.

Their comments about the rise of the Isthmus and its role as a barrier that separated the tropical marine fauna are fascinating. The striking similarity between fish species in the Pacific and the Atlantic led them to support the hypothesis that a salt-water channel had once united the two oceans.

"The ichthyologic evidence is overwhelmingly in favor," commented Meek and Hildebrand in 1923, "of the existence of a former open communication between the two oceans, which must have become closed at a period sufficiently remote from the present to have permitted the specific differentiation of a very large majority of the forms involved. That this differentiation progressed at varying rates became at once apparent. A small minority of the species remain wholly unchanged, so far. . . .A larger number have become distinguished from their representatives of the opposite coast by minute (but not 'trivial') differences, which are wholly constant."

The construction of the Panama Canal would open a new chapter in the role the Isthmus played on the evolution of marine species. After serving as a barrier that separated the fishes of the two oceans for millions of years, now the interoceanic route might reestablish the passage of fish from one ocean to the other.

In these volumes, treating the freshwater and marine fishes of Panama, Meek appears as first author and Hildebrand as second author. However, it was Hildebrand who edited both works. This shows his altruistic spirit and gratefulness toward his mentor, who initiated him in ichthyology and furthermore was his great friend. The following section summarizes a few biographical details about these two naturalists.

Seth E. Meek

Seth Eugene Meek was born in Hicksville, Ohio, in 1859. His father was Scottish and had served as a soldier in the U.S. Civil War. His mother, of English descent, was born at sea while her parents were immigrating to the United States. As a boy, Seth worked on his father's farm and attended a rural school. He wanted to be a teacher.

In 1881, Meek graduated from the normal school in Valparaíso, Indiana. His passion for zoology could be traced to one

of his professors at the University of Indiana, David Starr Jordan, who imparted a love for nature in his students by requiring that they choose an original problem to study or an individual field project. Starr recommended that Meek review the information about a group of tropical river fish, the *mojarras* or *mojarritas*. This task inspired Meek to dedicate his life to science; to collect and identify fish and to study fish systematics and problems concerning the

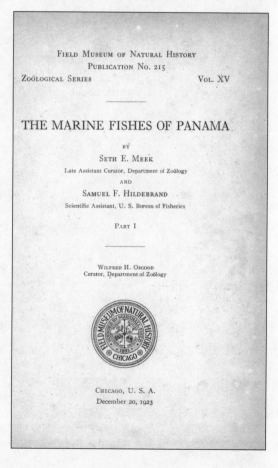

Cover of Meek and Hildebrand's book *The Marine Fishes of Panama*. Its three volumes were published by Chicago's Field Museum of Natural History between 1923 and 1928.

geographical distribution and life histories of fishes.

The University of Indiana granted Meek a Bachelor's degree in 1884, a Master's in 1886, and a doctorate in 1891. He married in 1886. He served as professor of natural sciences at Eureka College in Illinois, and at Coe College in Iowa. From 1892 to 1896, he was professor of biology and geology, and director of the Museum of Natural History, at the University of Arkansas. The Smithsonian Institution gave him a grant to study at the famous aquarium in Naples, Italy, from 1896–1897. When he returned to the United States, the Chicago Field Museum hired him as a fish specialist. He worked there until he died in 1914.

Meek and the Fisheries Commission

During the 1880s and 1890s, Meek studied the fishes and amphibians of North America during his vacations. He conducted field studies for the U.S. Fisheries Commission without pay, simply for the love of learning. He studied the river fish of Tennessee, North Carolina, Missouri, Arkansas, Iowa, Nebraska, and the Indian Territories, as well as the habits of the Columbia River salmon, and the fishes of coastal California.

A new phase would open up for Meek in 1902, when he began to study tropical fishes. He explored the Gulf of Tehuantepec in Mexico, and published *Distribution of the Fishes of the Isthmus of Tehuantepec* and

Seth E. Meek in the Chagres River, 1911. Photo by Samuel F. Hildebrand.
Source: *Explorations and Fieldwork of the Smithsonian Institution, 1912.*

Collection of Fishes from the Isthmus of Tehuantepec. Subsequently, he explored Central America, concentrating on lake fishes from Lakes Amatitlán and Atitlán in Guatemala, and lakes Nicaragua and Managua in Nicaragua, and the rivers of Costa Rica.

Samuel Fredrick Hildebrand

Hildebrand was born in Indiana on August 15, 1883. His parents, Herman Hildebrand and Sophia Weitkamp, were farmers from Munster, in Prussia. Poverty forced them to flee to the United States during the last years of the American Civil War. For years, his father farmed rented land. With great effort, he managed to buy a small farm near Zoar, a tiny town consisting of a Methodist church and a general store. The Hildebrands raised ten children there; Samuel was the youngest. He spent his childhood helping out on the farm and doing his schoolwork. As was the custom, he turned over all of his earnings to his father until he was 21 years old.

Because his parents lived in a community of German immigrants, they never learned to speak English; Samuel spoke German fluently. The Hildebrands were fervent Methodists. They instilled Methodist values in their children, especially a vigorous work ethic. Furthermore, like all of the Hildebrands, Samuel had a natural teaching ability.

In 1901, Samuel enrolled at Stendal College in order to study to become a schoolteacher; he graduated in 1905. To pay for his studies at the University of Indiana, he did different jobs, including teaching Ger-

Samuel F. Hildebrand (1883-1946). Student and colleague of Seth E. Meek. The pupil who surpassed his teacher. The field studies of both men established the basis for the contemporary ichthyology of Panama. Source: *Copeia*, March 1950.

man. In 1908, one of his professors, U. O. Cox, recommended him to Seth E. Meek, who was looking for a research assistant. It was Meek who inspired his enthusiasm for ichthyology.

The Trout of the Chiriquí Viejo River

Hildebrand would return to Panama in 1924, to explore the Chiriquí Viejo River, where, accompanied by a man named Foster, he stocked trout in the cold headwaters of the river. The fish that he introduced are still delicacies, enjoyed by visitors to the highlands around Volcán Barú. Hildebrand returned to the Chiriquí Viejo in 1937 to assess the condition of the trout that he had introduced in 1924.

Gorgas Laboratories

At the invitation of Dr. Herbert Clark, then director of Gorgas Laboratory, Hildebrand visited Panama in February 1935. He collected in Lake Gatún and its tributaries, and in the Gatún Locks, in order to determine the role of the Canal in the movement of fish species between the two oceans. He collected marine species in the Gulf of Panama and the Las Perlas Islands. At the request of Gorgas Laboratory, he surveyed Panamanian waters again in 1937. His final exploration of the Isthmus took place in 1944, as part of the biological surveys of the Las Perlas Islands.

In addition to his work on Panama, Hildebrand would publish other important works on the fishes of Central America, El Salvador, and Costa Rica, and a monumental work on the marine fishes of Peru.

How did Freshwater Fish colonize the Isthmus of Panama?

In 1938, Hildebrand published *A New Catalogue of the Fresh-Water Fishes of Panama*. He described the route followed by freshwater fish as they populated the rivers of the Isthmus:

> The information gained since our earlier work was printed. . . .seems to show more clearly that most of the fishes of eastern and central Panama are of South American origin. The principal route of migration apparently was from the Atlantic slope of Colombia to the Pacific slope of eastern and central Panama. The most probable route is from the Atrato to the Tuyra; from the Tuyra to the Bayano; and from the Bayano and neighboring coastal streams to the Chagres. . . . The fishes of far western Panama, however, are chiefly Central American.

In 1944, Hildebrand began a major undertaking which would remain unfinished: a more complete and updated catalogue of the marine fish of Panama, a project that would absorb him for years. By 1946, he had finished three quarters of the work. On March 16, after spending the day studying Panamanian fish, death suddenly claimed him.

Hildebrand's great humanity and scientific spirit, and his search for human welfare, are reflected in his work. Most of his publications are written to be understood and used not only by a few experts but also by the average citizen interested in nature and its intelligent use. Samuel F. Hildebrand understood that the best guarantee for the rational use and conservation of species would be to count on the enlightened participation of the public.

James Zetek:
Barro Colorado Biological Station
(1923-1953)

From an Unknown Hilltop
to a Famous Island

During the building of the Panama Canal, the Chagres River was dammed. It's rising waters flooded the valleys, forming Lake Gatún, and hilltops became islands. The highest hill, Barro Colorado ("red clay"), in the middle of the Isthmus, between the rainy Caribbean and the drier Pacific lowlands, became the largest island in the new lake. In 1923, the island became a nature reserve, and a tiny research station was established there. As time went by, naturalists from around the world would come to study its rich flora and fauna and reveal in hundreds of articles and books the secrets of a tropical forest.

In this epic of science in the tropics, in which the Biological Station on Barro Colorado became one of the foremost centers of tropical research in the world, James Zetek played a key role. Son of Czech parents, Zetek was born in Chicago on the 12th of December in 1886. He died in Panama in 1959 at the age of 73.

Today, there are more forests along the waterway than when it was completed over 90 years ago, most of them protected by law. Zetek was a forerunner in this conservation movement. Although Panama would award him the Vasco Núñez de Balboa Medal, and the Smithsonian Tropical Research Institute, STRI, would make him a Research Associate, his contributions are not well known to the general public. There is no bust of him, nor is there a plaque in his old house at Balboa, Number 0902, Amador Road.

Mosquito Expert

James Zetek arrived on the Isthmus in 1911, a 25 year-old recent graduate in entomology from the University of Illinois. He came to work for the Isthmian Canal Commission with Dr. William Gorgas, to study the great tropical killer yellow fever and its mosquito vector. He arrived just at the time

a major and unprecedented social ex-
periment was taking form: the U.S.
Canal Zone, a 10-mile wide area along
the Canal, was ceded to the U.S. by
Panama. It would eventually become
home of many U.S. citizens who would
come to be known as "Zonians."

In 1914, the year when the canal was
inaugurated, Zetek married his life-long
companion, María Luisa Gutiérrez,
daughter of a distinguished Panamanian
family. Both were fervent Catholics.
Their union would be one of the first in
a new social trend in Panama: marriages
between single U.S. men arriving on the
Isthmus and Panamanian women. For
Zetek, this union opened a window on
local customs and practices, and would
link him into the web of kinship and
social relations essential for getting
things done in Panama. Among his in-
laws he met Ignacio Molino, who would
become one of his few close friends and
furthermore his right hand man on a
number of projects.

In 1914, President Belisario Porras appointed Zetek to organize the National
Exposition, successfully celebrated in
Panama City from 1915 to 1916. Between 1916 and 1918, Zetek taught
natural sciences at the Instituto Nacional, then Panama's most prestigious
public high school. His photo, in the
Panama Blue Book for 1917, which
contained information on the most
prominent people in the Isthmus at the
time, shows him in a suit and tie, wearing a heavy mustache and an intense,
intelligent look.

James Zetek (1886-1959).
Entomologist and first director of the biological
station on Barro Colorado Island.
Photo by Alexander Wetmore.
Smithsonian Institution Archives,
Washington, D.C.

His specialty was mosquito biology and his first publications were in this field. However, he was fascinated by mollusks. His first publication in Spanish was *Los moluscos de la República de Panamá* (The mollusks of the Republic of Panama), which won a government prize, and was published by *Revista Nueva* in 1918.

An Expert on Flies

From 1918 to 1920, Zetek served as an entomologist for the Isthmian Canal Commission. In 1920, he was named by the U.S. Department of Agriculture "expert on the control of the black fly" (*Anastrepha*), which attacked tropical fruits. One of the few times he would leave Panama was in 1927, when he was sent to Texas to study fruit flies in the orange groves there. At the request of the Mexican government, he visited Cuernavaca, in order to choose a site for a fruit fly research laboratory.

Knowledge about Tropical Forests

Although the establishment of the laboratory on Barro Colorado was tied to the struggle against yellow fever, it is necessary to briefly outline the global context of tropical sciences at the time.

At the turn of the 20th Century, tropical forests were a great scientific enigma. The few tropical research laboratories in existence belonged to colonial European powers such as England, France, and the Netherlands. Even so, the Dutch research stations at Java and Sumatra were located in colonial administrative centers, far from the forest itself. In turn, the British station at Ceylon was surrounded by tea plantations.

Most of what was known about the tropics was a product of expeditions organized by museums and wealthy individuals from the industrialized countries of the day. The goal of these missions was not to study how species behaved in their natural environment, but to collect as many specimens as possible in order to classify and catalogue them back in their home institutions. Determining how many plant and animals existed in the tropics was of utmost interest to scientists.

A Natural Park on the Banks of the Canal

Although Zetek studied insects, he was also interested in plants and other animals. Arriving in Panama, he was struck by the impact of the canal works on the landscape: the extensive deforestation, the draining of vast wetlands, the excavation of a huge trench and the transportation of monstrous volumes of soil to other areas, the damming of a tropical river, and the formation of an enormous artificial lake to supply water in astronomical quantities to the locks.

The formation of Lake Gatún stimulated the local economy, aggravating deforestation. Firms based in Panama City selectively logged the most valuable timber species in the forest. Along the Chilibre River, it was not unusual for loggers to extract 1,500 mahagony trees per year. Growing bananas for export to the United States became an important business. *Campesinos* cleared thousands of hectares of forest to plant the fruit that was sold to foreign companies for shipment to ports on the eastern seaboard of the United States.

Faced with the advance of deforestation, Zetek proposed "to find a sufficiently large area of virgin tropical forest that will remain unaltered, where men of science can come to work." One of the few wild areas in the canal watershed with such characteristics was Barro Colorado. For 12 years Zetek sought support from within and outside of Panama to convert it into a "natural park": a forested area in good condition, with many plants and animals, where naturalists could expand their knowledge in all branches of the biological sciences.

Gradually, he obtaineed support from distinguished academics and scientists who either worked for the Canal or came to visit the work in progress: Wheeler, Strong, Barbour, Fairchild, and Piper. As in many human dramas, nationalism would play a role. Some men of science in the U.S., like Thomas Barbour from Harvard, felt that the United States should have its own tropical laboratory which could compete with those of Europe. Furthermore, Barbour proposed that tropical studies should be funded from a portion of canal revenues. His government responded that there were no funds for such an undertaking.

Porras and Morrow: Panama as a Center for Tropical Research

Zetek had two powerful allies in the Isthmus: Belisario Porras, President of Panama, and Jay Morrow, Governor of the Canal Zone. Both shared his vision of Panama as an important center for advanced scientific studies of the tropics.

Porras was one of the few Panamanian presidents who had a clear sense of the fundamental role of science in promoting growth and development. For Porras, the laboratory for terrestrial research that Zetek was proposing for Barro Colorado would be a jumping-off point from which naturalists from around the world would set out to

Jay J. Morrow, Governor of the Panama Canal Zone, 1921-1924.
In 1923, Morrow declared Barro Colorado Island a protected area for biological research.

study the rest of Panama and neighboring countries. *Don* Belisario's strategy also included two other components: founding a great marine research center in Panama City, where the statue of Vasco Núñez de Balboa now stands facing the Pacific, and a center for advanced studies of tropical medicine, the current Gorgas Memorial Laboratory.

Governor Morrow was an enlightened man who was interested in scientific progress and, above all, in its applications. He envisioned a great botanical garden whith tropical species from many different parts of the world, both ornamentals and plants of economic of the sciences.

People wishing to conduct studies on Barro Colorado had to be approved by Thomas Barbour, president of the executive committee. But in Panama, the telegraph office address for the laboratory was "Zetek, Balboa, Canal Zone" and the postal address: "James Zetek, Box 245, Ancon."

In 1946, the U.S. Congress transferred Barro Colorado to the Smithsonian Institution; Zetek would become the resident manager until his retirement in 1956. The next director of the biological station would be Martin H. Moynihan. As an outcome of the Torrijos-Carter Treaties in 1977, in 1979 Barro Colorado and the five surrounding mainland peninsulas would become the Barro Colorado Nature Monument, administered by the Smithsonian Tropical Research Institute.

"Laboratory from water," view by F. Chapman of the facilities at Barro Colorado in 1927.
Source: American Museum of Natural History Archives, New York, N.Y.
Page 176-77: The train station at Frijoles, Gatún Lake. Frijoles was the disembarkation point for naturalists going to Barro Colorado Island.
Photo: Smithsonian Institution Archives.

The boat landing at Frijoles, circa 1950, where those heading for BCI took the launch.
Source: Smithsonian Institution Archives, Washington, D.C.

To Attract Naturalists

From 1923 until 1953, Zetek would be the dedicated and visionary administrator of the Barro Colorado Island Biological Station. His contribution during the first years of the station was monumental. With a very limited and unpredictable budget, he would work miracles during the Great Depression and the Second World War, when the station's yearly income never exceeded $3,000 and the fate of Barro Colorado hung by a thread. For several years, before the island was declared a reserve, bananas had been grown in Barro Colorado; the bunches produced in these small plots became handy, and were sold to defray the station's expenses.

In the face of constant scarcity, Zetek assumed many responsibilities. While canal employees had the right to take 54 vacation days each year, Zetek was only offered 15 days, which he used in service to the laboratory. Furthermore, he covered certain island expenses out of his own pocket and helped out students short on cash.

His superiors always admired Zetek's ability to present impeccable, orderly accounts for the laboratory year after year. They wondered how he could "provide good food and comfort to our visitors at such extremely low cost." Although Zetek was shy, he was forced to beg for donations. He contracted and trained local labor to maintain the station's basic services. He built installations to provide minimal comforts that would attract naturalists: a roof, a clean bed, good food, potable water, and laboratories in healthy surroundings. He constructed miles of trails on the island, establishing the tradition of baptizing each trail with the name of a researcher, or a patron of the station. He was, in addition, the island's first meteorologist, librarian, contact between the scientists and authorities from Panama or the Canal Zone, and the first "resident naturalist" and guide to interpret tropical nature to visitors.

He convinced the Canal Commission to clear navigation channels around the island by dynamiting the huge trees submerged in the lake. The U.S. Army Air Force would take the first aerial photos showing the precise location of virgin forests and areas where timber had been extracted from Barro Colorado Island.

The boundaries of the island were marked with signs in English, Spanish, and French, the latter because many *campesinos* around Lake Gatún were former canal laborers from the French Antilles. The first foreman hired by Zetek was a labourer from Martinique who had worked for 20 years on the canal. He was an intelligent man, with no formal education, who spoke French, English, and Spanish. His wife, a *chiricana* (a native from Chiriquí province), would introduce hundreds of visiting scientists to local Creole cooking. Four *chiricano* campesinos served as *macheteros,* to clear the vegetation with machetes, and as boatmen and woodsmen.

The Library

A specialized library is vital to science. Zetek put his extensive private collection in the service of visiting scientists and established the rule that people who worked on Barro Colorado Island or in Panama, should submit two copies of their work for use by other researchers in the future. He placed the library on the mailing lists of great scientific institutions and obtained permission

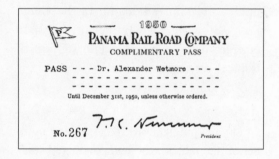

Naturalists doing research on Barro Colorado Island enjoyed complimentary passes from the Panama Railroad.
Source: Smithsonian Institution Archives, Washington, D.C.

for scientists to use the public health library in Ancón Hospital in Panama City. Meanwhile, Barbour and Fairchild paid for books bought in Europe and North America for use on the island.

Private and Public Support

Various steamship lines that transited the Panama Canal decided to give a 25% discount on the price of a ticket from the United States to Panama to naturalists whose proposals for research on Barro Colorado had been approved. United Fruit and Standard Fruit, who bought bananas in Gatún, and the Chilean *Compañía Sudamericana de Vapores*, were the first to give such discounts. The naturalists could also travel on the U.S. Navy supply vessels for $1.50 per day if there were space available. The Panama Railroad offered berths on their boats sailing from the east coast of the U.S. to Cristobal for $50, as well as free passage on their trains in Panama. The Canal Commission extended privileges to the scientists: use of commissaries, access to hospitals, and family housing in the Canal Zone. Slowly a novel framework began to emerge for private and public support of tropical research.

Publications

Gradually, publications by a growing number of naturalists, who had conducted studies in the forests of Barro Colorado, began to appear. By 1930, there were 118 published reports from the island: articles in both scientific and popular journals, and several books such as Frank Chapman's best seller *My Tropical Air Castle: Nature Studies in Panama*. In 1947, the bibliography had surpassed 600 titles, treating such diverse subjects as lichens, ferns, fungi, mosquitoes, ants, snakes, freshwater fish, frogs, coatimundis, monkeys, and bird behavior and the habits of sloths.

Applied Research:
Termites and Photographic Equipment

During the first decades, applied studies were also conducted on the island. One of the most important regarded termites. During canal construction days, a major problem for engineers and architects had been the speed with which termites devoured wooden structures. The timber industry in the U.S. financed studies of termites and their effects on different woods from 1923 until the 1940s.

Zetek and Thomas Snyder, entomologist with the U.S. Department of Agriculture, were in charge. They studied 57 species of Panamanian termites, 45 of these from Barro Colorado, and some capable of eating even the lead shielding on electrical wiring. They also tested termite resistance of hundreds of different types of wood, both native and exotic, with and without protective chemical treatment. A new construction material "Celotex" was subjected to its first tropical trials on the island.

The Eastman Kodak Company conducted extensive tests on Barro Colorado on the effects of tropical conditions on cameras; how a microscopic fungus etched lenses; how film behaved, especially regarding color retention; the storage and packaging of photographic materials. C. C. Soper, who was responsible for this research, became a very close friend of Zetek.

Students on the Island

An objective of the station was to stimulate student interest in tropical forest research. This goal has been accomplished many times over. In October 1946, Corina Rodríguez, a Panamanian high school student, would write her impressions of the exuberant landscape of Lake Gatún and Barro Colorado and of James Zetek in the local Panamanian magazine *Epocas*:

Solitude without depression! The smell of forest and humid soil! All on an Island that rises from Lake Gatún and bewitches and enthralls. . . . Barro Colorado is clad all in greens: lime green, olive green, jade green, emerald green, light green, blue green, sea green. . . . There, among the greens. . . . is a scientist, Zetek, who works day and night. A "Knight of Columbus", who lives for humanity, for God and for Science. The Island is a true arcadia, an enchanted place, an Eden! Zetek is the guardian. He is the scientist who knows all its nooks and crannies, its many trails, its streams and the immense variety of birds that inhabit it. He is a man who has something of Tolstoy about him, much of Favre, and the humility of St. Francis of Assisi. He is a researcher whose work should be known by young people: an exemplary life that reconciles us with humanity and returns our faith in education. On his island reign modesty, peace, research, truth, and love for all beings: from the most humble of God's creatures to the wisest sage, who comes from beyond the seas to know the flora and fauna of the tropics.

The Panama Canal Natural History Society

Zetek was deeply concerned with spreading scientific knowledge to the broader public. In 1931 he became a founding member and first president of The Panama Canal Natural History Society. Its goal, as stated in its motto, was: "For the promotion of scientific research, the unification and diffusion of such knowledge and spirit in the Republic of Panama and the Panama Canal Zone."

It was thought that there existed in the Isthmus a sufficient critical mass of men of science and interested laymen to establish a monthly program of motivating and valuable talks for both the people of Panama City and the Canal Zone. To enrichen the talks, Zetek was able to interest naturalists passing through the Isthmus and those working at Barro Colorado Island. Herbert C. Clark, Director of the Gorgas Memorial Laboratory in Panama City, who became president of the Natural History Society in 1934, offered the Gorgas auditorium as the venue for the monthly talks.

The membership included residents from Ancón, Balboa, Balboa Heights, Fort Clayton, Panama City, Pedro Miguel, Quarry Heights, Summit as well as Thomas Barbour of Cambridge, Massachusetts, and Frank Chapman of New York City.

Between 1931 and 1932, Zetek gave presentations on such topics as: "The Life of the Termite;" "The Economic Aspect and Means of Control of Termites;" "Monkeys as Plant Collectors;" "Notes on the Fer-de-Lance and Bushmaster;" "Why Scientific Names?," and "Red Ring Disease of Coconut Palms in Panama."

Zetek according to Adela Tapia de Gómez

Little has been written about Zetek's personality. Therefore, I interviewed Adela Tapia de Gómez, an institution in her own right at the Smithsonian Tropical Research Institute. She began to work as Zetek's secretary and eventually was responsible for millions of details that made this great research center function. "Zetek lived in Balboa, next to the YMCA. He would go to the Balboa post office three times a day. He wrote copiously and received lots of correspondence. He dressed formally, in suit and suspenders, a white, long-sleeved shirt, ironed and starched," remembers Adela, adding:

> He was very kind; he liked to give a hand to people who were short on cash. If someone didn't have a job, he would help to find one. Often, he would give little gifts to the fellows who worked on the Panama-Colon train.

He was very immersed in his studies, and read constantly. He was a bit dry. He had few friends; one of these was the head of Kodak in Panama, Cliff Soper, a chemist and the head of Kodak research laboratories here. Zetek rarely went to parties; he usually invited people to his own house. Among the scientists who came to Barro Colorado he had few friends, Dr. Alexander Wetmore and his wife

Comparative tests of wood preservatives for controlling termites began in 1928 in Barro Colorado, Canberra, Honolulu, and the Union of South Africa.
The photo shows Watson Perrygo from the U.S. National Museum, looking at test stakes at BCI in March 1946. Thomas E. Snyder and James Zetek led this project.
Photo by A. Wetmore. Source: Smithsonian Institution Archives, Washington, D.C.

Bea, who would come to work on his book about the birds of Panama. Another friend was T. C. Schnierla. Zetek spoke Spanish well, but traveled little within Panama; nor did he like to go to the United States. He was quiet, humble, he didn't let on that he knew about everything; he didn't show off, talk about himself, his family, or his origins.

Our entomologist preferred rum to scotch and liked to drink several times a day: one drink before lunch, and then at dusk. He didn't like to get drunk. He didn't listen to the radio or music. He liked to eat rice, beans, and *sancocho,* a local chicken soup made with root vegetables and lots of *cilantro*. Adela remembers that at the time "Panamanians had no interest in science, they were not keen in knowing about Panamanian natural history."

One wonders about Zetek's solitude, that certain bitterness, perhaps due to the fact that he only had a bachelor's degree. His lack of a Ph.D. had denied him certain possibilities for promotion and acknowledgement in the scientific world, where titles and diplomas meant everything. For those scientists who knew him, he was always "Mr. Zetek." For Panamanians and Zonians, he was always "Dr. Zetek." His death went unmentioned in the Barro Colorado Annual Report, which he had initiated and faithfully edited for 30 years.

C. W. Powell's Orchid Garden at Cerro Ancón (1910-1926)

In the 1910's and 1920's, the biggest tourist attraction in Panama (after the Canal) was Charles Wesley Powell's garden at his house on Ancon Hill. "The Powell orchid garden at Balboa," wrote Paul Standley enthusiastically in a 1924 report to the Smithsonian Institution, "is one of the most interesting sights of the Canal Zone, and botanically by far the most remarkable thing to be seen there. It is something unique in tropical America, if not in the whole world." Over 7,000 plants grew in this garden, including 400 different species of orchids unique to Panama.

In Powell's garden one could see and study all the well-known orchids of Panama. Furthermore, we owe most of our knowledge about Panamanian orchids at the beginning of the 20th Century to Charles Powell's hobby. He spent his free time gathering, cultivating, and studying orchids, an extraordinary achievement for someone who began as a layman.

His garden was surrounded by an eight-foot tall chicken wire fence covered by lianas and climbing plants that he arranged to achieve the optimum proportion of light and shade.

Most of his plants were epiphytes or plants that would usually grow on tree trunks and branches. Most tropical orchids belong to this group. The other group was the terrestrial orchids. Powell's epiphytes grew in baskets and boxes suspended from a great mango tree on the patio.

Powell arrived in Panama in January of 1907 and, like most North Americans, scarcely knew about the tropics. But he quickly realized how different tropical plants are from those of temperate zones. Naturally, tropical orchids, the aristocrats among flowers, attracted his attention. In Panama orchids are very diverse due to the major contrasts in the climates of two coasts so close to one other: the wet forests of the Atlantic, and the drier forests and savannas of the Pacific slope.

C. W. Powell (1854-1926).
Originally a quinine dispenser of the Isthmian Canal Commission, Powell became the most important orchidologist in Panama at the beginning of the 20th Century.
Photo by P. C. Standley. Source: *Annual Report of the Board of Regents of the Smithsonian Institution*, 1924.

Powell became interested in orchids in 1915, when he decided to build the most complete collection of orchid species from Panama. He was passionate about everything concerning these exotic plants, which to a large extent live on water and air and are as temperamental as opera singers. Years later he regretted that he had not become interested in orchid classification earlier, before the construction of the canal, which destroyed so many forests. Many species disappeared as a result of the canal works. Among these was one of the most beautiful orchids in Panama, *Sobralia powellii*, discovered and named in honor of Powell by Dr. Schlechter, the famous German botanist. This species, endemic to the Chagres River, was found by Powell in an area now under the waters of Lake Gatún. Although later he spent a great amount of time looking for it, he was unable to find it again.

Apparently, Powell's passion for orchids arose during a fishing trip to the recently formed Gatún Lake. According to an account by Robertus Love of the *St. Louis Daily Globe-Democrat* from May 1927:

> Down in the Panama Canal Zone two southerners from the United States chipped in and bought a motor boat. Gatún Lake, a part of the Panama Canal, was a comparatively new creation in its present form. The waters rose and rose until they presented at last a level surface through which the upper portions of thousands of tall trees protruded. The American motor-boating partners went fishing on the lake, their craft cutting paths between the treetops. The elder, C. W. Powell, was a most enthusiastic fisherman. A. A. Hunter, about twenty years younger, divided his affections between fishes and flowers.

> "Look, Powell – orchids! Oodles of orchids! Treefulls of orchids! Let's get some of 'em," said Hunter.

> "What's orchids?" innocently inquired Powell.

> Hunter smiled. The boat was steered close to a half-submerged tree and the younger man skillfully detached a beautifull orchid from the trunk; then another and another, and after visiting and "robbing" many trees the motor boat was full of wonderfull plants and blossoms. Fishing was forgotten. C. W. Powell had discovered what orchids are, where and how they grow, how to catch them instead of catching fish. It was a new sport to him, and before long it became the new ruling passion of his life.

Quinine Dispenser

Charles Wesley Powell was born in Richmond, Virginia, on May 5, 1854. As an adult, he planted cotton, and later worked for a newspaper in Memphis, Tennessee. For 15 years he lived in New Orleans, until he moved to Guatemala. He arrived in Panama in January 1907 at age 43 to work for the Isthmian Canal Commission. First he worked in the Atlantic division of the canal works, as assistant in a field clinic in Gatún, administering quinine pills to workers. Then he was transferred to Colón as a sanitary inspector, and then to Portobelo, to the big quarries from which stone was extracted for the huge Gatún dam and locks. Later he would work at the railroad camp at Gorgona, and was one of the last five people to be evacuated from this historical town in 1913, before it was flooded when the huge Gamboa dike was blown up to allow the water from Gatún Lake to flow into the Culebra Cut and then into the Pacific. From 1913 onwards he would work as pharmacist on the Pacific side, until his retirement in 1926.

Orchid collecting was extremely difficult then, for Panama had no road system. Powell spent most of his free time collecting and cultivating orchids. On his vacations, accompanied by another orchid enthusiast, his great friend A. A. Hunter, he would go deep into the forest, especially in the mountains of Chiriquí, because orchids are more common at higher altitudes. He also hired people from nearby towns to facilitate collecting in the forest. His most trusted assistant was a West Indian, Christopher Cheeseman, who gradually became the most prominent local orchid expert. From the forests, plants were transplanted into Powell's garden at Cerro Ancón, where, with utmost care and attention, they flourished and reproduced. Thanks to Powell's perseverance, world specialists could study the orchids at their leisure. Only the careful cultivation techniques that Powell employed in his garden made it possible to gather this record number of isthmian orchids in a single place.

Powell honestly believed his orchids knew him by feeling his presence upon entering the garden. "I know this sounds odd," he once said, "but it is true, and I have seen it with my own eyes too often to be mistaken. When I used to return from a trip into the Jungle, I'd go into my garden and all the flowers would look tired and dejected. Then I used to wander about, speaking to this plant and that one, removing a twig, feeling the stem, and noticing any changes. And before I had been in the garden ten minutes I would notice a marked change in the plants, which seemed to spruce up and stiffen their wilted petals."

Powell's Contribution to Panamanian Orchideology

Although Panama and Central America are a paradise for orchid collectors, it was not until the end of the 19th Century that a detailed study of local orchids began.

According to Standley, the first plant collector who visited Central America was the Frenchman Luis Née, botanist aboard the famous Spanish navy expedition led by Commander Malespina which circumnavigated the globe between 1789 and 1794. Neé visited Panama and described some of the most common tropical plants in America for the first time. He collected plants on Ancón Hill, a promontory of volcanic origin, where Panama City was relocated after the English pirate Henry Morgan destroyed the Old City (*Panama Viejo*).

Later came the Pole Warscewicz, an orchidologist who traveled around Central America beginning in 1846 arriving in Veraguas, at that time a territory that encompassed most of western Panama including the contemporary provinces of Veraguas, Chiriquí and Bocas del Toro. Warscewicz devoted quite some time to exploring Chiriquí, considered to be Panama's richest region for orchid collection by the botanists of the time.

Ironically, only small patches of the extraordinary forests of Chiriquí survive today, and even those designated as protected areas such as Volcán Barú still suffer the constant onslaught of man. In 1852, Berthold Seemann arrived to study the plants of the Chagres River and other areas of the Isthmus. He published the first list of orchids of Panama, with 104 entries. Later, Henry Pittier and William Maxon collected many orchids around the canal, Chiriquí and other parts of Panamanian territory as part of the Smithsonian Institution's 1910–1912 Biological Survey.

beautiful and diverse tropical plants. Studying the literature available at the time, he soon realized that many of the plants in his garden were not known. He sent samples to the English orchidologist Rolfe, who unfortunately died before he was able to study

Oncidium Powellii, one of the many Panamanian orchids discovered by Powell. Photo by C. W. Powell. Source: *Annual Report of the Board of regents of the Smithsonian Institution, 1924.*

Powell's effort was admirable. When he acquired his orchid hobby, he earned a small wage of $60 per month, ignored the literature on these plants, and did not have any relationships with specialists. But, mastering these challenges, he transformed his garden into a unique living collection, and assembled an excellent library on these

the Panamanian orchids. Powell then sent another collection to the orchidologist Rudolf Schlechter from the Berlin Botanical Museum, who in 1922 published an article on the orchids of Panama. This work described 184 species, of which 75 were new to science. Later, when Powell sent his samples to Oakes Ames from the University of Harvard, the principal U.S. authority on orchids, the number of Panamanian orchids discovered by Powell had increased to 341. There has hardly ever been a similar record for a tropical country in which a single person has discovered so many orchids or has built such a complete collection of these plants.

Powell died on August 18, 1927, at age 72. In his last will he asked to be cremated and have his ashes spread at Cerro Ancón, but instead he was buried in Corozal, next to the Panama Canal and the railroad, beside his daughter's tomb. After his death, his friend A. A. Hunter, chief of the Balboa's post office, took charge of the Powell Orchid Garden, which he had donated to the Missouri Botanical Garden in 1926 for one dollar. Renamed the Missouri Shaw's Garden, this would become a Mecca for orchidologist from around the world.

The Missouri Botanical Garden and the *Flora of Panama*

However, the history of Powell's orchid garden does not end here. The Missouri Botanical Garden transformed it into the nucleus of its famous Tropical Station at Balboa, to be administered by A. A. Hunter until 1936, when it was transferred to the Canal Zone government and orchidologist Paul Allen was placed in charge of its administration.

The closing of the Tropical Station in 1936 opened another chapter in the Missouri Botanical Garden's relationships with Panama. It marked the beginning of a series of field expeditions, culminating in the publication of the monumental *Flora of Panama*. Begun in 1943 and concluded in 1981, this work adds up to more than 6,800 pages and describes 7,345 species of flowering plants from Panama.

Frank M. Chapman: From Banker to a Student of Nature in Panama (1912-1935)

Frank M. Chapman was born in New Jersey in the United States in 1864. In time, he would become one of the great specialists on the tropics of the early 20th Century. Chapman was part of that group of naturalists that arrived in Panama in the years following immediately the construction of the Panama Canal. Between 1912 and 1935, he investigated and published profusely on the Panamanian flora and fauna. As a product of his expeditions and natural history studies around the world he wrote sixteen books and hundreds of articles. This extra-ordinary legacy of work, documenting the nature of the Isthmus and the way in which naturalists of his time operated, is not well known.

The son of a northern veteran of the U.S. Civil War, he went to school in Baltimore but was not a particularly good student. However, in time he would earn a doctorate in science and become a curator at the American Museum of Natural History in New York and president of the American Ornithologists' Union.

After finishing his elementary studies, he first worked at the American Exchange National Bank, with a drudging commute between his home in New Jersey and his desk as a clerk. Quite early he would discover his two greatest sources of pleasure: birds and solitude. Every day, before going to work, he would wake up at dawn to observe migratory birds. His heart told him that his destiny was not to spend his life behind a teller's window, but to search out Nature's secrets.

In the dedication of his 1895 book *Birds of Eastern North America* he warmly and fondly acknowledges the person who stimulated his first interest in nature in these words: "To my mother who has ever encouraged her son in his natural history studies this book is affectionately dedicated." At the professional level, Elliot Coues, William Brewster, Dr. A. K. Fisher would stimulate

Frank M. Chapman (1864-1945).
A leading ornithologist of the early 20th Century, working on his field notes at "Chapman House", on Barro Colorado Island, 1935-1936.
Source: American Museum of Natural History Archives, New York, N.Y.

the ornithological interest of the young man noted for his sensibility. "It was about this time,"wrote D. R. Barton, "that a prize was offered for the best paper tracing the migratory movements of birds in various sections of the country. The prize for the Eastern Seaboard was awarded to a young bank clerk who was, of course, Frank Chapman and who accumulated nearly all his data from sundown to dark and between daybreak and the parting whistle of the 7:30 a.m. train to West Englewood station! This involved rising before dawn to tramp in the neighboring woods via a route planned to bring him to the station just in time to catch his train." With this prize, banking lost a clerk and ornithology gained a legendary figure.

In 1886, at age 22, he began to work at the American Museum of Natural History in New York, where he would remain for 50 years. One of his key interests was the indoor portrayals of the natural life of birds. He wanted the Museum to offer birdlovers the greatest information possible on local forms. One of his first successful exhibits was titled "Birds Within 50 Miles of New York City." Besides his pioneer work in the display of birds in museums he also helped to lay the foundations of scientific ornithology in our hemisphere. By 1908 he was in charge of the Ornithology Department. In the United States he is considered to be the second most important figure, after the famous naturalist painter John James Audubon, to encourage public interest in birds. In 1895 he would publish his book on the birds of Eastern North America. The early 20th Century found him carrying out extensive fieldwork for the American Museum of Natural History throughout Colombia and Ecuador. These impressive expeditions produced two formidable, groundbreaking publications.

Chapman's passion for the Panamanian forest arose gradually during his work in South America, especially after visiting the Isthmus for the first time in 1912. He would publish two books about his research in Panama that became best sellers. Both works described, for an English-speaking public of the temperate zones, the marvels

An early aerial view of Barro Colorado, the largest island in Gatún Lake, seen at bottom, in June 1927. The view taken by a U.S. Army airplane based at France Field, Colón, looks north, toward Gatún Locks and the city of Colón on the Caribbean entrance to the Panama Canal.
Photo: American Museum of Natural History Archives, New York, N.Y.

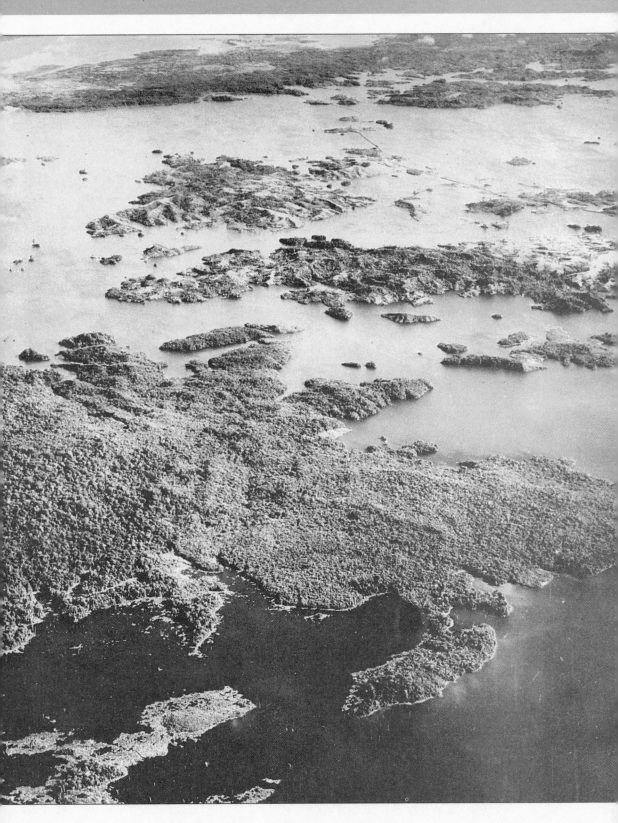

"Chapman House", on Barro Colorado Island (BCI) in 1927.
Photo by F. M. Chapman. Source: American Museum of Natural History Archives,
New York, N.Y.

of the flora and fauna of Barro Colorado, an exotic Panamanian island covered by jungle in the middle of the Panama Canal. For fifteen years he lived and studied this site, a magic corner that he called "my tropical castle." Thus, his first book in 1929 is entitled *My Tropical Air Castle: Nature Studies in Panama*. In 1938, he published his second masterpiece on the flora and fauna of Panama: *Life in an Air Castle: Nature Studies in the Tropics*.

Sometimes Chapman brought his wife on his sojourns to the Isthmus. However, due to an unwritten policy of barring women from the Island, Mrs. Chapman would stay at the Tivoli Hotel in Ancón in Panama City. Frank joined her on Sundays, returning promptly to BCI on Mondays, "with an ever increased appreciation of its charms," as he would later write.

Chapman's passion for Barro Colorado clearly shows in a letter he sent from the Island to Professor Osborn in January 1926:

"It [the New Year] finds me in the most fascinating place I have ever visited, a place where man may associate with tropical nature primeval on equal terms. Here every prospect pleases and the only men are the monkeys! No motor cars; no radio; no jazz; no movies; nothing that makes life objectionable and everything in nature that one could

Chapman on the balcony of "Chapman House" at BCI, 1934-1935.
Panamanian workers, usually half his age, fondly called him *Papá* Chapman.
Source: American Museum of Natural History Archives, New York, N.Y.

Chapman in his dugout *Evan
Evans* among the jungle-covered
islands of Gatún Lake, 1926.
His canoe was named after a
patron who payed the yearly fee
of the American Museum of
Natural History on BCI.
Photo: American Museum of
Natural History Archives,
New York, N. Y.

ask for to make it interesting. I lay awake last night listening to the silence! The innumerable noises, which have become an inescapable adjunct of modern life, seemed to belong to another phase of my existence. I had washed the slate clean; had returned to primitive conditions where the only sound came from the forest. . . .

Thanks to the founders of this laboratory enough of the normal environment of my species has been brought here to make me feel and act as though I were in my own habitat. The screens enclose a well-ventilated house with comfortable sleeping quarters and well arranged working space. The food and water are excellent; we have a shower bath and even ice! In short, everything has been done to keep the individuals of the genus Homo who are introduced and released on this island in good physical condition, but, it is of the utmost importance to observe, without in any way encroaching on the rights and privileges of the natives with whom we wish to reestablish relations long since severed. I don't ask the monkeys (howlers) to share my cot, nor do they insist that I pass the nights on a limb where I have seen them curl in evident comfort. Man, then, comes here not to improve and de-

"José," the coati, and F. M.
Chapman at BCI, 1935-36.
Opposite page:
The "great *almendro*" tree, BCI,
1931.
Photo by F. Chapman.
Source: American Museum of
Natural History Archives,
New York, N.Y.

Donato Carrillo, c. 1927, a *campesino* from Chiriquí and indispensable field hand of the early
days of Barro Colorado Island.
Photo on opposite page: Nemisia, BCI's cook and cleaning woman, 1928.
This peasant girl from Chiriquí introduced naturalists from around the world to Panamanian
cooking. The only trail on Barro Colorado Island named after a woman bears her name.
Photos (2): F. Chapman.
Source: American Museum of Natural History Archives, New York, N.Y.

velop (which means destroy) but to regain his place in nature.

Although his primary interest was to understand the incomparable diversity of birds that inhabit the Panamanian forests, Chapman had an inexhaustible curiosity for all the life forms in the forest: he studied the behavior of monkeys, ocelots, jaguars, tapirs, opossums, and pacas. For three years, patiently and with a sort of oriental dedication, he observed the behavior of José, a friendly wild coati to whom he dedicated delightful pages.

In one of the most beautiful chapters of his 1929 book, he describes one of the most extraordinary and important trees in the tropical forest: the great mountain almond tree (*Dipteryx panamensis*).

"Trees," says Chapman:

have so many human-like attributes, that someone who is responsive to their influences inevitably endows them with a personality. Their placement, their size and shape, the appearance of their bark, the form and color of their leaves and blossoms, the nature of their wood, their sap, their fruit, even the movement of their limbs, and the sound of the wind

in their foliage, are combined to create the character through which a tree speaks to us – for that trees have voices, no tree-lover will deny. It is their endless diversity, and the confusion of their voices that overwhelm us in a tropical forest. The luxuriance of the vegetation sets no limit to their powers of expression.

For Chapman, the best way to explore the forest of Gatún Lake and its many islands was by traveling in a *cayuco* or dugout canoe, an extraordinary Panamanian cultural artifact. *Cayucos* were made from a single tree trunk. Chapman dedicated very interesting pages to describe the construction process and its use by Panama's forest dwelling people. What a striking figure is a Panamanian from Gatún Lake and its tributaries! When on land, he is of small stature and poorly dressed, but as soon as he uses his *cayuco*, grace and dignity de-

scend upon him and Chapman was obliged to confess and admit his envy and feeling of inferiority. Every year, upon returning to Barro Colorado, the sensation that he yearned for with the greatest anticipation was "to renew relations with my cayuco. These are not to be reestablished in a day. As between two friends long-parted, the approaches are gradual and reciprocal. Finally, seated in my place, in full control of the sensitive creature beneath me, it glides forward under the impulse of my paddle, so easily, so smoothly, so noiselessly, that we seem to be one and the same organism."

Panamanians hold a great debt to Frank Chapman. Throughout many years of hard work, monastic dedication, patience, and talent, he and other notable naturalists of the time transformed the island of Barro Colorado into the most famous outdoor natural laboratory for the study of tropical flora and fauna. He was one of the key figures in this achievement. Before arriving in Panama, he already had a world-class reputation as ornithologist, and this fame served as a magnet that attracted other connoted investigators to study nature at Barro Colorado. Today, among biologists and naturalists, Barro Colorado Island is as famous around the world as the Panama Canal is for engineers.

In the early 1920s, the research center that Chapman helped to consolidate was called the Institute for Research in Tropical America. The original founding institutions of the only research station held by the United States in the tropics were the University of Michigan, Harvard, John Hopkins University, the Missouri Botanical Garden, and the American Association for the Advancement of Science. Shortly they were joined by American Museum of Natural History and the Smithsonian Institution. Decades later, Martin Moynihan would change its name to the Smithsonian Tropical Research Institute.

In the early days of BCI each member institution paid an annual fee of $300 for the upkeep of the Laboratory. This contribution was known as the "table fee." It granted bench space to researchers of the member institution. Chapman's work on Barro Colorado was made possible by generous patrons such as the Marcia Tucker Foundation, who year after year paid the annual contribution of the American Museum of Natural History to Barro Colorado.

In closing, another of Chapman's contributions should be mentioned: raising public interest in sciences and tropical ecosystems such as tropical forests by means of dioramas. These were artistic and scientific recreations—windows, so to speak—on some of our planet's once pristine ecosystems. Many of these ecosystems are now irreversibly disfigured. As Neal Smith of STRI recently commented on these illusions of wilderness: "Nothing was more influential to me as a teenager than the magnificent dioramas of the American Museum of Natural History—period!" Its Hall of Birds had 14 dioramas and Barro Colorado was the model for the diorama on tropical forests of the Americas. It recreated for visitors the magnificent diversity and complex interrelationships between plants, animals, and soils in the tropics.

Frank Michler Chapman died at age 81, in November of 1945.

Ludlow Griscom
and his Studies on the Birds of Panama
(1917-1927)

During his life as an ornithologist, Ludlow Griscom was considered the dean of bird-watchers in Central and South America. He conducted three expeditions to study the birds of Panama. He personally analyzed 16,637 Panamanian specimens, some obtained during his expeditions, others by his collectors, and still others he examined at the main collections of Isthmian birds from natural history museums in the United States and Europe. His numerous writings on the birds of Panama were published between 1924 and 1934.

Griscom was born in New York in 1890. His parents, wealthy, cosmopolitan travelers, belonged to the high society of the East Coast of the United States. And since they joined esoteric cults, they opted to educate him at home until he reached the age of 11. Before his 28th birthday, Ludlow had traveled to Europe 15 times, spoke five languages and could read another ten.

Despite the strong desire of his father to study diplomacy or law, Ludlow stubbornly chose ornithology. Early on, he developed a great interest for the birds of the American tropics, for he considered that this region held the most interesting ornithological problems. He finished his master degree at Cornell University in 1915, under the tutorship of Arthur A. Allen, the first professor of ornithology in the United States. But Griscom would never complete a doctorate, a fact that would limit his career in the institutions of natural sciences in his country. He worked at the American Museum of Natural History in New York until 1927, under the guidance of Frank Chapman, one of the driving spirits of Barro Colorado.

From Shotguns to Binoculars

Griscom's professional life encompassed two stages in the scientific study of birds.

Ludlow Griscom (1890-1959) in 1917.
From W. E. Davis: *Dean of Birdwatchers: A Biography of Ludlow Griscom.*
Smithsonian Institution Press, Washington, D.C., 1994.

During the primitive era, known as the "shotgun school," birds were hunted with firearms, prepared as specimens, and sent to museums; thus, taxonomist could systematically study their characteristics and geographical distribution. Later on, modern field ornithology emerged, based on the study of live birds and their behavior in natural habitats.

Griscom's first expedition to the Caribbean and Central America was in 1917. He visited Cuba, Panama, Costa Rica, and Nicaragua. Although he spent only two days in Panama, crossing the Isthmus by train and traveling through the Canal Zone, the experience made an impact on him. Years later, he wrote these lines on the genesis of his passion for Isthmian birds:

I first became interested in Panama birds in the early winter of 1917, when the late Waldron de Witt Miller and I spent a couple of days in the Canal Zone, en route for Nicaragua. During the next few years, my chief contact with Panama birds was the final identification and distribution of the great collection from the Rio Tuira Valley and Mt. Tacarcuna in eastern Darien, made by Richardson, Anthony, and Ball for the American Museum of Natural History. By 1924, however, it became apparent that the Republic of Panama was lagging behind other Central American States in thorough modern collecting. With Dr. Frank M. Chapman's advice and approval, I made plans for the explorations of various neglected parts of the country, work which continued through the next eight years. At that time, I compiled a bibliography of Panama ornithology, and prepared a checklist of all the birds recorded from the country. The explorations of the past two decades have increased the list of Panama's birds by about 23%.

Griscom understood that Panama's political borders had nothing to do with zoogeographical boundaries. He was intrigued by the "curious coincidence" displayed by the Isthmus, whose avifauna was divided into tho distinct parts by the Chagres valley. In 1935 he wrote:

Western Panama is the southern end of the Central American sub-region, and its mountain avifauna is practically identical with that of the Costa Rica highlands. Eastern Panama, or Darien, is the northern apex of the humid rain forest Colombian-Pacific and Magdalena Faunas of Colombia, and its montane avifauna is a continuation of that of the western Andes of Colombia. . . . The lowland depression of the Isthmus is a transition area between these two sub-regions, and the bird-life of the Isthmus itself is a mixture, which can be easily explained on topographical and ecological grounds. On the Caribbean coast the approach of the mountains to the coast just east of Almirante Bay apparently act as a final barrier southward to the characteristic species peculiar to the Central American Humid Tropical Zone. The humid northern half of the Canal Zone consequently possesses a decided element of South American birds, but scarcely one bird that is purely Central American. This situation is reversed on the Pacific or dry side of the Canal Zone. Here the savannas and scrub forests of western Panama extend right across the Isthmus at least as far east as Chepo, and consequently birds characteristic of the Central American Subregion come much nearer to South America than they do on the Caribbean slope.

In 1917, after returning from his field expedition to Panama, the army called on the young 27 year-old ornithologist. The United States had become engaged in the First World War. Given his language skills, Ludlow was assigned to military intelligence.

Veraguas and the Tabasará Mountains, 1924

Griscom returned to Panama in 1924, to continue the work started by the Guatemalan Enrique Arcé, who in the 19th Century had already collected birds in Veraguas, suggesting important differences between birds there and birds in the western highlands of Chiriquí.

On February 5, he departed from New York aboard a yacht, with three assistants: Rudyard Boulton, from the Department of Zoology of the University of Pittsburgh who also carried a movie camera; George Seaman, a collector; and Manson Valentine, a Yale draftsman and taxidermist. In Panama, R. R. Benson, who had lived in Veraguas, joined them. At Balboa, Griscom received support from James Zetek, manager of the recently created Biological Station on Barro Colorado Island. Belisario Porras, President of Panama, facilitated collection and gun permits, and became most interested in the expedition.

They landed at Aguadulce and traveled on horseback to Santiago de Veraguas. In Santiago, they received by Mr. A. R. Wilcox, a lumberman, who took them in as houseguests. After five days of hard riding, they arrived at the town of Remedios. They lodged in the cozy household of Rafael Grajales, a merchant friend of Zetek's, who had been forewarned by telegraph about the expedition. Grajales provided vital support so the expedition could enter the Serranía del Tabasará, riding across Guaymí territory, to reach their goal, Cerro Santiago.

Unfortunately, in Remedios no one knew where Cerro Santiago was. "Between the Volcan de Chiriqui and the Pico Calovévora in Veraguas," commented Griscom on the local people's abysmal lack of geographical knowledge and the appalling inaccuracy of available maps, "lies a mountainous country unexplored and unvisited by white men, inhabited only by wild Indians. No knowledge exists regarding its topography. The courses of the rivers of the interior and their tributaries are pure guesswork, the location of the higher peaks varies from map to map as much as twenty miles, and their altitude as much as 2,000 feet!"

According to Griscom, two years prior to his arrival at Remedios, the Indians had killed two Panamanians who had entered Guaymí territory to carry out a census. Centuries of harsh exploitation had generated a deep mistrust of the *latinos*, Spanish-speakers of mixed European and Indian ancestry, among these indigenous people. Grajales, who, due to his honest dealings with them, had gained the trust of the Guaymí, wrote a letter of recommendation to the *cacique* or chief of the Guaymí, Aquile Sánchez, of the highlands of Remedios. He was a very intelligent man, spoke Spanish, and lived in Cerro Iglesias. The letter explained that the visitors were explorers, Americans and friends of President Porras, who would not stay more than 30 days, and far more importantly, were not looking for gold but instead studying birds.

Given the appalling trails, it took them a full day to arrive at Cerro Iglesias. The *cacique*, his face painted blue, received them with hospitality, telling them that he had been told of their arrival three days ago. After reading the recommendation letter,

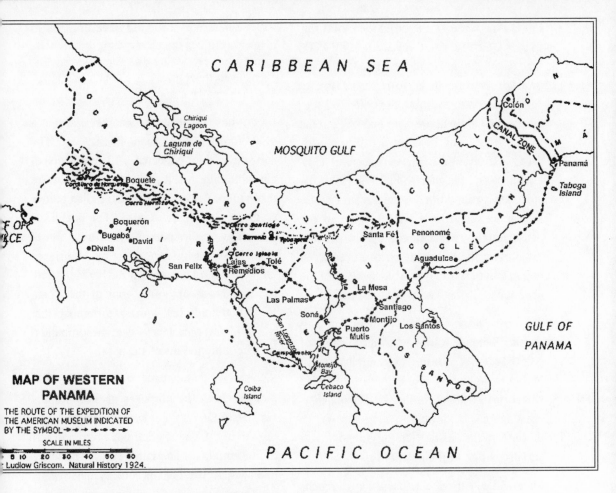

MAP OF WESTERN PANAMA

THE ROUTE OF THE EXPEDITION OF
THE AMERICAN MUSEUM INDICATED
BY THE SYMBOL ➡ ➡ ➡   ➡ ➡ ➡

SCALE IN MILES

5 10   20   30   40   50   60

Ludlow Griscom. Natural History 1924.

drinking *chicha* (a local fermented beverage) and curing some ailment of the chief's wife with aspirin, Ludlow and his group were granted permission to enter the mountains, accompanied by a guide by the name of Toribio.

From Cerro Iglesias they began the rough ascent up the Tabasará Range, the name given locally to the Talamanca Mountains. First they crossed a broad strip of land devoid of trees and covered by harsh grass, turned brown due to the action of the hot northerly winds of the dry season. Here and there reddish patches of soil marked the sites of multiple landslides. Suddenly, just be-

Map of Western Panama. It shows the Griscom expedition route in 1924, from Panama City to the Tabasará Mountains in Chiriquí. Griscom was hoping to establish in Panama the geographical division between the birds of South and North America.
Source: W. E. Davis, *Dean of Bird Watchers: A Biograophy of Ludlow Griscom*. Smithsonian Institution Press, 1994.

fore reaching the continental divide, the dry grasslands gave way to a thick green carpet of forest, extending northward across the summit of the mountains, and then all the way down to the coast on the Caribbean slope.

For ten days, they camped in the cloud forests of Cerro Flores at an altitude of 3,700 feet. Each day the explorers headed in four or five separate directions, returning to camp at noon to examine the collected specimens and to compare who had bagged the most. Every day brought a different surprise, with strange and novel species. "Collecting was," he later remembered, "difficult. The ground birds were shy and secretive and exceedingly hard to find in the dense jungle. Most of the others were in the tops of the tallest trees, practically out of gunshot or scarcely visible because of the abundance of the intervening leaves."

Griscom, accompanied by Benson and Aquile Sánchez, climbed a nearby hill of 6,000 feet, its summit covered by small bushes wrapped by mosses and ferns. He was surprised at not finding birds from eastern Panama, but rather species similar to those from the Costa Rican highlands, with variations due to their isolation.

Meanwhile he tried to devise a way of reaching the cloud forest above their camp:

> A day's scouting trip with Benson and the Indian chief furnished experiences which any naturalist might envy. We reached the continental divide at 6,000 feet, and could look for forty miles or so to the north-west, where lay the Caribbean lowlands. To the west about ten miles rose a cone-shaped peak about 1,000 feet higher than the crest on which we were standing. . . .Perhaps it was the real Cerro Santiago. The forest had changed with the altitude to a gnarled and stunted one, and every tree was loaded with parasitic plants of many kinds. Above 5,000 feet the very ground had been left behind and we struggled upward in a gigantic bed of moss of unknown depth, with manholes between the roots of the trees,

> through which we could have dropped as much as fifteen feet. Everything dripped with moisture, everything was slimy and moldy, and everything gave way at one's touch. . . . A camp in the cloud forest was impossible.

Later, they would set up another camp at a cloud forest, at an altitude of 4,500 feet. The specimens they collected—12 new subspecies and three species new to science—were taken to the lower camp by the Indian guides so they could be dried out. "The bird life," according to Griscom, "was utterly unexpected. Not a single one of the mountain species found farther east occurred here. Instead, the fauna was obviously that of the Costa Rican highlands, but, with this difference, that isolation and remoteness were accompanied by a certain amount of variation."

Short on food and aware of the natives' suspicions about the purposes of their studies since their Guaymí guides had departed during the night, Griscom broke camp and left the mountains. The chief Aquile Sánchez had been accused by his countrymen of selling Cerro Flores to Griscom because it was said to contain gold. People refused to believe the foreigners were really interested in birds. After resting at Remedios for several days free of charge thanks to the hospitality of Grajales, they boarded a launch to the port of Santiago de Veraguas. They passed by the beaches of San Lorenzo, where Griscom took photos of the spectacular forests of southern Soná and the Gulf of Montijo, now covered by pastures. At San Lorenzo they stayed for two weeks as guests of A. R. Wilcox, president of the Tropical Lumber Company. "The camp," as Griscom described it, "was in the heart of a heavy primeval forest, and one of the commonest trees was a recently discovered species of mahogany of gigantic size. . . . At least 200 species of birds occurred in the surrounding country. Howling monkeys were heard daily, and wild peccary was a welcome addition to our bill of fare. When tired of the forest we took the launch and had an interesting day with aquatic birds and sea snakes. . . .Three days later in the bustle of Panama City, the mountains and wild forest seemed far away, like the incidents in a pleasant dream."

Griscom was a grateful man. Upon returning to New York he obtained a resolution from the Executive Committee of the American Museum, dated October 15, 1924, stating:

"That the Trustees desire to express their thanks to Señor Don Rafael Grajales for the many courtesies which he extended to the Museum's expedition to Panama, under the leadership of Mr. Ludlow Griscom. His advice and experience made it practical for the expedition to enter regions that would otherwise have been impossible, while his generous hospitality made it possible to greatly extend the work of the expedition. In recognition of Señor Grajales's services and interest, the Trustees take pleasure in hereby electing him an honorary Life Member."

Private Collectors:
Henry Wedel and Rex Benson

It was common in that period for museums in developed countries to use specialists in the tropics to enrich their collections. These collectors received money and supplies in advance. In Panama, Griscom hired two field experts to obtain birds for the Harvard Museum of Comparative Zoology: Henry Wedel, a German who explored the highlands of Chiriquí and Bocas del Toro, and Rex Benson, who for three years had collected birds in Panama's central region to clarify how far into Veraguas species of birds from Chiriquí extended. Sometimes freelance collectors were unreliable. Benson, for example, received several cash installments from Frank Chapman to collect birds in eastern Panama, however, for varios reasons he failed to deliver. After returning he offered Chapman over one thousand specimens from western Panama. When this offer was rejected, Benson sold the collection to another U.S. institution for a higher price.

Benson worked for Griscom around Santiago as far as the Gulf of Montijo. At the beginning of 1925, he traveled through the cloud forests of Santa Fe in the central cordillera of the Isthmus collecting 1,000 bird specimens. To the east he found many quetzals. At the beginning of the rainy season of 1925, he worked in the vicinity of Macaracas and then Punta Mala in the Azuero Peninsula, broken terrain then still covered by forests but now all cattle pasture. Later, he headed to Aguadulce, exploring its plains and mangroves, where he obtained aquatic birds previously unknown to Panama.

In 1926, Benson ventured into the mountains of Chitrá, east of Santa Fe. It was a difficult expedition; the rains had started early, with incredibly strong thundershowers. Provisions and equipment had to be carried in backpacks because the deep muddy trails made the use of horses impossible. When the weather worsened, slowing even more the pace of the expedition, the *campesinos,* who had to return home to tend their rice and maize crops, left him. Only a young boy, who did not know they way back, remained with Benson.

In his expeditions, Benson received help from naval aviators at France Field, a naval base in Colón, the Caribbean entrance to the Panama Canal. Particularly useful was lieutenant Dale V. Gaffney, who in 1926 would accompany Benson in an expedition that required 12 men to serve as porters. They crossed the continental divide from Santa Fe on the Pacific to the Calovébora River on the Atlantic.

At the end of the 1920s, Griscom decided it was time to study the birds of eastern Panama in detail. Sponsored by the American Museum of Natural History, he conducted his last expedition to the Isthmus. He was accompanied by his wife, five months pregnant, who served as a camerawoman; Rex Benson, a collector, and Paul Covel, a taxidermist. A wealthy traveller by the name of Maunsel Crosby came with them, able to realize his dream of visiting the legendary Darién in return for funding a third of the expedition's costs.

The expedition lasted from February 9 to March 13, 1927. Griscom visited Frank Chapman on Barro Colorado Island. Then, in the yacht *Big Bill*, Griscom headed toward the Las Perlas Archipelago, collecting local birds and studying the large colonies of marine birds on these beautiful islands.

After, they entered the Gulf of Garanchiné and went up the Sambú River. Punta Garachiné turned out to be a collector's paradise. The avifauna of Darién seemed to Griscom "inexhaustible." He described the coasts of the Gulf of San Miguel and Garachiné as being covered by a belt of dry tropical forest, full of huge *cuipo* trees. Anchored at the bay, they could see to the north, above the thatched and tin roofs of the village of Garachiné, the massive bulk of Cerro Sapo. On its lower slopes, the contrast between the belt of brownish dry coastal forests and the deep green tonalities of the humid forests were clearly demarcated.

Moving westward along the coast, in the region of Chimán, they found a few man-made slash and burn clearings. Griscom describes the region as mostly covered by a thick, vast carpet of humid forest, without any signs of the dry forest found at Garachiné or of its avifauna. Most of the species of birds seen or collected were species of South America. On clear mornings, they could catch a glimpse of the unexplored region extending between the headwaters of the Bayano and Chucunaque rivers.

Griscom promised himself to return in the future to collect birds at the sources of both of these two large rivers of eastern Panama. But this was a promise he was unable to keep: he would spend the rest of his professional life working at Harvard's Museum of Comparative Zoology. Griscom died at the age of 69, on May 28, 1959.

Paul C. Standley and the Flora of Panama's Interoceanic Region (1923-1925)

On December 1921, Jay Morrow, Governor of the Panama Canal Zone, requested the U.S. Secretary of Agriculture to send the best tropical plant expert that could be found to the Isthmus to prepare a book on the vegetation along the Panama Canal. All experts consulted agreed that the best qualified person for such a task was a botanist from the Smithsonian Institution who, after exploring Mexico extensively, had published a book on Mexico's woody plants. He was a man of small stature, spoke Spanish very well and wrote even better in Latin. His name was Paul Carpenter Standley.

Standley disembarked in Panama in November 1923. During the next five months, he collected 7,500 specimens of plants from the Canal Zone and the surrounding countryside. He returned to Panama City in November in 1925 to study the flora of Barro Colorado Island situated in the Panama Canal, recently established as a protected natural reserve.

The Smithsonian Institute would publish two of his studies on Panama: *The Flora of Barro Colorado Island*, in 1927, and later his monumental *Flora of the Panama Canal Zone*, in 1928.

Botanist of the Transit Region

Paul C. Standley was born in Missouri in 1884, in the tiny town of Avalon in the Ozark Mountains. He began his undergraduate studies at Drury College and continued at New Mexico State College, where he obtain his bachelor's degree in 1907 and his master's degree in 1908. In 1909, he went to work at the Smithsonian Institution's National Herbarium. He was Pittier's assistant in the analysis of plants collected in Panama by the Smithsonian's Panama Biological Survey.

In 1928, he became a specialist in plant classification at the Field Museum of Natural History, Chicago, until his retirement in 1950.

Paul C. Standley (1884-1963).
Great student of the plants of Central America and Panama. Botanist at the Smithsonian
Institution, Washington, D.C., and the Field Museum of Natural History, Chicago.
This photo by Huron H. Smith shows Standley at work in his laboratory at Chicago.
Source: L. O. Williams (ed.), *Homage to Standley*, Chicago, 1963.

To write about the flora of the canal, Standley studied his own vast collections, as well as thousands of specimens gathered by other naturalists in Panama and housed in the National Herbarium of the United States, perhaps the best collection of Isthmian plant specimens in the world. He also analyzed specimens obtained in the 19th Century by Fendler along the Chagres River, and those collected by R. S. Williams. He reviewed the 6,000 specimens brought from the Isthmus by Henri Pittier, W. Maxon and A. S. Hitchcock during the Smithsonian Institution Biological Survey of Panama, 1910-1912. Additionally, he studied hundreds of plants obtained by Killip; those collected near Panama City by the Christian Brothers, Celestino and Gervais; MacBride's collection, and an additional 1,500 specimens obtained by C. V. Piper of the U.S. Department of Agriculture.

Standley would become, after Paul Allen from the Missouri Botanical Garden, the naturalist who collected the largest number of plants from Panama. Allen collected in various places around the Isthmus. Standley was the botanist *par excellence* of Panama's transit region, the historical corridor of interoceanic communication crossing the Isthmus from the Atlantic to the Pacific. At the same time he is perhaps the best chronicler of land use before and after construction of the waterway.

For Standley the best way to appreciate the natural history of tropical America was to cross Panama by train. In its 80 km journey the track crossed from the dry slopes of the Pacific, dominated by savannas and dry forests, to the wetter Atlantic watershed, covered by moist lowland rain forests. In his words: "Even those who have no direct interest in natural history must notice, as they cross the Isthmus on the railroad connecting Colon to Panama, the striking change in the superficial aspect of the country that takes place within a very few miles of the divide, near Summit Station. The transition is most evident during the dry season, when the vegetation of the Atlantic watershed is everywhere fresh and green, while that on the Pacific slope is dry and brown. The abrupt decrease in the density of the vegetation as the Pacific is approached is also obvious."

Research Along the Canal, 1923-1924

Standley was passionate about the history of interoceanic communication and its botanical implications. "A hundred years before the English colony of Jamestown was founded," he wrote in 1928,

the Spaniards, with that zeal which characterized their exploration and conquest of America, had established in southeastern Panama the first European settlement upon the American Continent. The isthmus is very important in the history of the Western Hemisphere, for the narrow neck of land joining North and South America. . . .became the gateway to the gold and silver mines of Peru and Bolivia, and provided a convenient means of communication with the west coast of Central America and Mexico, and with the East Indies.

Panama thus assumed at the very outset of its modern history the most important place in the New World. When the Pilgrims landed on the Massachusetts coast, Panama already had a history of over. . . .a century, filled with events of the most entrancing interest.

Standley marveled at the fact that Panama City, founded in 1519, had played a key role in the discovery, conquest and trade of the Americas. "Here in Panama," he added, "the people of Europe first made acquaintance with the natural products of the American mainland. . . . How strange must everything have seemed to the early explorers, fresh from Spain! How fortunate were they, if they took more than a passing interest in their surroundings, to find themselves in a world where every plant and animal was new!"

Although his specific task was to study the flowering plants of the Canal Zone, he quickly expanded his collecting elsewhere: to Taboga Island; to the natural savannas west and east of Panama City and to the dry forest belt, extending eastward parallel to the coast from the outskirts of Panama City to Tocumen and Chepo. He explored the stunningly beautiful gallery forests of the rivers near the capital, streams that later, due to unchecked urban growth, have become sewers: the Matías Hernandez, Matasnillo, Juan Díaz, Tapia, and Tocumen. He found the Paraíso River an excellent collecting site, for even though in the lower terrain West Indian workers had small parcels planted with plantain, banana, and manioc, the steeper slopes were still forested. He also studied the forests of the Chagres River up to Alhajuela, a limestone site where Madden Dam would be built in 1930-1935.

He sketched the deforestation that took place on the Pacific side, close to Panama City, long before the canal was built, north of Balboa toward Corozal, Paraíso, and Summit, areas that gradually had become

potreros, man-made pasturelands for cattle and dominated by guinea grass. Today, these same areas are forested. Standley detailed the impact on nature of the canal and the great complex of military bases to defend it.

In 1928 he wrote:

Comparatively little virgin vegetation remains. The construction of the canal, with the necessary excavation of vast quantities of earth and its deposit at distant places, modified both the land and its plant covering. The scars left by the engineering feat are now almost obliterated, as is always true of humid tropical regions where exposed earth is soon hid under a luxuriant growth of plants. Work about the several military posts also has had a considerable effect on plant life. Extensive low tracts have been cleared and either leveled or filled, to provide drill grounds and aviation fields; while even the remaining swamps have been ditched in order to control the mosquitoes. In the forests that survive, many trees have been cut to supply lumber and charcoal. There can be little land close to the canal whose vegetation has not changed in some respect.

Among the sites, where limited tracts of forest had survived, which allowed to have an idea of what the primeval forests of the Isthmus were like, he mentioned Frijoles, Gamboa, Obispo, and Barro Colorado Island.

Standley documented the extensive deforestation for the cultivation of bananas for export that had occurred around the newly formed Lake Gatún. A destruction caused not so much by small peasants, who planted a few hectares, but rather by "the large lease holders, who during the past few years have cleared wide stretches of forest and planted the land with bananas. Banana growing has

Alhajuela, a banana-growing village on the jungle-covered banks of the Chagres River, in 1901. At this site Madden Dam was built between 1930-35, creating Lake Alhajuela, to store water for the canal, generate electricity and controle the floods of the river.
Source: *Report of the Isthmian Canal Commission 1899-1901.* Washington, D.C.

become an important industry. . . .and has wrought a substantial change in the aspect of the Atlantic slope."

Within the historic Isthmian region of transit, two areas of the Pacific drew his botanical interest: Ancón Hill and Taboga Island. "Ancón Hill," Standley would write in 1928, "seemed to be a replica of the hills of Taboga, and must be geologically related."

The Vegetation of Ancón Hill

Panama City's most distinctive landmark is Ancón Hill, a volcanic promontory on the pacific entrance to the Panama Canal, with the smaller Sosa Hill rising nearby. According to Standley:

Ancón Hill, with an altitude of about 600 feet, covers only a small base, hence its sides are steep. On the western side, where the rock has been quarried, they are precipitous, and overhang Balboa and Quarry Heights. There is no indication that the vegetation of this hill has changed greatly in the past 400 years, except as some of the trees may have been cut for firewood. Even this is doubtful, because the sides are so steep that woodcutters would naturally prefer to prepare firewood and charcoal in more convenient places. There is at the present a military road for vehicles which ascends almost to the summit.

From a botanical standpoint, Ancón Hill is a locality full of surprises. It is a small hill, easy to climb, and accessible in only a few minutes from Panama, Ancón, or Balboa. Nearly every botanist visiting the Isthmus must have ascended it, yet its flora seems inexhaustible. During several short excursions to the summit, I found a few species not previously reported from this part of Panama, and one new to science. Piper collected here one or two plants unknown elsewhere in the region. . . .

There is no obvious reason for such localized flora. On the lower slopes of Ancón Hill, all the original vegetation has been destroyed to make room for buildings, and in the unoccupied places about its base, there are only the usual guarumos and balsas, with other weedy trees and shrubs. Along the northwestern slope, extending nearly to the top, there are remnants of forest hitherto little disturbed except by the annual grass fires. Several of the trees are interesting. *Vochysia*, for example, besides other species of rare occurrence elsewhere. In these residual groves one happens every now and then upon some shrub or herb which previously has eluded collectors. Such a plant is *Selenipedium*, one of Panama's rarest and strangest orchids, an herb sometimes 10 feet high, discovered here a few years ago by Killip.

On the steep slopes above the groves of trees stretch patches of grasslands whose flora is essentially that of the savannas beyond Panama. It is curious, but perhaps not especially significant, to find on a hilltop this savanna flora. The same type of vegetation exists also on the high slopes of Taboga Island, for Ancón Hill is almost a replica of the hills of that island, to which it must be related geologically.

In contrast to Ancón, Sosa Hill seemed to him uninteresting, as it was more exten-

sively deforested, and had sizeable areas under cultivation.

The Flora of Taboga Island

Taboga became for Standley not only a picturesque spot, but botanically extremely interesting. These are some of his observations on the people and the flora of this island within Panama Bay:

> Taboga Island is not a part of the Canal Zone, but it is too closely associated with the canal to be excluded from the present treatment. Although of no great extent, it is the largest of the islands of Panama Bay, lying about 10 miles of the shore. It is from every standpoint one of the most interesting locations of the Isthmus, particularly because it is more typically Latin or Central American than any other place that the visitor to the zone is likely to see.
>
> Taboga has long been one of the best-known stations of the Pacific coast. For centuries it was visited by ships, which anchored to take on water, which here was of better quality than that to be obtained elsewhere along the coast. The island has a more agreeable climate than the mainland, and the merit of being free from malarial mosquitoes. During the canal construction days the United States Government maintained here a sanitarium for convalescent patients from Ancón Hospital. . . .
>
> Taboga is a rugged mass of rocky hills, which rise from the sea to a height of nearly 1,000 feet, and constitute the most elevated land in the neighborhood of the zone. There is practically no level ground, but the parts of the steep slopes are fit for cultivation. In general the shores are rocky, yet in sheltered coves there are delightful beaches. . . .
>
> The whole population of Taboga is concentrated in a single settlement, a sleepy little village situated on the shore facing the main-

land. . . . The town, with its low white stuccoed buildings, is quite unlike Panama or Colon, two cities which have little in common with others of Central America.

The people also are distinctly different from those of the mainland, especially because they speak only Spanish. They have two occupations, fishing and agriculture.

Taboga is noted locally for its vegetables and fruits; above all, for its pineapples, which, being practically the only good fruit grown in the region (except papayas, in which Panama is unequaled). . . . The villagers have small patches of cultivated ground on distant parts of the island, going out each day to tend them. The plantations of pineapples are the most important and extensive, but there are many fruit trees of different kinds and, strangely enough, even a little coffee is grown for local consumption. It is rarely that coffee is planted in Central America at sea level.

On the main peak of Taboga there still remains some forests, and, although the island is well drained and the climate comparatively dry, this forest is rather wet, conserving a few small springs and insignificant trickles of water, about which grow tree ferns. The forest has not been well explored, nor the vegetation of other parts of the island, for that matter, and it is likely that a good many addi-

tional species would be revealed by a thorough search of the hillsides.

Standley found out that, botanically, the most interesting part was the hill located at the extreme east end of the island:

Its vegetation is almost identical with that of the top of Ancón Hill, but is developed on an ampler scale. The soil of the hilltops is apparently too sterile for cultivation. The steep slopes support a sparse growth of stunted bushes, especially sandpaper-tree (*Curatella*) and nance (*Byrsonima*).

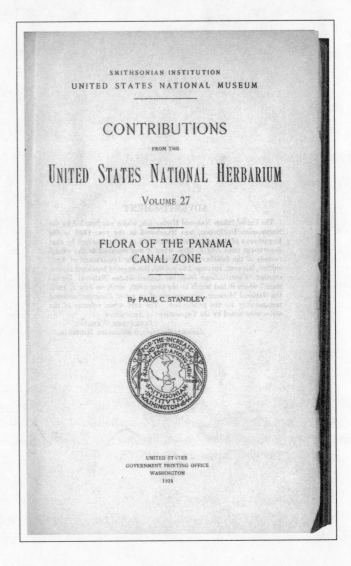

Standley's book about on the flora of the Panama Canal Zone, published by the Smithsonian Institution in 1928.

Don Pablito Standley during a botanical expedition in Honduras in the 1950s. From left to right: Pablo Caceres, Paul Shank, Paul Standley, Antonio Molina, and Louis O. Williams. Photo by Paul Allen. From: *Homage to Standley*, op. cit., 1963.

The whole aspect and composition of the flora is essentially that of the savannas, yet there grow here a few plants absent from the level savannas, and in the latter there are many species not found on these exposed well-drained slopes.

Standley was impressed by the existence of nearly a dozen Tabogan species otherwise unknown elsewhere in the region. Also, he stressed that the flora of other islands in the Bay of Panama remained unknown.

Vernacular Names of Plants in Central America and Panama

In his travels throughout Latin America, Standley was fascinated by, and loved to jot down, the different vernacular variations of the Spanish language existing from one country to the next. He attributed these linguistic differences to the indigenous substratum of the people. He considered that the differences in Spanish as spoken in Latin America were greater than those separating English as spoken in England and the United States.

Standley was passionate about linguistics. He wanted to know the origins of the names country people gave to local plants. Plant collectors in Central America had largely overlooked this aspect. Henri Pitttier had been an exception. These are some of Standley's observations regarding the roots of the names given to plants in Latin America, and the deep linguistic divide between Central America and Panama:

> Collecting vernacular names is a branch of botanical work neglected by most collectors visiting Central America, and naturally it can not be prosecuted intelligently without a speaking knowledge of Spanish. Even with a reasonably thorough acquaintance with that language it is easy to make mistakes, for the educated native people of Central America themselves differ as to the proper spelling and interpretation of many vernacular names.

> A knowledge of the plant names employed in Central America is often useful in identifying inadequate plant specimens, and a full list of such names would indeed be valuable in other ways; for example to the lumberman, whose operations depend largely upon a familiarity with the local names of the trees. As a rule, the names of trees are much more stable than those of herbaceous plants, doubtless because the special uses of the trees are more accurately and generally known. . . .Some persons have the impression that in Latin America a plant has an indefinite number of vernacular names, but this belief is ill founded.

For many plants, the names are uniform almost or quite throughout their range. As examples may be cited the Cecropias, known everywhere in Central America under the name of *guarumo,* the Spanish-cedars (*Cedrelas*) or *cedros,* and mahogany or *caoba.*

The variation in speech in Mexico and the Central American countries is a fascinating study. The differences depend largely upon the stock of the aboriginal inhabitants of the respective regions. In every country there are many local words for common objects, words universally used in each country but without meaning in the adjoining ones. The differences are, I should say, ordinarily much greater than those between the English of England and that of the United States. Aztec influence is widely spread in Central America, certainly as far south as Costa Rica, and many of the articles of daily use bear names of Aztec origin quite distinct from the words used in Spain for the same objects. The Nahuatl or Aztec language was extraordinarily rich in plant names; therefore it is not remarkable to find a large Nahuatl element in the Central American plant vocabulary. This is not true of Panama, however.

Assembling vernacular names about the Canal Zone is a difficult and discouraging task. The Spanish spoken in Panama City more nearly resembles literary Castilian and probably freer from vulgarisms than any other part of Central America. No doubt this results from the fact that the local Panamanians [Standley refers to people from Panama City] have mostly been city dwellers and not agriculturalists, and have either descended from natives of the Iberian Peninsula, or remained in constant association with them. They have had comparatively little intercourse with the native aborigines, the source from which other Central Americans have adopted their peculiar words. It is strange that in Panama the intensive mingling of the races for four generations has not introduced a larger element of foreign words; yet it has had little apparent effect, if we exclude the English of recent years, which threatens to exterminate the speaking of Spanish in Panama City. Dozens of the most important and widely used words of Central America are not understood in Panama City; for example, *petate*, mat, *metate*, grinding stone, *zacate*, grass, *zopilote*, turkey vulture; and even *frijoles* or black beans, next to maize the most important food of Mexico and Central America, will be sought in vain in the market.

The Flora of Central America

After concluding his studies of the plants of Panama, Standley explored and wrote for the next 30 years on the plants of Central America, becoming the authority on the subject. Based on his field explorations and work in herbariums he wrote his great works, still classic as reference texts today: *The Flora of the Yucatan* (1930), *The Flora of the Lancetilla Valley, Honduras* (1931), *The Forests and Flora of British Honduras* (1936), *The Flora of Costa Rica* (1937-1938), and finally, *The Flora of Guatemala* (1946).

A look at his list of publications may lead to the question how he could have achieved so much in a lifetime. Standley was a hard-working man with iron discipline. He kept a strict rhythm, working 12 to 14 hours daily. He never married and chain-smoked, the cause of his death. He collected more than 130,000 plant specimens. The only plants that he did not like were petunias. In addition to his brilliant and productive career, dedicated to the classification of the plants of Central America, he was a simple and modest man with a rare capacity to extract good empirical information from *campesinos* known by few others. In all of his work, one appreciates his love for the people and countries of Latin America.

Standley would serve as a model for many young botanists. Robert Woodson of the Missouri Botanical Gardens confessed that Standley's floras motivated him to take on his monumental *Flora of Panama*.

Retirement in Honduras

Retiring in 1950, the United Fruit Company invited Standley to their great research station at Lancetilla, Honduras. He spent his last days as honorary botanist in the herbarium of the Escuela Agrícola Panamericana, better known as Zamorano. Upon his death in Tegucigalpa in 1963, he was buried at his request in the valley of the Yeguare River, in a small plot at the town of San Antonio de Oriente.

The Expeditions of George Proctor Cooper to the Forests of Bocas del Toro and Chiriquí (1926-1928)

Panama has an incredibly rich biodiversity. For example, there are more than 2,000 species of tree growing in the Isthmus, more than for the whole of Europe or North America. Toward the end of the 19th and beginning of the 20th Century, most of the scientific information that existed on Panama's forests was gathered by foreign researchers. One such expedition was carried out in the forests of Western Panama between 1926 and 1928, specifically those of the Province of Bocas del Toro on the humid Atlantic coast and those along the Chiriquí Viejo River in Chiriquí Province, on the dry Pacific slope. The Field Museum of Natural History, the New York Botanical Garden, and the United Fruit Company also supported the mission, led by Yale University scientists.

The Yale Forestry School Expedition, 1926-1928

The expedition led by George Proctor Cooper, a specialist in tropical forests at Yale School of Forestry, included George Slater from the United Fruit Company (UFCO). The survey began in the mid rainy season of 1926 in Bocas del Toro, in forests next to the Company's plantations around Changuinola. United Fruit was closing these plantations because of the *mal de Panamá*, a deadly banana disease caused by a fungus, with the intention of moving most operations to Chiriquí on the drier Pacific side. After studying the areas next to the banana belt on the Atlantic, Cooper focused his attention on the fascinating forests of the archipelago of Bocas del Toro, especially Isla Colón or Columbus Island, seat of the provincial capital. Cooper found the island "to be an ideal region for many unusual trees."

In essence, Cooper and Slater conducted the first systematic study of the forests of Bocas del Toro in the 20th Century, concentrating around the two large coastal lagoons of Almirante and Chiriquí Grande, the islands of the archipelago of Bocas del Toro, and the

Cricamola River, home of the Guaymí people.

The flora of Bocas del Toro had remained largely unknown. It was not until the end of 1885 that the English botanist John H. Hart had arrived by steamer from Jamaica at the invitation of a Protestant mission. Hart, at the time director of the Royal Botanical Garden at Kingston, would study the forest on the islands of Colón, Nancy's Cay or Isla Solarte, and Bastimentos or Old Bank. He penetrated the mainland along the Guariviara River, then inhabited by the Guaymí Indians.

In July 1927, the Yale-UFCO mission began its survey of western Chiriquí province on the Pacific. They set up camp at Progreso, a banana farm that the United Fruit, also locally known as the Chiriqui Land Company, had recently opened in the middle of forests at 80 feet above sea level near the banks of the Chiriquí Viejo River. First, they explored the forest from the seacoast up to La Cuesta, at 300 feet altitude, on the border with Costa Rica. Then they headed eastward toward the Divalá River at the end of the great Pacific savanna. Their survey of the forests and their sample collection of trees was completed in the dry season of 1928. It was the first in-depth study of the middle and lower course of the Chiriquí Viejo River.

In 1928, Panama's President was Rodolfo Chiari, who was soon to be suceeded by Florencio H. Arosemena. In one way or another, both of these Liberal Party presidents would continue in the footsteps of Belisario Porras, whose three presidential terms did much to consolidate Panama's institutions and to complete major public works such as the Chiriquí Railroad running from David to Puerto Armuelles, the new banana headquarters and port on the Pacific. This engineering project, carried out by the J. G. White Company, was completed in 1928. Ernesto Jaén Guardia received it on behalf of the government. The first Superintendent of the Chiriquí Railroad was Alberto Vallarino.

The railroad and the banana plantations radically altered Chiriquí. Along the tracks sprouted new stations, or "towns of the Line": Aserrío, Gariché, Jacú, Santa Marta, and others. Simultaneously, the jungle gave way to the *zona bananera*, the banana zone with it's epicenter in Progreso, which began to expand, opening up new plantations baptized with the names of native trees: *Bonga, Balsa, Malagueto, Sigua*. Towards these camps migrated thousands of peasants from Chiriquí and Central America, especially Nicaraguans and Salvadorians, initiating their gradual assimilation into a rural proletariat. Later on, they would be joined by Guaymí Indians.

The expedition leader, George Proctor Cooper, noted in his mission reports that striking differences existed between the rainforests of the Caribbean, where soils are nutrient-poor and badly drained, and those of the drier Pacific slope, with more fertile soils. He recorded the tight correlation holding between soils and forest types, describing the popular terms for the different soil categories (*yulial, catival, manglar*). "In contrast to the Pacific," noted Cooper in 1928, "the mountain slopes running down the Caribbean are mostly of red clay, and unfit for cultivation. The continual heavy precipitation over this region gives it a rank, impenetrable jungle. The rather evenly distributed rainfall in the north coast seems also to affect the wood of forest trees, in that they are generally less dense and not considered as strong or durable as identical species from the Pacific side, where an annual dry season occurs." The same species on the Pacific fetched higher prices than those in the Caribbean. He furthermore added: "Many more species are made use of on the Pacific side than on the Caribbean, perhaps because the woods are more accessible and the population greater in the former region, aside from the better quality of the woods themselves."

In Bocas del Toro still exists today a striking linguistic richness in the names given by local people to diverse tree species, resembling a bilingual dictionary of timber trees. This reflects the cultural and ethnic mix of its population: *latino* or Spanish-speaking mestizos, various Indian groups, and *criollo* or creole English-speaking people.

Among Cooper's observations of Bocas del Toro, the following passages stand out:

Bocas del Toro

On the Caribbean Coast, the climate is regulated by the trade winds, generally heavily moisture-laden during the winter months. The precipitation is heavy at this time, and flood conditions often prevail on the low coastal banana lands. But on the Pacific Coast. . . this period [January to April] is the dry season, and in places it does not rain for two or three months' duration. The grasses and small plants often turn brown from lack of water and the cattle ranges have a semi-

arid appearance. Naturally, this difference in the precipitation has a marked effect on the plants and forests of each region. The more open park-like stands above the mangrove fringe on the Pacific Coast is nowhere to be found in the north, which has an evenly distributed rainfall. . . and consequently a heavy, luxurious tropical forest growth throughout.

The moisture factor clearly determined land uses. Cattle ranching prevailed on the drier pacific and bananas on the opposite side of the mountains, to the north.

The Province of Bocas del Toro has a population of about 30,000, mostly West Indians (imported many years ago by the banana companies for work on the farms), and Indians living in the bush. The latter often raise small patches of bananas for sale, to provide such of their requirements, as they cannot readily supply from the forest and the soil. In the two or three towns there are some Panamanians of the upper classes, mostly in charge of government administration. Bocas del Toro, the provincial capital, has a population of about 3,000. An English patois is more generally spoken than Spanish.

The only means of transportation on land is by the banana railroad and a few poor horse-trails. The main railroad runs from the deep-water port of Almirante, up the coast 20 miles, and then turns inland along both sides of the Rio Sixaola, which, at the moment, forms the international boundary between Panama and Costa Rica. The end of the line is not far from the foothills, and has an elevation of 300 feet. Several kinds of trees grow at this altitude that are not found in the coastal plain.

The Changuinola region is made of four kinds of lands: (1) The old abandoned banana plantations, and pastures that are now cleared, all above the lower Changuinola River; (2) a strip that could be called marginal land, not good enough for bananas, though not swampy; (3) the "catival", where the stand is almost pure

Cativo in places; (4) and the "yulial", which is under water most of the year.

In the first type are found Chaperno or Dogwood, Guácimo Molenillo, Guácimo del Ternero or Bastard Cedar, Guarumo or Trumpet Trees, Balsa, Ceiba, Sandbox or Javillo, Guavo, Guayabo, Wild Fig, Jobo or Hog Plum, Capulín, Wild Tamarind, Laurel Negro, Lagarto or Prickly Holly, Ramóon, Burío or Majagua, Bribri, Stinking-toe or Carao, Ebo or Almendro (left because it is too hard co cut), Breadnut (left for same reason), and a few others.

In the second type there are some trees also present in the first type, there being a gradual transition throughout; some Cativo, Tamarind, Figs, Cedro Macho, Sangrillo, Mastate, Bogum or Barillo, Madró, Mata-palo, Garoche, Fruta Dorado or Bogamaní, Fidlewood or Llema de Huevo, John Crow Wood, Camfine or Fosforito, Anona, Mata Cansada, Ajoche Macho, Guayatil Blanco and G[ayatil] Colorado, Cabbage Palm, Pilón, Palo de Leche, Zapote de Mono, Jagua, Aguacatillo, Wild Cacao, Wild Guavo, Monkey Tamarind, Manwood, Níspero, Bully Tree, María (rare), Cedro (rare), and several others for which no vernacular names were learned.

In the third type the stand is over 75 per cent Cativo, with Bogum, Tamarind, Guayatil, Cedro Macho, Sílica Palm and Sangrillo scattered with others throughout.

In the fourth type [of terrain], which is called "yulial" by the Indians because of the pre-

The construction in the 1920s of the Chiriquí railroad encouraged the development of banana plantations and lead to the extinction of the lowland forests of the Chiriquí Viejo River.
Photo: *Memoria de Agricultura y Obras Públicas.* Panama, 1920.

dominance of Sílica Palms, there are few trees of importance. This area extends to the mangrove swamps on the coast.

There is no export trade in the woods of this region, and only a few find local use in the operations of the United Fruit Company. Ties are cut from Níspero, Bully Tree, Manwood (at least three woods by this name), Llema de Huevo, Fiddlewood, Sigua Canelo, Cabbage Bark, Alcornoque, Sur Espino, and Guayácan (from the hills back of Talamanca, where it is called Yellow Manwood). Fence posts split from the shell of an old log on the ground proved to be identical with the cuajada (*Vitex Cooperi*) of Chiriqui. The majority of posts and piles for houses and also some railway ties are made from this wood or from the Black Manwood. Orey and Mangrove are used for most of the pilings in salt water. For rough construction lumber a wood called Cedro Macho or Saba (probably two woods) is now generally used since the Spanish Cedar (*Cedrela*) has been exhausted. This wood is also used for bridge boards, as are Bogum or Barillo, and Laurel. For finer constructions and furniture, Spanish Cedar and Mahogany, which is brought in, and the Laurel Negro is also used to a limited extent. Most of the buildings, that is, the "white houses" [for white people], are made of Georgia pine, as it was found cheaper to import this lumber than to log and mill the questionable local timber.

An examination of the banana ports on one short spur showed no less than seven different woods used as posts, namely the Black Manwood, the Yellow Manwood, Sur Espino or Alcornoque, *Clarisia sp.* (new for Panama), *Mouriria parvifloria*, and two unidentified woods.

The Province of Chiriquí

The Province of Chiriquí runs from the Montañas de Santa Clara, a range lying north and south, and forming a part of the disputed Costa Rica-Panama border, to the Río Tabasará, in the provincial boundary with Veraguas. It is separated from Bocas del Toro on the north by the Serranía de Tabasará or the Cordillera. Beginning at the Costa Rican frontier, the high peaks are Cerro Pando, Cerro Picacho, Volcán de Chiriquí (the highest point in Panama), Cerro Horqueta, Cerro Hornito, and Cerro Santiago (the second highest peak).

In contrast to the high percentage of West Indians in Bocas del Toro, there are scarcely any in Chiriquí. The government discourages blacks from settling in the country preferring to keep the blood as near Spanish and Indian as possible. The Chiriquí Indians have been living in the region for hundreds of years, and remains of their pottery in burial mounds show that in the past they were more cultured than today. The towns have a good class of Panamanians and a lower mixed peon type. Spanish is the only language spoken, although there are many natives who speak some English. The Chiricano considers himself quite aristocratic, claiming descent from the family of Christopher Columbus through the Duke of Veraguas. The land has passed from family to family for many generations—even the squatter Indian lands. The federal [central] government, when it came into existence, recognized most of the rights of the inhabitants of the province. There is probably less federal land in Chiriquí than in any other province of the republic. When one wishes to purchase a tract he must first buy out the squatter and record the deed, and then pay the federal government charge of six pesos per hectare. Of course, all the large cattle ranches are now titled land.

The region around and below the Volcan contains the bulk of the total population of the province—76,000. David, the capital, with over 6,000 people, is a cattle and coffee exporting center. It is reached through the tidal port of Pedregal, and the small steamers and schooners which risk the breakers and reefs

Sîlica palms (*Manacaria saccifera*) near the mouth of the Cricamola River, 1940.
This river flows into the Chiriquí Lagoon, Bocas del Toro.
Photo on opposite page: The vegetation of the swampy lowlands along the old mule tram in an abandoned banana plantation on the Guarumo River, Bocas del Toro, 1940.
Photos (2): Russell Siebert Papers, Missouri Botanical Garden Archives.

can go up and down the channel only at the crest of the tides.

The Forests of the Chiriquí Viejo River

From David, a government narrow-gage railroad runs north to Boquete, over 4,000 feet above the sea, and west to La Concepción, at an elevation of 800 feet. Large motor trucks mounted on iron wheels are used for most passenger service, and low-geared engine takes two or three small freight cars at one haul up the Boquete line. The Panamanian government is now building a deep sea-port at Puerto Armuelles or Rabo de Puerco, where an old abandoned sugar-company railroad formerly started inland to Progreso. From this new port, which will accommodate all large ocean-going vessels, a government railroad is being built by the J. G. White Company to run north through Progreso, where the new banana operations are underway, and then swing east to join the present line at Concepción. Upon completion of this double project, a large, heavily forested area will be thrown open, between the Port and La Cuesta, beyond Progreso. It should be possible to bring out many valuable woods, such as the Espavé, Cero or Bogum, María, Chuchupate, Cedro Bateo, Guayacán, Mora, Cedro, and others, which are at present inaccessible.

The largest and most frequent tree of the upper story is the Espavé, which grows to 150 feet in rare instances, but is generally not over 100 feet tall, with an unbutressed bole 4 or 5 feet through, and clear of limbs for about 50 feet, except when grown in the open. This wood, although inferior to the Spanish Cedar, should make satisfactory building mate-

rial in all places not exposed to the direct effect of the rains. The sapwood is thick, sometimes over 6 inches, and is brownish in color. As many as ten trees per acre can be found over fairly large areas. Where the soil is heavier and wetter, trees grow poorly, and to a smaller size. The Cedars are still scattered over the area, there being at least two varieties, the red and the brown. Cedro Cebolla, C. Granadine, and C. Real are the common names. A tree called here Cedro Bateo is identical with the Cedro Macho of the Bocas region. Aguacatón is almost as durable as the cedar, and is used for the same purposes. It grows to a larger size and more abundantly in the mountains, where it almost entirely replaces cedar for building. Chuchupate is a

beautiful wood used for furniture and building; the trees are not over 50 or 60 feet tall and 12 inches in diameter, and are scattered. Zapatero is used for lumber, but warps badly. Arenillo and Cañafístulo are used for interiors. María is a good wood for building and furniture, but is not plentiful. Railway ties are made from several woods, notably Cuajada, Guayacán, Mora, Níspero, María, Quira, Cañafístulo and Guachapeli.

The region around Progreso, from the Montañas de Santa Clara to Divalá, is fortunately protected from the high winds which often sweep through mountain passes, and down into the David valley. For these reasons, it is possible to grow bananas there without danger of wind damage. This area is less susceptible to drought than the land on the other side of the Volcán. . . .In the immediate vicinity of Progreso the land is quite sandy, and in two hours after a heavy downpour one can walk around dry-shod. During the months of July and August, when the writer was in the country, it rained almost daily, generally commencing about four o'clock in the afternoon and ceasing about eight in the evening or earlier. Only rarely did a shower come in the morning.

The incredible diversity of species of lumber trees extracted from the forests of Western Panama is astonishing. And we cannot but admire the depth of empirical knowledge that the *bocatoreños* and *chiricanos* of those days had regarding the properties of these local woods. Many of these species bore lovely names, whose origins clearly goes back to Panama's indigenous history.

Cooper, without knowing it, wrote the epitaph of the forested treasures of westernmost Chiriquí. Today, they have nearly vanished, with only small patches surviving. Most of the timber species used then have now disappeared, or are in danger of becoming locally extinct.

Rather than stimulating a national interest in managing this priceless resource, Panama's exuberant forests seems to have weakened this drive. The country has neglected its forestry vocation; it lacks a school of forestry to train the professionals that this economic sector requires. Investment in research, public or private, is almost nil. Although late, there is still time to establish a forestry research program that would recover information and genetic material from threatened timber tree species. George Proctor Cooper's report may one day contribute to this objective in the case of Bocas del Toro and Chiriquí. A forestry school is a necessity for Panama.

Paul Allen's Botanical and Forestry Studies in Panama (1934-1954)

Paul Allen was one of the great botanists of the flora of Panama and Central America during the first half of the 20th Century. He was born in Enid, Oklahoma, in August 1911. Between 1934 and 1947, he made 17 expeditions to Panama's forests under the auspices of the Missouri Botanical Garden, collecting 7,000 species of plants. He was, after Henri Pittier, the naturalist who has studied more nooks and crannies of the isthmian geography.

Expeditions of the Missouri Botanical Garden, 1934-1947

A passionate orchidologist, an expert ecologist and taxonomist of tropical rainforests, Allen was also a specialist in bananas, avocados, and tropical palms, especially the *pixbae*. Allen also made forays into anthropology, archeology, and geology. His attachment to Panamanian forests arose by chance. In 1935, as a 26-year old student at the Missouri Botanical Garden, he was sent to Panama as an assistant to the botanical survey led by Carrol Dodge and Julian Steyermark, to study the flora of the mid and upper Chagres river in the wake of the construction of Madden Dam. The dam gave rise to Madden Lake or Lago Alhajuela, flooding some 50 km² of tropical forests. Its purpose was to store water for canal operations in the dry season, prevent the devastating floods of the rainy months, and generate power for Panama and the Canal Zone. It was the second damming of the Chagres, the first one had been at Gatún during construction of the canal.

In 1936, after the death of A. A. Hunter, Allen became resident manager of the Missouri Botanical Garden Tropical Station at Cerro Ancón, home of the famous Powell orchid collection. Since the 1920s the station was headquarters to a series of botanical expeditions that lead to the publication of the great work *The Flora of Panama*. In 1937 Allen began the methodical exploration of Panama's forests. In 1937 and 1938, for example, he botanized in eastern Panama. "Of the entire republic of Panama," he wrote in the *Missouri Botanical Garden Bulletin* of 1939, "the vast province of Darien, lying on the border of Colombia, probably offers the richest field for plant collecting." He explored the Tuira River as far up as Boca de Cupe. In the dry season of 1938 he made the first of many trips to the highlands of western Panamá, in Boquete and Volcán.

By 1941 he had discovered one of his favorite isthmian plant hunting places in an extinct volcano. "About a week ago," he reported to the Missouri Botanical Garden,

> I had the opportunity of spending four days in El Valle, in Coclé Province, and I am astonished at the tremendous wealth of the place. This time I was able to get into the high plateau regions to the north, and never in all my collecting experience have I seen such a fantastic region or such fascinating plants. After leaving the crater proper, there is a line of buffer hills to the north, rising in three rounded domes topped with an elfin forest and over which a steady cascade of fog and misty rain pours. To the north of these hills is a maze of valleys, with a most curious set of plateaus, some not over an acre or two and others probably forty or more acres. The tops are almost perfectly flat, with deep rich black soil, sup-

porting a growth of giant trees which literally drip with epiphytes of all descriptions. . . .Occasionally the mists would clear for a bit, and far off the Atlantic Ocean could be seen.

Paul Allen also served as botanical consultant to the former Canal Zone schools, and later as "Superintendent for the Experimental Gardens at the Canal Zone," today's

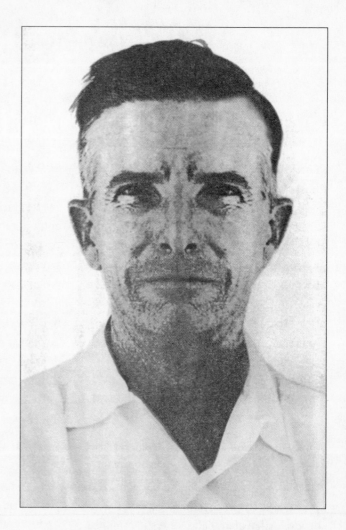

Paul Hamilton Allen (1911-1963), July 1962. Allen directed the Missouri Botanical Garden's Tropical Station at Cerro Ancón and the Summit Botanical Garden in Panama City.

Summit Botanical Gardens, a rainforest jewel on the banks of the canal, now administered by the office of the mayor of Panama City.

The Second World War turned many rainforest products into strategic materials, such as rubber latex and the bark of the *cinchona,* from which quinine is extracted. Allen was in charge of securing supplies of natural rubber in the Amazon and Orinoco basins for the Allies.

The construction of Maden Dam across the Chagres River (1930-35) led to the formation of Lake Alhajuela to store water for the canal. This view by Paul Allen shows the rising waters of the new lake in 1935.
Source: Missouri Botanical Garden Archives.

Panamanian Orchids and their Relationships with those of Colombia and Costa Rica

At the end of the war, Allen returned to Panama to gather information for a book on the taxonomy of local orchids; for Allen's true love was the Central American orchids. In a letter written in 1947, he joyfully described to Oakes Ames of Harvard University the discoveries he made during his orchid-collecting expeditions through Panama:

> Work continues on the collection of Panama orchids, which seems to be endless, with new species, or extensions of range coming to light in almost every trip. Such slight deviations from the beaten track as the Pearl Islands, and the wet mountain peaks north of El Valle, in Coclé province, have recently produced plants of *Cyrtopodium punctatum* and *Polyeyeni barbata,* both genera previously unrecorded from Panama. Although I have not seen New Guinea, or the mountains of Brazil, I would set the area covered by Costa Rica, Panama and Colombia against any in the world for wealth of species.

During the 1940s it was thought that Panamanian orchids shared more similarities with those from Costa Rica than those from Colombia. Allen believed this was not true, but was a consequence of how little the rich flora of Panama had been studied, particularly that of the eastern region, from Panama City to Darién. In a letter from September 14, 1947, he commented to C. Schweinfurt from Harvard University:

> The other evening I spent several hours entertaining myself with a sort of botanical idiot's delight that sometimes fascinates me, making a chart of the geographical range and

relationships of the Panaman orchids, and the results were in some ways startling. . . .For example, I find that 108 species are presumed to be endemic to Panama, mostly known from single collections and hence somewhat open to question. Also, while 135 species are common to Panama and Costa Rica, only six are common to Panama and Colombia! This is simply incredible, since it would indicate a profound biological break between Panama and Colombia, territories that on the Darien-Chocó boundary share common lands for more than one hundred and twenty five miles. After some consideration and consultation of my rainfall map of Panama, and charting areas from which collections have been taken, I am slowly coming to the conclusion that parts of Panama which would be likeliest to have a Choco-type flora have as yet, for the most part, to be seen by a botanists, even from afar. All of the highland area of the boundary is completely unknown, as are the mountains of the San Blas coast as far as the Canal. The parts of Panama best known and best collected are the Canal area, the dry Pacific Coast for thirty miles east, and sixty miles west of Panama City, the wet highlands of Coclé, and the highlands of Chiriquí, all of which would be expected to have affinities with the flora of Costa Rica.

Years at the United Fruit Company

At the beginning of the 1950s, the United Fruit Company contracted Allen as director of the Experimental Station at Golfito, a banana port on the Pacific Coast of Costa Rica. There, he studied the potential of tropical timber trees. These studies resulted

Photo on opposite page:
The famous Tropical Station of the Missouri Botanical Garden at the foot of Cerro Ancón, Panama, 1935.
Source: Missouri Botanical Garden Archives.

in the publication of his classic work *The Rain Forest of Golfo Dulce*.

In 1953 he was named director of the Fairchild Tropical Garden in Miami but only stayed a year, for he missed the nature and culture of the tropics. In 1954, he accepted a post as teacher and researcher at the Escuela Agrícola Panamericana, Honduras, better known as Zamorano, which at the time held one of the largest collections of tropical plants in Central America. For four years he taught botany, agriculture, and horticulture. His free time was spent improving the herbarium, founded by Juvenal Valerio and enlarged by Paul Standley and

L. O. Williams, which held thousands of plants from his previous explorations in Panama and Costa Rica. From his years at Zamorano emerged his work *The Timber Woods of Panama*, edited in Honduras.

In 1958, at the request of Francisco de Sola, he accepted an invitation to study the timber resources of El Salvador. After concluding this work, the United Fruit Company put him in charge of the Experimental Station at Lancetilla, in Tela, Honduras. This renowned station had been founded in 1926 by a group of researchers transferred there from Panama after the company closed its banana farms in Changuinola. In time, Lancetilla acquired the largest collection ever made of plants from the American tropics with economic potential.

In 1959, the United Fruit Company once again asked Allen to help and entrusted him with its ambitious research project: the production of a commercial "super-banana." As stated by the company's managerial office, the object of the investigation was "the combining in one commercial banana variety of all possible desirable qualities such as disease resistance, insect resistance, improved growth habit, better quality fruit, and other favorable characteristics." In Asia researchers had to collect as many samples as possible of wild and cultivated species of *Musa*, the banana genus.

For two years, Allen and his team combed the far corners of the Philippines, Taiwan, Borneo, Sarawak, Malaya, Java, Bali, Thailand, and Ceylon. Not only did they obtain for Lancetilla the largest collection of banana plants in the world, but they also established the Genetic Reference Bank of the Far East and left collections in many Asian countries.

El Valle de Antón, circa 1937, looking north. Allen's favourite orchid hunting site in the Isthmus was the crater of this extinct volcano. Photo: Missouri Botanical Garden, Archives.

Tropical Palms and *Pifá*

After orchids, palms were the plants that interested Allen the most. He helped organize the International Palm Society, of which he was elected president. He was fascinated by the that although it was a wild palm, it showed great variability in the color and size of its fruits, as well as how easy it was to propagate. He worried about the lack of measures aimed at propagating the cultivation of superior varieties of *pixbae*, and the deficit

Paul Allen and Robert Woodson at lunch after pressing plants, 1937.
Photo by Russell Siebert. Source: Russel Siebert Papers, Missouri Botanical Garden Archives.

"peach palm" or *pixbae* or *pifá* (*Bactris gusipaes*), as this palm is popularly known in Panama. This noble rainforest palm produces an excellent fruit, a very nutritious and important food source in Panama and Costa Rica, countries in which it is cultivated and the fruit sold in the streets after being boiled in salty water. Nevertheless, its usage is almost unknown in the rest of Central America.

According to Allen, the distribution of *pifá* northward to Central America took place after the Conquest. He marveled at the fact

of commercial nurseries. To promote among the people an acquaintance with, and love for the rainforest, Allen recommended the publication of simple illustrated manuals, focusing on improving the knowledge of living plants. This first step would allow an interested individual to access the existing literature, until then locked in the jargon of the specialists.

When he died in 1963, at the age of 52, he was at the height of his professional career, leaving many unfinished publications on the flora of Panama.

Alexander Wetmore and the Birds of Panama (1944-1966)

In 1944, a tall, graying man landed in Panama. He was quietly modest and of great internal fortitude. He was a man of few words, who spoke only if he had something important to say. Although he enjoyed the company of people, he was happiest in the field studying birds. He was one of the most famous ornithologists in the world. His myriad high-quality scientific publications included: *The Birds of Argentina, Paraguay, Uruguay, and Chile* (1926), *Classification and Systematics of the Birds of the World* (1930), and *Birds of Puerto Rico and the Dominican Republic* (1931). Almost 58 years of age, at a time when most people think of retirement, he had come to study the birds of the Las Perlas Archipelago and to begin, at the time unknown even to himself, a new and creative stage in his life that would forever and indelibly associate his name with Panama. This man was Alexander Wetmore.

For the next 22 years, from 1944 until 1966, Wetmore would return to investigate the avifauna of the entire Isthmus. From these researches arose his magnum opus, *The Birds of the Republic of Panama*. "My personal studies," said Wetmore in the 1965 Introduction to this work, "began in 1944, and have continued annually for approximately three months each year since 1946, with laboratory investigations of specimens, and a survey of the published works of others who have made contributions in this region."

The Birds of the Republic Panama was published by the Smithsonian Institution in four volumes. The first was released in 1965, when Wetmore turned 80 years old. The second volume appeared in 1968, and the third in 1972. The fourth was published posthumously in 1984, having been completed by others after his death.

Initially, Wetmore had not intended to start a project that would take 22 years to complete. Along the way he was captured by the biological wealth of this land. "The

Alexander Wetmore (1886-1978).
From 1944 until 1966 Wetmore organized 22 expeditions to study the birds of Panama. He was
research associate, and later, sixth Secretary of the Smithsonian Institution in Washington, DC.
Photo: Smithsonian Institution Archives, Washington, D.C.

number and kinds of birds known from the isthmus is so large," he said modestly of his long-time effort, "and materials available are so extensive, that completion of the report has required more time than originally contemplated."

An Early Interest in Science

Alexander Wetmore was born in Wisconsin in 1886, and died in 1978. He knew, even as a child, what he wanted to do when he grew up. From a very early age he decided to be a naturalist and to study birds, thanks to the encouragement of his mother. In the little rural town where he lived as a child he walked 6 miles to school. He studied at the University of Kansas and, in 1920, received his doctoral degree from George Washington University. His dissertation was entitled *The Birds of Puerto Rico*.

Wetmore began his career in 1910 as field assistant to the U.S. Biological Survey. In 1925, he was named director of the United States National Museum in Washington, D.C., a position he held until 1945, when he was named sixth Secretary of the Smithsonian Institution. During his tenure at the Smithsonian, the Institution added two organizations: the National Air Museum and the Canal Zone Biological Area (now the Smithsonian Tropical Research Institute).

Wetmore sat on the board of directors of numerous scientific, academic, and cultural institutions. He was president of the American Ornithologists' Union, the U.S. Academy of Sciences, the Washington Biologists' Field Club, and the Academy of Medicine, also in Washington, D.C. In 1948, President Truman appointed him chairman of the Interdepartmental Committee on Research and Development, a high-level group that was to determine the direction to be taken by scientific research in the United States after the Second World War. For years, he sat on the board of directors of the National Geographic Society and the Cosmos Club. He presided over North American delegations to international ornithological congresses and to the Inter-American Commission of Experts for the Protection of Nature and Wildlife, a board that in 1940 set guidelines for international conservation in the hemisphere.

Although Wetmore retired at 66 years of age, he continued to work daily in his laboratory nearly until his death. He always had time to guide young researchers.

Research in Latin America and the Caribbean

Wetmore's initial studies of the birds of Latin America took place in Puerto Rico, in 1911. Later on, he analyzed avian mortality rates at the Great Salt Lake, Utah. In 1920 he traveled to South America to observe the annual migration of North American birds southward. During the 1920s and 1930s, he occupied himself with the birds of Canada, Mexico, the Caribbean Islands, and Central and South America. He worked in Haiti and the Dominican Republic (1927), Guatemala (1936), and Venezuela (1937). In 1939, he traveled through Mexico, in 1940 across Costa Rica, and in 1941 around Colombia.

During his travels, he collected an impressive number of birds for the U.S. National Museum: 26,058 specimens, of which

14,291 were from Panama. In total, he described 189 species and subspecies of birds new to science, the majority from Central and South America. Fifty-six new species bore his name. As Storrs Olson would comment, "Dr. Wetmore's collections seem large in retrospect; but they form part of the fundamental resource on which present and future work will depend. The very magnitude of these collections would tend to make further collecting in most areas where he has worked superfluous."

Studies of Fossil Birds

Wetmore was interested in living birds as well as those that inhabited the earth long ago. For decades, he was nearly the only scientist to study the fossils of prehistoric birds. He is considered one of the founders of paleornithology, publishing more than 150 articles about fossil birds. People from Mongolia to Java, Panama, Bermuda, and elsewhere sent him fossils.

He considered the study of fossil birds from oceanic islands to be exceptionally important. Many species had been rapidly driven to extinction as humans introduced exotic predators. Since these introductions took place prior to the age of scientific exploration, we could learn about these vanished species only from their fossil remains.

Wetmore focused considerable attention on extinct Caribbean birds. In the Virgin Islands he found his first fossil, a huge flightless bird. He discovered bird species that had disappeared from Puerto Rico, a giant owl from Haiti, and several enormous birds of prey from Cuba. Wetmore collected 4,363 fossil birds, 540 of these from Panama. Among these were a *pato real*, a duck that had inhabited the Isthmus a million years earlier.

Twenty-two years Studying the Isthmian Land Bridge

From the beginning, Wetmore set forth the origin for his fascination with Panamanian biodiversity. In the first volume of *The Birds of the Republic of Panama* he wrote:

> The long, narrow Isthmus of Panama, which unites North America on the one hand and South America on the other, is a geographic area outstanding in its interest to biologists in the systematics field as the land connection between these two regions of the Northern and Southern Hemispheres. Present understanding of geologic history indicates that the two areas were separated by open sea in the Tertiary period for a vast space of time that began in the Paleocene Epoch and extended toward the end of the Pliocene. For 50 million years, South America remained isolated from other lands, while North America had periodic union with Asia through land connections in the present region of Bering Sea. The great diversity in plant and animal life that now marks the Panamanian land bridge is a reflection of invasions from the two adjacent continental areas. Study of present-day distribution, variation, and relationship in any group is of deep interest and valuable in scientific information.

Wetmore traveled to nearly all corners of Panama. After his major study of the Las Perlas archipelago he returned to Barro Colorado Island in 1944, and Jaqué, near the Colombian border, in 1946. Thereafter, he would come back every dry season to Panama until 1966. Once in the Isthmus, well installed at the Tivoli Hotel, his first order of business was in the Canal Zone, tending to matters regarding the operations at Barro Colorado Island (BCI). In the early 1950s, for example, a most pressing need was improving the electrical system by replacing the island's two old diesel generators with an underwater cable that could bring a more reliable power supply from the mainland. Once BCI business was concluded, he would then head out to do field work in some part of the Panamanian landscape.

Usually he would arrive from Washington, D.C. with his wife Bea and his field assistant W. M. Perrygo, from the U.S. National Museum. In Panama, his native guide and woodsman, Ratibor Hartmann, a young man from the highlands of Chiriquí who worked for the Gorgas Memorial Laboratory, would join him. The commandant of the Caribbean Air Command with headquarters in Albrook Field, was a priceless source of logistical support, be it a jeep, a plane to land Wetmore's team at some forgotten jungle strip, or a fast boat to take them to a distant island and return to pick them up weeks later.

Thanks to Storrs Olson we now have a detailed reconstruction of Wetmore's field trips across Panama. In 1947, he was on Barro Colorado, then he headed to the Jaqué River in Darién. A C-47 dropped him on the morning of March 25 at an airstrip built in the jungle during the war. As he commented in a letter to Major General H. R. Harmon, chief of the Caribbean Air Command:

> In brief report, we reached Jaqué expeditiously, thanks to your kindness in arranging for us in a C-47, in the early morning of March 25. By good fortune, I was able to get in touch immediately with Panamanians that I had known last year, so that at 4:00p.m. on March 26 we were on our way up the Jaqué River with four men and two dugout canoes [*piraguas*]. I was intent on getting out of the town that afternoon, as the tide was running up the river and I wanted to get the outfit out of town before any farewell drinking on part of our helpers!

SMITHSONIAN MISCELLANEOUS COLLECTIONS
VOLUME 150 (WHOLE VOLUME)

THE BIRDS OF THE REPUBLIC OF PANAMÁ

Part 1.—T INAMIDAE (Tinamous) to R YNCHOPIDAE (Skimmers)

By
ALEXANDER WETMORE
Research Associate
Smithsonian Institution

(PUBLICATION 4617)

CITY OF WASHINGTON
PUBLISHED BY THE SMITHSONIAN INSTITUTION
DECEMBER 27, 1965

Cover of *The Birds of the Republic of Panama, Part I*, initiating Alexander Wetmore's classic work on the avifauna of the Isthmus.
Its four volumes were published by the Smithsonian Institution between 1965 and 1984.

Lunch at Cerro Campana. Beatrice "Bea" Thielen Wetmore, second from left; in the middle,
Alexander Wetmore takes notes; Watson Perrygo, front right.
Source: Alexander Wetmore Papers, Smithsonian Institution Archives, Washington, D.C.

We spent that night on the gravel bar at the mouth of the Río Pavarondó, which enters the Jaqué, from the north, and is near the head of the tidewater. From here on the men were using push poles up through rapids, with occasional stretches of flat water. The evening of May 27 found us within the second line of hills, and we spent that night at the mouth of the Arroyo Tortadó. On this second day, we passed a few fincas of Panamanians and occasional clearings of the Chocó Indians. From the Tortadó on there were only scattered groups of Indians, with the forest unbroken except for their clearings. In the late afternoon of March 28 we came, with some difficulty, to the mouth of the Rio Imamadó, the point for which I had been aiming. The rapids had been swifter and the river shallower all through this day. Here we found the last Indians located on the Jaqué River. By good fortune the headman in the group was Conejo, whom I had met last year, and at whose invitation I had come up here. . . .We reached this point, just ahead of a terrific rain, got our canoes into the mouth of the Imamadó, part of the outfit covered with a waterproof tarpaulin, and the rest and ourselves at Conejo's house. The storm gave us the opportunity to talk and become friendly. It developed that Conejos' brother is godson to old Gerónimo who was with me as one of the helpers from Jaqué. At the end of an hour I had made a bargain to rent the house for $5.00 for a month, and here we located.

This point is in the heart of a tremendous unbroken green forest, with openings only along the streams, and trees from 100 to 175 feet high elsewhere. The undergrowth was heavy in places, more open in others, and there were large areas grown with the tagua palms, which form the palm nuts of commerce. Our house was a platform six feet above the ground in posts, had a good thatched roof but no sides. The Indians are all small people so that one of the first necessities was to strengthen the underpinnings because of my weight. . . .In this space the six of us lived for four days with 25 plus or minus Indians of assorted ages, sexes and sizes. Perrygo and I never succeeded in making a complete count that we could depend upon as the flock of small youngsters circulated too rapidly to make this practicable. Finally, our Indian friends moved down river and from then on came back to visit us Sundays. . . .

Forest birds were tremendously abundant and in good variety. The Indian trails in the main followed the streams, through the water itself where this was shallow, and on the banks only around the deeper holes . . . .our first task was to cut hunting trails until in the end we had about eight miles available for hunting. . . .

In the period of a little less than four weeks we made a fairly large collection of birds of this region, securing much that is supplemental to what we got last year near Jaqué. We started down the river in the early morning of April 18, and the following morning reached the Jaqué Airfield.

The map Wetmore used, prepared by the Engineers of the US Army based at Corozal, was found to be inaccurate. It did not show the true meanderings of the Jaqué River or its tributaries: "As nearly as I could estimate," he continued in his letter to General Harmon, "our camp lay back somewhere between 50 and 60 miles, by river, from Jaqué at the river mouth." He was surprised that the Jaqué River valley was the terminus of many jungle routes used by Panamanians and Colombians to travel back and forth between both countries.

At the time, malaria was rampant in the Jaqué region, as well as other diseases. Several deaths had occurred and "the Choco Indians," according to Wetmore, "are friendly but do not welcome strangers. We did not have the slightest difficulty with them. In fact, I am now the 'compadre' with all the Indians in this river! They told me that they were getting poisoned arrows ready to use on some witch doctor over on the headwaters on the Sambú to the north. The story was that these brujos had gone into Colombia, had learned some new witchcraft, and that the people were dying because of it so they were going to get rid of the witch doctor as the easiest way to settle the difficulty."

Most of Wetmore's fieldwork for 1948 was in the provinces of Herrera and Los Santos. In a letter thanking Major General Willis Hale, Commanding General of the Caribbean Air Command, he described his trip to the Azuero peninsula as follows:

Darién, 1947. Wetmore in front of an embará household on the Imamadó, a tributary
of the Jaqué River.
Source: Smithsonian Institution Archives, Washington, D.C.

Under date of 17 April 1948, I forwarded a letter to general Carl Spaatz, Chief of Staff, United States Air Force, expressing my thanks, and that of the Smithsonian Institution, for your kindness in making available by loan a jeep for official travel during my recent scientific expedition in western Panama. This car made it possible to cover a considerable area that would not have otherwise have been available, and so added measurably to the results of the work. In fact, through this transportation the value of the data secured was more than doubled.

My headquarters for this work was located in the village of Parita in the province of Herrera, where I joined a party of archeologists from the Smithsonian Institution engaged in excavations of the Indian deposits in that area. With Parita as a base, I worked intensively throughout the eastern two thirds of the province of Herrera, and the northern third of the province of Los Santos. In addition, I made a trip down through eastern Los Santos as far as Punta Mala.

The work may be considered under three divisions, the first concerned with the sea coast, with its sandy beaches and extensive mangrove swamps found at the mouths of the principal streams. Inland, there was the coastal plain from four to six miles in width, narrowing considerably below Pedasí. And inland from there to a somewhat more elevated region of rolling hills that became higher toward the interior. An isolated group of hills between Paris and La Cabuya known as Los Voladores was especially interesting since these were completely isolated and were still covered with forests.

In the north of Herrera, near Santa María and La Concepción, there are extensive savannas on which are found several species of birds, notably the Panama pipit, the meadowlark, the red-breasted blackbird, and certain species of hawks, that find the southern limits of their distribution on the coastal plain. There are also a few fresh water lagoons. Particularly one called Ciénaga Macana. . . .where water birds were especially abundant. There were certain species found only in the coastal mangrove swamps and beaches, others restricted to the coastal plain, and still others that did not extend eastward beyond the hilly region of the interior.

Wetmore collected 850 birds from 170 species on this trip. In his letter, he commented on the water supply of the region, which was bad. Although the government had begun to dig wells: "We lived mainly off native food which was plentiful and of good variety. As this is a cattle country, fresh beef was constantly available though it is not refrigerated, being freshly killed each day. Deer are common and venison was sold to us regularly. We also had quail and other game birds brought to us constantly." Finally, he noted the accelerating process of conversion of forest to pasture:

The rainfall here is decidedly less than in Balboa. The precipitation is extremely little in the dry season from the end of December to May, and I was told that ordinarily little rain might fall until July. The region is primarily a cattle country, which is run by fairly large holdings, and of small farms owned by people living in the villages. The pastures in most cases are over grazed and the cattle become thin and a good many die toward the end of the dry season. There is no understanding of soil conservation, and the clearing of brush and forests cover to make new pastures was proceeding steadily back toward the heads of the streams. This [Wetmore pointed out with almost uncanny foresight] naturally will decrease the water supply, so that unless some conservation is undertaken soon land resources will become badly depleted. This is unfortunately the common story throughout wide areas of Latin America.

By 1949, Wetmore had explored Cerro Azul, Chepo, Utivé, and Pacora, east of Panama City. The following year, he visited Chimán, Río Majé and Cerro Chucantí. In 1951, he was west of Panama City, in Cerro Campana, Bejuco and El Valle. During 1952, he was on the Caribbean side, up the Río Indio and Uracillo. Then he moved to the small islands of Panama Bay: Taboga, Taboguilla and Urabá. The next year found him in Veraguas, traveling around Soná, Puerto Vidal, Río de Jesús and Puerto Mutis, and then on to Quebrada de Piedra in Chiriquí. He then was off to Coclé, collecting near Río Hato, El Valle, and Antón.

In 1954—1955, Wetmore concentrated on Chiriquí, around Volcán, Sereno, and Cerro Punta. By 1954 the idea of a book on the birds of Panama was clearly in his mind. "At the present time," said an article from The Panama Canal Review, "Dr. Wetmore and his wife are in Chiriquí, on the tenth field trip he has made to Panama. Out of these trips - and future trips -he hopes- will come a book on the birds of Panama, but for that he is not yet ready." For those interested in learning more about birds around the canal he recommended seeking a copy of the book by Bertha Sturgis *Birds of the Panama Canal Zone.*

In 1956, Bolivar Vallarino, head of the National Guard, arranged for him to study the birds of Coiba, the largest island off the Pacific coast of Latin America and the site of a Panamanian penal colony. In 1957, he was back to Los Santos, covering the Tonosí Valley, Isla Iguana, La Villa, and Pedasí. The following year, in 1957, he returned to Bocas del Toro, boating to Escudo de Veraguas, Tiger Rock, Swan Key, and inland into the Changuinola region. In 1959, after exploring Juan Mina and Gamboa in the Canal Zone, he went to the Paya and Chucunaque rivers, in Darién. The dry season of 1960 was a busy one. Within the Zone, he collected around Gamboa, Chiva-Chiva, and Cerro Galera. Then he went out to the Las Perlas archipelago, visiting most of the islands, and finishing this trip in the highlands of Chiriquí: Volcán, Cerro Punta, Buena Vista, Concepción, Alanje, and Boquete. During 1961, his work took him into the Panama Canal Watershed, to Cerro Pirre in Darién, and to the lowlands east of Panama City. In 1962 he was back in Coclé, Los Santos, and Veraguas, including such small islands off the Pacific coast as Frailes del Sur, Canal de Afuera, Afuerita, Brincanco, and Cébaco. The following year he was again in Coclé, the islands of Chiriquí, and the San Blas archipelago. In 1964 he returned to Darién, into the region of El Real, Pucro, Tacarcuna, Malí, and Boca de Cupe. In 1965, he collected on the islands of Cé-

baco and Gobernadora, and then headed for the Chiriquí highlands. His final season in Panama, in 1966, took him again to Chiriquí. By then he was 80 years old. He collected around Puerto Armuelles and Punta Balsa, on the Burica Peninsula, where deforestation was progressing rapidly.

Throughout his numerous field seasons in Panama, Wetmore's headquarters were at the Gorgas Memorial Laboratory of Tropical and Preventative Medicine. He was a research associate there, and a board member from 1949 to 1976. There he had met his lifetime local field guide and companion, a native woodsman and pathfinder from the highlands of Chiriquí, Ratibor Hartmann. In 1973, Gorgas Laboratory named a 150 feet long suspension bridge, anchored to the tops of three huge trees in the Bayano River, the "Alexander Wetmore Canopy Bridge." This was the first bridge in the Western Hemisphere designed specifically for studying life in the canopy, and also served to facilitate many bio-medical studies. Personnel from the Panama Canal built it with funds from the National Geographic Society.

Wetmore maintained a close relationship with distinguished Panamanians interested in Panama's tropical environment who supported his work. Thanks to their key contacts they helped to overcome numerous local bureaucratic obstacles. Among them were Pedro Galindo Vallarino of the Gorgas Memorial Laboratory; Alejandro Méndez Pereira, director of Panama's National Museum, and Eugene Eisenmann, the great Panamanian ornithologist and lawyer, who placed a great deal of data on Isthmian birds at Wetmore's disposal.

Alexander Wetmore preparing bird specimens in Soná, 1953.
Source: Smithsonian Institution Archives, Washington, D.C.

Environmental Concerns

Throughout a lifetime dedicated to research, Wetmore would acquire a profound understanding and appreciation for nature. On many of his field excursions he observed the dramatic destruction of the tropical forests. For example, to the construction of roads he reacted with preoccupation and warned of "continued change in access to more remote areas, clearing of forest with an alarming rapidity, in steady pressure in restriction of the native fauna and flora." His concern compelled him to become a pioneer in the Panamerican branch of the International Council for Preservation of Birds.

At the same time, he was pleased by the 1967 decision of the Minister of Agriculture to establish the first protected area in Panama. "In this connection it is a pleasure," he said in the second volume of the *The Birds of the Republic of Panama*, published the following year, "to record the establishment of the National Park and Biological Reserve of Cerro Campana, an interesting region that marks the southern boundary of the mountain flora and fauna of the highlands of western Panama. With this important beginning it is hoped that other areas also might be set aside for the preservation of their natural features." He also noted with pleasure the legislative Decree No. 23 of 1967 which established measures to conserve Panama's native fauna.

In the sunset of his life, the tall naturalist Panamanians liked to call *"Don Alejandro,"* leaves us the following and final acknowledgment: "In my travels in the course of my studies, which have taken me widely throughout the Republic, from the Costa Rican border in Chiriquí and Bocas del Toro to the Colombian frontier in Darién and San Blas, I have had courteous and friendly reception everywhere from residents of the country, and I owe much to many for their assistance."

Studies by Alexander Wetmore on the Birds of Panama's Pacific Islands (1944-1956)

During his long studies on Panama's avifauna, Alexander Wetmore paid considerable attention to the birds on the numerous islands of the Isthmus. On the Pacific side, for example, he studied the Las Perlas Archipelago in 1944; Taboga, Taboguilla, and Urabá in 1952, and Coiba in 1956. The natural history of these islands was practically unknown until the 1940s, because the incredible biological wealth of avifauna on the mainland may have diverted attention from efforts to study the islands. Wetmore was also intrigued by the possibilities that these islands offered as habitats for bird species that had been only scantily reported upon; furthermore, people assumed that only marine species nested there.

Based on the available information, Wetmore speculated that the islands were connected to the mainland during the last glaciation, some 11,000 years ago, when the Isthmus was far broader than it is today. Later, as polar caps melted and sea levels rose, the seas advanced and cut the islands off. He thought that the islands close to Panama City today—Taboga, Taboguilla, and Urabá—had first been isolated rocky outcrops. Gradually, soils formed and vegetation increased, covering these barren islands and creating a favorable environment for mainland birds. He also wondered about how the water barrier might have prevented most common mainland birds from crossing onto the islands. Finally, he also asked himself whether or not humans had been responsible for the extinction of some species of birds.

The Las Perlas Archipelago, 1944

The Las Perlas Archipelago, guarding the entrance to the broad Gulf of Panama, was well known to sailors and explorers. Nevertheless, its natural history was nearly unknown. World War II would rescue their flora and fauna from anonymity. Suddenly, as a result of military activity, San José was transformed from an uninhabited island into one of the most studied areas in tropical America, appearing frequently in the scientific literature of the 1940s.

The Las Perlas or Pearl Islands are an archipelago composed of three main islands with sparkling white beaches and black volcanic rocks—Rey, San José, and Pedro González—, plus dozens of small islands and rocky promontories. San José, the southernmost of the major islands, lies 60 miles from Panama City. The climate, similar to the Pacific coast of Central America, consists of sharply defined wet and dry seasons.

When Balboa first discovered the islands of Las Perlas in 1513, they already were one of the most important centers of pearl diving in the Americas. Tararequí was the name given by the native Indian inhabitants to the largest island. When the Indian population was decimated in the mid 16th Century, black people were brought in to replace them as pearl divers. Their descendants are the current island inhabitants. However, the population on the islands has always been sparse. Gradually, pearl diving disappeared and during World War II the islanders lived by fishing during the dry season and subsistence slash and burn agriculture during the rainy months.

Alexander Wetmore gave particular attention to the study of Panama's islands. This photo was taken in 1944, during his research on San José, Las Perlas Archipelago. Source: Smithsonian Institution Archives, Washington, D.C. Page 249: View of San José Island, Las Perlas Archipelago, in 1944. Source: Alexander Wetmore, Smithsonian Institution Archives, 1946.

World War II and
Scientific Surveys of San José

The island of San José, seven miles long and three miles wide, had been largely uninhabited since the 1850s. Its last occupant had been an eccentric Englishman, who after buying the island had deforested half of it to introduce cattle. For unknown reasons, he was murdered. People said that San José was bewitched and avoided the island at night.

In 1943 the U.S. Navy established a station on San José. In 1944 Army engineers arrived and, in six months, constructed camps, airstrips, and many kilometers of roads. Thousands of soldiers were stationed there.

The Chemical Warfare Service would conduct a significant number of tests as part of the preparations for a future invasion of Japan. Everyone was convinced that it would be a bloody replica, in a far grander scale, of the carnage that was taking place during amphibious assaults on Japanese-held islands in the Pacific. The secret testing of deadly gases under tropical conditions, received the code name "San José Project." Col. Robert D. McLeod was Chief of the Project.

With the roads came a small unusual vehicle that would change the world, the jeep. This sturdy, manoeuverable, four-wheel-

drive car greatly facilitated the exploration and study of most of San José. After the war, the olive-green jeep, loaned to the Smithsonian by the U.S. Caribbean Air Command, became Wetmore's vehicle of choice for his yearly field trips throughout Panama.

Because the island had been abandoned for the past 80 years, it conserved most of its tropical vegetation. Half of it was virgin forest, the other half secondary growth due to previous deforestation. There were also small patches of natural savannas. To study the flora and fauna, an impressive group of naturalists was assembled: C. O. Earlanson and I. M. Johnson to study the vegetation and collect botanical specimens; Austin Clark, marine mollusks; J. P. E. Morrison, freshwater mollusks; Doris Chochran, reptiles and amphibians; and Samuel F. Hildebrand, freshwater fishes. Alexander Wetmore would study the birds from February 7 until March 14, 1944.

The archipelago is a paradise for marine birds. The first naturalist to study the birds of San José was the Swedish ornithologist Carl Bovallius from the University of Uppsala, in 1882. In February 1927, Ludlow Griscom collected 39 bird specimens from San José. In September 1937 and February 1941, Robert Cushman Murphy collected birds on the island. Other naturalists who had observed the local bird life were Thomas Barbour and James Zetek. Wetmore found that in Las Perlas the number of species of birds was small in comparison to the mainland. Fifty species were counted on San José, 46 nesting there.

The Islands of Taboga, Taboguilla, and Urabá, in 1952

In the dry season of 1952, upon returning from the *costa abajo* of Colón, and from canoeing up the Río Indio, Wetmore returned to the Pacific side, to visit the islands of Taboga, Taboguilla, and Urabá. Because he was Secretary of the Smithsonian Institution in Washington, D.C., an official governmental agency, the U.S. Army provided him with a fast boat used to rescue downed pilots at sea, to take him to these spots, drop him, and return for him later. He stayed at Taboga from March 14 to March 24. He was accompanied by W. M. Perrygo of the U.S. National Museum, and by his two trackers and hunters from Chiriquí, the Hartmann brothers, Armagedon and Ratibor, his field companions on most of his Panama expeditions. In Taboga, they stayed at Julio Chu's "Hotel Taboga."

In 1952, Taboga, two and a half miles long and four miles wide, had large forested areas on its steepest southern slopes. Above 800 feet, the soil was poor, with bare, rocky outcrops, covered by grasslands similar to the ones Wetmore had seen in the mainland, at Cerro Campana. Taboguilla, the smallest island of the three, was completely forested, save for a few clearings made by Taboga farmers to plant their slash and burn crops.

Like Naos, Perico, and Flamenco, the islands at the Pacific entrance to the Canal, Taboga had been extensively fortified during World War II. Naval bases and forts had been built, and thousands of U.S. troops had been stationed there. Fortunately, the need to camouflage the installations required leaving much of the vegetation intact, helping to preserve the landscape. In 1952, these defense sites had been abandoned and the strong rains and vigorous plant growth rapidly began to heal the scars of man's preparations for war.

Little was known of Taboga's birds. Fred Hicks was among the first to collect here in 1865. In 1888, the Reverend Thomas Heyde collected hummingbirds. Later, in 1915, Thomas Hallinan collected birds which can be found today in the American Museum of Natural History in New York. In 1924, Thomas Barbour and Ludlow Griscom visited briefly. Apparently, the only Panamanian who had studied these islands was Eugene Eisenmann, who visited Taboga during several rainy seasons and generously offered Wetmore his notes and observations. Wetmore collected 127 bird specimens, of which 21 were migrants passing through. In terms of their relationships, these birds seemed to Wetmore closer to those of the Las Perlas than to those on the mainland.

Coiba Island, 1956

On January 6, 1956, at 1:30 pm, a fast U.S. vessel, known as a crash boat, anchored at Las Damas Bay, across the headquarters of the Coiba penal colony, known as "La Central." The craft had set off the previous day from Rodman Naval base, 220 miles away on the Pacific entrance to the canal. It departed after leaving off Alexander Wetmore and his two field assistants, Armagedon Hartmann, and Vicente Alvarez, a U.S. Army technician from the malaria control outfit.

Captain Juan A. Souza, director of the penal colony, quartered them in the new hospital, and assigned a trusted prisoner as cook and another as operator of the outboard-powered dugout canoe. Wetmore stayed in Coiba until February 6, 1956.

Coiba, 540 km² in surface area and the largest island in the Pacific coast of Central America, has always dazzled voyagers due to its luxuriant vegetation, its beaches, and its reefs. It appears in early maps under such exotic names as Cobaya, Quibo, and Coiba. Bartolomé Hurtado, the first Spaniard to visit it in 1516, found it densely inhabited. According to the Spanish Chroniclers, the people of Coiba were large in stature and spoke Guaymí. In warfare, they used thick cotton vests and heavy lances with points made of shark teeth. These indigenous people were exterminated; the last ones were taken to Darién and sold as slaves in 1550 to work in the gold mines.

During the Spanish colonial period, Coiba remained uninhabited, but was visited frequently by Spanish vessels and corsairs, attracted by its excellent fresh water streams, forests, and abundant game. William Dampier visited Coiba in June 1685. "It is all over plentifully stored with great tall flourishing Trees of many sorts," he says, "and there is good Water."

George Shelvocke, of the English navy, came in January 1720, and in December 1741 the fleet of Admiral George Anson anchored in Las Damas Bay on its expedition around the world. Anson described great flocks of macaws, parakeets, and parrots, as well as an infinite number of marine turtles.

Pearls were Coiba's most magnificent natural asset. Its oyster beds yielded some of the most striking pearls found along the Pacific coast of the Americas. At the beginning of the 20th Century, pearl diving was still going on, and at Observatory Point there was a bar, a store, and other buildings. Eventually, the over-fished oyster beds gave out, and with them vanished the exploits of the pearl divers, legendary for centuries. In 1919, the government of president Belisario Porras turned all private lands into public property and established on Coiba a penal colony that still exists today. During World War II, the U.S. Army installed a radar tower and a camp as part of the outward ring protecting the canal.

The fascinating history of pearl diving in Coiba is intimately linked to the history of the provinces of Chiriquí and Veraguas. As a child in Chiriquí, I can still remember the gripping tales recounted by old "Marquitos," the last of the legendary hardhat pearl divers. He would tell us endless stories about the mortal dangers of the sea and the souls of dead divers wandering in the "land of the *chiricanos*," a long forgotten cemetery on the sands of Jícara Island, where pearl divers from Chiriquí were buried after meeting death in quest of the "tears of the sea," as pearls were called then.

In spite of the prison camps and the clearing of forest for pasture and croplands, Wetmore found Coiba covered by a vegetation only comparable to the one he had seen along the Jaqué River in Darién. On Coiba, Wetmore discovered another hidden treasure: 133 species of birds, among them 16 new to science.

Eugene Eisenmann Brandon: Lawyer and Student of the Birds of Panama (1939-1981)

Eugene Eisenmann Brandon was born in 1906 in Panama City, within the walled *intramuros* of the colonial neighborhood of San Felipe. He was the first of six children of Gustave Eisenmann Ehrman and Ethel Brandon Maduro. Eugene came into the world with a serious handicap in one arm but nature compensated for his disability with the gift of a brilliant mind and a profound curiosity about the natural world of the tropics.

Upon completing his doctoral degree with honors in law at Harvard University, he became a successful lawyer in a prestigious New York firm. In his free time, Eugene studied the tropical birds of the New World, becoming one of the most respected authorities on this subject in the 20th Century. When he retired from his practice of law in 1956, he began a new career as ornithologist with the American Museum of Natural History in New York, serving as mentor and role model for countless young ornitholo-gists. He worked as a research associate at the museum until his death in 1981. Eisenmann was, according to Frank Graham, an example of how a serious amateur could contribute significantly to the advancement of the biological sciences.

His books were few but considered to be milestones, especially his work on the birds of Barro Colorado Island (1952) and his monograph on the taxonomy and distribution of Central American birds from Mexico to Panama (1955).

In 1983, his colleagues edited a volume in his honor, *Neotropical Ornithology*, with contributions from the foremost specialists on Central and South American birds. In this publication, Thomas Howell, ex-president of the American Ornithological Union, referred to Eisenmann as ". . . .a remarkable person who had a profound impact on ornithology in the Americas and influenced generations of investigators of the birds of that region."

His Ancestors

Gustave Eisenmann Ehrman, Eugene's father, was born in New Iberia, Louisiana. The Eisenmanns, a Jewish family from Alsace-Lorraine, had immigrated to this French colony with a *laissez-passer* signed by Emperor Napoleon Bonaparte himself. At the age of 18, Gustave Eisenmann arrived in Panama to work at the Ehrman Bank, owned by his maternal uncle, Henri Ehrman. Henri, born in France, had come to Panama as a young man, penniless but with aspirations. With tenacity and vision he would become a successful businessman, owner of the Hotel Central (the best in its day in Panama City), banker, and agent of the French Interoceanic Canal Company.

At the beginning of the 20th Century, Gustave Eisenmann was already a well-known businessman in Panama City. His two companies, the American Bazar, with Carlos Eleta, sr. as partner, and the Universal Ex-

Eugene Eisenmann Brandon (1906-1981).
Born in Panama City, Eugene Eisenmann became a successful New York City lawyer and one of the most notable scholars of tropical birds of the New World during the mid-20th Century.
Photo: Courtesy of Audrey Eisenmann de Kline.

port Corporation, located near the Cathedral, were at the economic and political epicenter of the capital. While unable to attend college, he was well-read and firmly believed in the role of education as a means to liberate the human spirit. Also an athlete, Guatave Eisenmann was one of the pioneers of baseball in Panama, together with Ernesto "Neco" De la Guardia.

Eugene Eisenmann's mother, Ethel Brandon Maduro, was the daughter of David Henry Brandon and Judith Maduro, both from Panamanian families of old Sephardim Jewish stock, who had contributed substantially to progress in Panama. "Estelita" Brandon, born in Panama, studied at what was then the best private school on the Isthmus, "La Escuela de Marina", and was later sent to a finishing school in New York.

Eugene's curiosity about birds developed early in his life. As he would comment in 1977: "My own modest contribution to ornithology were the result of an interest stimulated during my childhood in Panama."

The Plazas of *Intramuros* and the Savannahs of *Extramuros*

Following the sacking and burning of the original city of Panama by Henry Morgan in the 1680s, the Spanish relocated its site some six miles to the west at the foot of Ancón Hill and constructed a wall around the new city. Within the walls or *intramuros* stood the seat of political, religious and economic power, home to the white and upper clerical and merchant class. Outside the walls or *extramuros*, especially around the Plaza of Santana, lived the poorer masses.

Eugene spent his childhood in the classrooms of the "Escuela de Marina" and in the *plazas* and parks of colonial Panama City. It was the American era of canal construction. He lived on 4th Street, near the plazas of San Francisco, the Cathedral, and Las Bóvedas. The residents of this small city of some 20,000 inhabitants got around in coaches and the tram. The streetcar began its route in the walled section of the colonial quarter, passed through the old West Indian neighborhood of Calidonia, and ended up at El Casino. There began the lovely countryside called "La Sabana." The savannah extended from the capital city to Chepo, some 50 kilometers to the east, a narrow band of rolling grasslands sandwiched between the mangroves on the Pacific coast to the south, and the forested mountains of the continental divide to the north. Crystalline streams crisscrossed the mostly flat countryside, their banks lined with splendid, lush forest.

Eugene loved the dry season. His family spent summers at La Sabana, in a simple wooden house on stilts, with its well, its horses and its chickens. In the savannahs, Eugene would go horseback riding, swimming in the streams or simply exploring the countryside. It is here that the sensitive and observant youngster came to love this landscape of forest and grasslands. He became acquainted with wild animals: opossums, which people blamed for stealing chickens, and sloths. It amazed him to watch how, when an *iguana* was sighted, all hired hands on the farm would suddenly vanish, off on the chase. They were heirs to a Pre-Columbian tradition that regards the meat of this reptile as a delicacy.

His innate curiosity soon fixed on birds, which attracted his attention: "I found the hummingbirds fascinating, as they fed on floral nectar, on wings beating so fast that they seemed as translucent as those of the bees and dragonflies." Awed by the existence of so many varied birds, he was frustrated when he was unable to find answers to his questions in the books of his day.

New York and Harvard

When Eugene was 10, his mother died while giving birth to her sixth child. His father moved the family to New York City in 1916, where he opened a branch of his import/export firm. Eugene would not return to Panama until he was 17 years old.

His interest in birds revived while attending public high school in New York, where he found other children whose pastime was also bird watching. In 1923 he entered Harvard University, where he obtained a doctor of laws degree with honors, a solid foundation for a promising career as a lawyer in a New York legal firm.

In the 1930s, Eugene rediscovered his avocation for birds, expanding and deepening his ornithological knowledge. He went on field trips with the New York Audubon Society. His restless intellect was nurtured at meetings of the Linnaean Society at the American Museum of Natural History in New York. Ernest Mayr, the great biologist and editor of the society's publications, captivated him with his lectures and his book *Systematics and the Origin of Species* (1942), mostly on the subject of bird evolution. Influenced by Ernest Mayr, Eisenmann came to realize the great contributions serious amateurs had made to the field of ornithology.

Barro Colorado Island

Apparently, Eugene's first trip to Barro Colorado Island in the Canal of Panama was in 1939, motivated by his intention to study the birds along the island's trails. In the visitors' log he wrote: "I wanted to have the opportunity to really get to know this impressive site. However, I spent less time on the trails than I would have liked, given [that] the activity and variety of birds that can be seen from the porch of the laboratory was overwhelming."

The Second World War limited biological research. According to his sister Audrey, soon after the attack on Pearl Harbor, Eugene had an unusual experience. He went bird watching in Punta Paitilla, then an uninhabited, strategic promontory overlooking the Pacific, where the U.S. Army was building fortifications to defend the canal. Suddenly, he came upon a camouflaged battery of guns, across from the site currently occupied by the Sonesta building. A soldier held him at gunpoint. Seeing that he had Japanese-made binoculars, a German camera, and a notebook full of apparently suspicious notes, the soldier shouted: "Oh, a secret code, a spy!" He was taken prisoner and transported to the Navy base at Fort Amador, at the Pacific entrance to the canal. He was interrogated by the base commander, who eventually set him free upon concluding that he was not an Axis spy. The commander confessed that he, like President Franklin Roosevelt, was also a bird-watcher.

At the end of the War, Eugene spent more time visiting Barro Colorado. When a lawyer friend of his died at the age of 50, he decided to retire and to live longer by doing more bird watching.

In 1952, the Smithsonian Institution published his work *Annotated List of Birds of Barro Colorado Island, Panama Canal Zone,* which became an essential reference for zoogeographers, ecologists, and ornithologists interested in Barro Colorado. Eisenmann underscored the importance of the island as an ideal site for research on the ecology of tropical species. Later he analyzed and reported on the causes which had led to the gradual extinction or disappearence of 38 bird species from the island between 1926 and 1955. Eugene supported Barro Colorado intellectually and as a generous patron of the laboratory. A cove was named in his honor.

Cerro Campana, La Jagua, and Volcán Barú

During the 1960s, Eugene and Horace Loftin, of the Center for Tropical Studies at Florida State University, published several bird lists. In 1967, they co-authored *A list of birds known from the Cerro Campana area - Panama.* Later that year, Campana was declared Panama's first National Park. They also published a bird list for La Jagua, an old 7,200-hectare *hacienda* in the Río Pacora area to the east of Panama City. Its owners, the Huertematte family, permitted the Center for Tropical Studies to establish a field station here, to study the savannah and gallery forest ecosystems of Eastern Panama Province. The *hacienda*, which included the La Jagua marsh, bordered on the mangroves of the Pacific coast. Alexander Wetmore and Neal Smith also contributed to the La Jagua bird list. In 1972, Eisenmann and Loftin published a list of the birds of Volcán Barú and Boquete, on the Chiriquí Highlands of Western Panama.

Central and South America

As transportation through Central America improved and more ornithologists arrived, there still was no complete accurate list of the bird species of the region. In 1955, Eisenmann published *The Species of Middle American Birds*, enumerating 1,400 forms known from Mexico to Panama. This was the first brief and concise compendium of the taxonomy and distribution of the Central American avifauna. This work, resulting from an extensive review of the literature, suggested standard English names for each bird species, which became the accepted norm. Experts preparing books sought his advice and sent him their manuscripts for revision. Eugene advised Rodolfe Meyer de Schauensee as he prepared *The Birds of Colombia* (1964), *Species of South American Birds and their Distribution* (1966), and *Guide to the Birds of Venezuela* (1978).

Eugene also played a key role in the publication of the *Guide to the Birds of Panama,* co-authored by Robert Ridgeley and John Gwynne (1976). Ridgeley acknowledged in his introduction: "The two men who have contributed most to the study of the birds of Panama in the XXth Century are Alexander Wetmore and Dr. Eugene Eisenmann."

An Intellectual Bridge

Because he was bilingual and on account of his great interest in tropical America, Eugene Eisenmann served as an intellectual bridge between the Spanish and English-speaking ornithologists of our hemisphere. He maintained continuous contact with specialists and students of birds throughout the region. He offered advice and support to those who sought him. Among them was Francisco Delgado, a student of the birds on the Azuero Peninsula. Delgado named a new subspecies of painted parakeet he discovered in this region after Eisenmann (*Pyrrhura picta eisenmanni*). This subspecies has recently been recommended to be recognized as a full species.

A serious problem confronting the biological sciences in Latin America is the paucity of specialized libraries, particularly when it comes to finding information about birds. Eisenmann supplied existing collections with the latest literature in English, while keeping North American colleagues up to date on the latest publications from Latin America. Because they were published in Spanish in journals with limited circulation, for the most part these findings were not accessible to the international scientific community.

His colleagues held him in such esteem that four bird species new to science bear Eisenmann´s name. One of them, *Thryothorus eisenmanni*, was a species discovered in 1965 by John O'Neill and George Lowery while studying the birds near the Inca ruins of Machu Picchu, Peru.

Like all of the Eisenmanns, Eugene had a talent for teaching. He always gave more than he received. He read constantly. And in addition to being good-natured, he possessed a strict sense of ethics.

Biodiversity and Ecotourism

Eisenmann was a pioneering proponent of what today would be called sustainable de-

TRANSACTIONS

OF THE

LINNAEAN SOCIETY

OF

NEW YORK

Volume VII

The Species of
Middle American Birds

A list of all species recorded
from Mexico to Panama, with
suggested English names, outlines of range,
and a distributional bibliography.

By Eugene Eisenmann

With the collaboration in the selection
of English names of Emmet R. Blake
and Edward L. Chalif

New York
APRIL, 1955

Cover of Eisenmann's book on the distribution of tropical birds from Mexico to Panama, published by the New York Linnean Society.

velopment and ecotourism. Very early on, he envisioned the forests of Panama with their incredible diversity of birds as a major resource for the future development of the country. He pointed out that there would be an increasing number of bird watchers for whom Panama with its diversity of habitats and birds would be a paradise.

In 1959, his sister Audrey, then head of public relations at the Panama Hilton Hotel, wanted to publish a pamphlet for tour-

ists about the natural beauties of the Isthmus. She asked Eugene to write the section about birds. Here, for the first time, we share these unpublished notes written by Eisenmann on 30 September 1959:

Panama is admirable for its variety of birds. More than 800 species have been identified, and others will certainly be added as a result of additional ornithological expeditions. Panama's species list is more extensive than the most complete lists from the United States and Canada combined. This great bird spe-

La Jagua Hunting Club, established in 1926, was located in a large cattle ranch of the Heurtematte family south of Pacora and parallel to the Pacific Ocean. The property held extensive marshes and lagoons. For decades its clubhouse catered to hunters and naturalists. Photo by A. Wetmore. Source: Smithsonian Institution, Archives. Washington, D.C. Alexander Wetmore Papers, 1898-1976.

cies diversity is primarily the result of the fortunate location of Panama at the crossroads of two continents and its diverse habitats. Its resident birds include Central and South American species. And its avifauna mushrooms as North American birds, fleeing the northern winter, arrive to spend the season in Panama every year. Even some bird species that nest in the coldest parts of South America avoid the Austral winter (June-September) by visiting the Isthmus. Therefore, Panama is a Mecca for avian as well as for human tourists. Wherever you go in Panama, you will find lots of birds, but to see a great variety you will have to visit different environments. Again, Panama is unusual in the sense that it offers many attractive scenic areas that are easy to visit without traveling long distances.

Roads and Conservation

As he worked in the field during the three decades following World War II, Eugene watched the relentless deforestation of Panama, especially in the wake of the construction of roads into the forest—even passing through extremely steep areas, clearly far better suited to remain as forest. "Roads are essential for rural development," he said, ". . . .but, for the future of Panama, it is vital to preserve substantial areas of forest, especially in the mountains and the foothills close to water sources. . . .This will maintain the biological value and the value for tourism of these resources . . . .while preserving soil and water reserves."

For Eugene, this destructive style of development manifested an implicit and profound disrespect for the aesthetic value of nature. Only the shortsighted would harm Panama's beautiful landscape.

Biological Wealth and Healthy Patriotism

Eisenmann's profound knowledge of Panama's biological wealth led him to state that this diversity could serve as the basis for the development of a healthy self-esteem and a national pride. "Pride," he once said, "based on the unique beauty and the diversity of the landscape, as well as for our distinctive flora and fauna, affects the social attitudes about our country and stimulates civic spirit, in the sense that truly patriotic citizens appreciate the grandeur of the best of our natural resources."

A Reflection on the Harpy Eagle

Paradoxically, Panama, a country based on interoceanic trade, is afflicted by a long-standing inferiority complex regarding foreigners, at the same time that it continues to ignore the obvious—its incomparable biological diversity, which is rejected as a source of national pride. A good example of this phenomenon is the national symbol, the Harpy Eagle. Recently, the Summit Botanical Garden, under the direction of the Panama City Mayor's Office, began a project to breed and protect this magnificent animal, the largest bird of prey in the world, and an endangered species. When support was sought among members of the local business community, only two companies responded: the Japanese Sony corporation, and American Airlines, who should be congratulated.

Bibliography

❖

1. BERTHOLD SEEMANN AND THE EXPEDITION OF THE HMS *HERALD* TO PANAMA (1846-1851),

p. 31

BELCHER, Edward. 1843. Narrative of a Voyage Round the World performed in Her Majesty's Ship Sulphur, During the Years 1836-1842, including Details of the Naval Operations in China from December 1840 to November 1841. Henry Colburn Publishers, London, 2 vols.

BENTHAM, George. 1844. The Botany of the Voyage of H.M.S. Sulphur, under the Command of Captain Sir Edward Belcher; R.N. During the Years 1836-1842. Smith Elder and Co., London. (Second edition, Verlag Cramer Sons, New York, 1968)

MOWICKE, Joan W. 1970. Type-Photographs of the Panamanian Collections of B. C. Seemann. *Annals of the Missouri Botanical Garden, 57.*

PIERCE, Richard A. and John H. Winslow. 1979. H.M.S. Sulphur on the Northwest and California Coast, 1837 and 1839. *Materials for the Study of Alaska History*, 12. The Limestone Press, Ontario, Canada.

REICHENBACH, H. G. 1872. "Obituary. Berthold Seemann" in *Botanische Zeitung, 30.* Jahrgang. Verlag von Arthur Felix, Leipzig.

SEEMANN, Berthold. 1852-1857. The Botany of the Voyage of H.M.S. Herald, under the Command of Captain Henry Kellet, during the Years 1845-51. Lovell Reeve, London.

1849. "Notes on the Recent Voyage of H.M.S. Herald" in *Hooker's Journal of Botany and Kew Garden Miscellany*, I: 144-149, 185-188. London.

1853. Narrative of the Voyage of H.M.S. Herald during the Years 1845-51 under the Command of Captain Henry Kellet being a Circumnavigation of the Globe, and Three Cruizes to the Arctic Regions in Search of Sir John Franklin. Reeve and Co., London, 2 vols.

1959. "Historia del Istmo" in *Revista "Lotería"*, 6: 91. (Translation from the English by Santiago Mackay.) Imprenta de la Academia, Panamá.

TRIMEN, Henry. 1872. "Berthold Seemann" in *The Journal of Botany, British and Foreign,* I: 1-7. Taylor and Co., London.

2. BERTHOLD SEEMANN AND THE FLORA OF PANAMA (1848), p. 40

SEEMANN, Berthold. 1928. Introducción a la flora del Istmo de Panamá. Imprenta Nacional.
Panamá. (Translated from the English by Maria Luisa Meléndez and Henri Pittier.)
1853. Narrative of the Voyage of the H.M.S. Herald during the Years 1845-51. Vol. 1, Chapter XVII, op.cit.

3. BERTHOLD SEEMANN'S NOTES ON THE PANAMANIAN FAUNA (1848), p. 49

FORBES, Edward. (ed). 1854. The zoology of the voyage of H.M.S. Herald, under the Command
of Captain Henry Kellet. During the Years 1845-51. London: Lovell Reeve, Covent Garden. 171 pp.
SEEMANN, Berthold. 1853. Narrative of the Voyage of the H.M.S. Herald... Vol. I, Chapter XVII,
op.cit.

4. THE GEOGRAPHY AND POPULATION OF PANAMA ACCORDING TO BERTHOLD SEEMANN (1849), p. 56

SEEMANN, Berthold. 1853. Narrative of the Voyage of the H.M.S. Herald. Vol. I, Chapter XVII,
op.cit.
1867. "Dotting on the Roadside. Chontales, Nicaragua" in Star and Herald (July 27th),
XIX(2917). Panama City, Panama.

5. THE NATURALIST JOSEPH VON WARSCEWICZ IN PANAMA (1848-1851), p. 69

ESCOBAR, Novencido. 1987. "El Desarrollo de las Ciencias Naturales y la Medicina en Panamá"
in Biblioteca de la Cultura Panameña, 13: XV-CIX. Universidad de Panamá, Panamá.
PENNELL, F. W. 1945. "Historical Sketch" in Frans Verdoorn (ed.): Plants and Plant Science in
Latin America, pp. 35-48. The Chronica Botanica Company, Waltham, Massachusetts.
REGEL, Eduard. 1867. "J. V. Warscewicz" in Gartenflora, 16: 95-96. Erlangen, Germany.
SAVAGE, Jay M. 1970. "On the Trail of the Golden Frog: With Warscewicz and Gabb in Central
America" in Proceedings of the California Academy of Sciences, XXXVIII(14): 273-288. California Academy of Sciences. San Francisco, Ca.
SEEMANN, Berthold (ed.). 1845. "Julius von Warscewicz" in Bonplandia. Zeitschrift für die gesammte Botanik, Jahrgang II(8). Verlag Carl Rümpler, Hannover, Germany.
STANDLEY, Paul. 1924. "Orchid Collecting in Central America" in Annual Report of the Board
of Regents of the Smithsonian Institution. Washington, D.C.
WAGNER, Moritz. 1853. "Die Provinz Chiriqui (West-Veragua) in Mittel-Amerika" in Petermann's Geographische Mitteilungen, 13: 16-24.

6. THE EXPLORATIONS OF WILMOT BROWN, JR. (1900-1904), p. 75

BANGS, Outram. 1900. "List of Birds Collected by W. W. Brown, Jr., at Loma del León, Panamá"
in Proceedings of the New England Zoological Club, II: 13-34. Boston, Massachusetts.
1901. "On a Collection of Birds Made by W. W. Brown Jr., at David and Divala, Chiriqui"
in The Auk, XVIII: 355-370. The American Ornithologists' Union, Lawrence, Kansas.
1902. "On a Second Collection of Birds Made in Chiriqui, by W. W. Brown Jr." in Proceedings of the New England Zoological Club, III: 15-70. Ibid.

1903. "A New Wren from San Miguel Island, Bay of Panama" in *Proceedings of the New England Zoological Club*, IV: 3-4. Ibid.

BARBOUR, Thomas. 1946. A Naturalist's Scrapbook. Harvard University Press, Cambridge, Massachusetts.

GOLDMAN, Edward Alphonso. 1920. Mammals of Panama. *Smithsonian Miscellaneous Collections*, 69(5). Smithsonian Institution, Washington, D.C.

PETERS, James L. 1933. "Outram Bangs, 1863-1932" in *The Auk*, L(3) (July): 265-275. The American Ornithologists' Union, Lawrence, Kansas.

THAYER, John and Outram Bangs. 1905. "The Mammals and Birds of the Pearl Islands, Bay of Panama" in *Bulletin of the Museum of Comparative Zoology at Harvard College*, XLVI(8). Museum of Comparative Zoology, Cambridge, Massachusetts.

7. The Smithsonian Institution and the Biological Survey of Panama (1910-1912), p. 81

BUSCK, August. 1912. "Descriptions of New Genus and Species of Microlepidoptera from Panama" in *Smithsonian Miscellaneous Collections*, 59(4). Smithsonian Institution, Washington, D.C.

DWYER, John D. 1973. "Henri Pittier's Botanical Activity in Panama" in *Taxon*, 22(5/6): 557-576. The International Bureau for Plant Taxonomy and Nomenclature, Utrecht, Holland.

ESCOBAR, Novencido. 1987. "El Desarrollo de las Ciencias Naturales y la Medicina en Panamá" in *Biblioteca de la Cultura Panameña*, 13. Universidad de Panamá, Panamá.

GOLDMAN, Edward A. 1920. "Mammals of Panama" in *Smithsonian Miscellaneous Collections*, 69(5). Smithsonian Institution, Washington, D.C.

ISTHMIAN CANAL COMMISSION (U.S.). 1913. Annual Report of the Isthmian Canal Commission. U.S. G.P.O., Washington, D.C.

MARSH, C. Dwight. 1913. "Report on Fresh-Water Copepoda from Panama, With Descriptions of New Species" in *Smithsonian Miscellaneous Collections*, 61(3). Smithsonian Institution, Washington, D.C.

MEEK, Seth and Hildebrand F. Samuel. 1923. "The Marine Fishes of Panama" in *Field Museum of Natural History*, 215 (*Zoological Series*, XV, I). Chicago, Ill.

NELSON, Edward 1912. "Descriptions of New Genus and Species of Hummingbirds from Panama" in *Smithsonian Miscellaneous Collections*, 56(21). Smithsonian Institution, Washington, D.C.

PITTIER, Henri. Unpublished Reports from 1911-1912 to the Secretary of the Smithsonian Institution. Smithsonian Institution Archives, Washington, D.C.

SMITHSONIAN INSTITUTION. Annual Reports, 1910, 1911, 1912, 1913. Washington, D.C.
1912. "Expeditions organized and participated in by the Smithsonian Institution in 1910 and 1911" in *Smithsonian Miscellaneous Collections*, 59(11): 15-26. Smithsonian Institution, Washington, D.C.
1913. "Explorations and Field Work of the Smithsonian Institution in 1912" in *Smithsonian Miscellaneous Collections*, 60(30): 62-74. Smithsonian Institution, Washington, D.C.

8. Henri Pittier: Botanical Studies in Panama (1897-1916), p. 90

BERNARDI, Luciano. 1980. "Vies paralleles de Mosé Bertoni et de Henri Pittier" in *Musées de Genève*, 201 (janvier): 19-22. Musée d'histoire naturelle, Genève, Suisse.

CHASE, Agnes. 1950. "Henry Pittier in Washington" in *Ceiba*, 1(2): 139-140. Escuela Agrícola Panamericana, Tegucigalpa, Honduras.

DWYER, John D. 1973. "Henry Pittier's Botanical Activity in Panama" in *Taxon*, 22(5/6):556-576.

EAKIN, Marshall C. 1999. "The Origins of Modern Science in Costa Rica: The Instituto Físico-Geográfico Nacional, 1887-1904" in *Latin American Research Review*, 34(1): 123-150. Vanderbilt University, Nashville, Tennessee.

JAHN, A. 1938. "Prof. Dr. Henry Pittier: Esbozo biográfico" in *Boletín de la Sociedad Venezolana de Ciencias Naturales*, IV(30): 18. Caracas, Venezuela.

LASSER, Tobías. 1950. "Henri Pittier: a man with a dream" in *Ceiba*, 1(2): 135-138. Escuela Agrícola Panamericana, Tegucigalpa, Honduras.

1951. "Apuntes sobre la vida y obra de Henri Pittier" ("Notes on the life and works of Henri Pittier") in *Boletín de la Sociedad Venezolana de Ciencias Naturales*, XIII(76). Ibid.

MARTI-HENNENBERG, Jordi and Anne Radeff. 1986. "Henri Francois Pittier 1857-1959" in *Geographers Bibliographical Studies*, 10: 135-142.

PITTIER, Henri. 1914. "Informe del Ingeniero encargado de la Estación Experimental de Agricultura" in *Memoria de Fomento*, pp. 51-69. Ibid.

1916. "Our present knowledge of forest formations of the Isthmus of Panama" in *Journal of Forestry*, XVI: 76-84. 1918.

PITTIER, Henri and C. D. Mell. 1931. A Century of Trees of Panama. (No place of publication.)

REPÚBLICA DE PANAMÁ. Memoria que el Secretario de Estado en el Despacho de Fomento presenta a la Asamblea Nacional de 1914. Tipografía Diario de Panamá, Panamá.

STANDLEY, Paul. 1950. "Henri Francois Pittier in Costa Rica" in *Ceiba*,1(2) (October): 129-135. Escuela Agrícola Panamericana, Tegucigalpa, Honduras.

SEEMANN, Berthold. 1928. Introducción a la Flora del Istmo de Panamá. Imprenta Nacional, Panamá. (Translated by María Luisa de Meléndez and Henri Pittier).

TEXERA-ARNAL, Yolanda. 1994. "Henri Pittier en Venezuela" in *Historia para todos*, 10. Historiadores, s.c., Caracas, Venezuela.

9. Henri Pittier:
Botanical and Ethnographic Studies on the Coasts of Colón, San Blas, and Puerto Obaldía (1911), p. 101

EAKIN, Marshall C. 1999. "The Origins of Modern Science in Costa Rica: The Instituto Físico-Geográfico Nacional, 1887-1904" in *Latin American Research Review*, 34(1): 123-150. Vanderbilt University, Nashville, Tennessee.

PITTIER, Henri. 1911-1912. The Unedited Field Reports of Henry Pittier in 1911 and 1912 to the Secretary of Smithsonian Institution Charles D. Walcott. Smithsonian Institution, Archives, Washington, D.C.

10. Henri Pittier: Chiriquí in the Dry Season of 1911, p. 113

PITTIER, Henri. 1911-1912. Field Reports to the Secretary of the Smithsonian Institution Charles D. Walcott. Smithsonian Institution, Archives, Washington, D.C. (unedited)

WILLIAMS, R. S. 1912. "New or interesting mosses from Panama" in *Contributions from the United States National Herbarium*,16, Part 1: 23-24. Smithsonian Institution, Washington, D.C.: U.S. G.P.O.

11. Henri Pittier: The Guaymies of Chiriquí (1911-1912), p. 121

PITTIER, Henri. 1912. "Little known parts of Panama" in *National Geographic*, 23(7): 628-643. Washington, D.C.

12. THE CHEPO SAVANNAS AND THE BAYANO FORESTS ACCORDING TO HENRI PITTIER (1911), p. 128

PITTIER, Henri. 1911-1912. Field Reports to the Secretary of the Smithsonian Institution Charles D. Walcott. Smithsonian Institution, Archives, Washington, D.C. (unedited)

TEXERA, Yolanda (ed.). 1998. La Modernización Difícil: Henri Pittier en Venezuela 1920-1950. Fundación Polar, Caracas, 704pp.

13. THE ZOOLOGICAL EXPLORATIONS OF EDWARD A. GOLDMAN (1910-1912), p. 134

GOLDMAN, Edward A. 1910/1911. E. A. Goldman Panama Field Journals. Transcribed by S. L. Olson in 1990. Smithsonian Institute, Washington, D.C.

   1912. E. A. Goldman Panama Field Journals. Op.cit.

   1912. "New Mammals from Eastern Panama" in *Smithsonian Miscellaneous Collections*, 60(2). Smithsonian Institute, Washington, D.C.

   1913. "Descriptions of New Mammals from Panama and Mexico" in *Smithsonian Miscellaneous Collections*, 60(22). Ibid.

   1914. "Descriptions of Five New Mammals from Panama" in *Smithsonian Miscellaneous Collections*, 63(5). Ibid.

   1915. "Biological Explorations in Eastern Panama" in *Journal of the Washington Academy of Sciences*, 51(11). Washington, D.C.

   1920. "Mammals of Panama" in *Smithsonian Miscellaneous Collections*, 69(5). Ibid.

REPÚBLICA DE PANAMÁ. 1910. "Decreto Número 128 de 1909 por el cual se declara provisionalmente inadjudicables unas tierras baldías" in *Memoria del Ministerio de Hacienda y Tesoro*, p. 29. Imprenta Nacional, Panamá.

   1910. "Asuntos Relacionados con la Zona del Canal" in *Memoria del Ministerio de Relaciones Exteriores*. Documentos Anexos a la Memoria, pp. 232-265. Tipografía Excelsior, Panamá.

   1911. "Demarcación Material de la Zona del Canal. Sección tercera. Zona del Canal" in *Memoria del Ministerio de Relaciones Exteriores*. Imprenta Nacional, Panamá.

RESTREPO, Vicente. 1952. (4th ed.) Estudio sobre las Minas de Oro y Plata de Colombia. Publicaciones del Banco de la República. Bogotá, Colombia.

WOZENCRAFT, O. M. 1881. "The Wilds of Darien" in *The Californian*, 4: 80-86, 163-171, 250-256. The California Publishing Company, San Francisco, Cal.

YOUNG, Stanley P. 1947. "Edward Alphonso Goldman: 1873-1946" in *Journal of Mammalogy*, 28(2): 91-109. American Society of Mammalogists.

14. SETH E. MEEK AND SAMUEL F. HILDEBRAND: THE FISHES OF PANAMA (1910-1944), p. 156

EVERMANN, Barton Warren. 1914. "Tribute" in Ella Tourner Meek, op.cit. 1915.

HIGGINS, E. 1950. "Samuel F. Hildebrand as a government scientist" in *Copeia*, 1: 8-11. The American Society of Ichthyologists and Herpetologists, Miami, Fla.

HILDEBRAND, S. F. 1938. "A New Catalogue of the Fresh Water Fishes of Panama" in *Zoological Series*, XXII(4). Field Museum of Natural History, Chicago, Ill.

   1939. The Panama Canal as a passageway for fishes. New York Zoological Society, New York, N.Y.

   1946. "A List of Fresh-Water Fishes from San Jose Island, Pearl Islands, Panama" in *Smithsonian Miscellaneous Collections*, 106(3). Smithsonian Institution, Washington, D.C.

HUBBS, Carl L. 1950. "Samuel F. Hildebrand, Ichthyologist and Herpetologist" in *Copeia*, 1: 12-21. The American Society of Ichthyologists and Herpetologists, Miami, Fla.

MEEK, S. and S. F. Hildebrand. 1912. "Descriptions of new fishes from Panama" in *Zoological Series*, 10(8): 77-91. Field Museum of Natural History, Chicago, Ill.

1913. "New species of fishes from Panama" in *Fildiana Zoology*, 10(8): 77-91. Field Museum of Natural History, Chicago, Ill.

1923-1926. "The Marine Fishes of Panama" in *Zoological Series*, 15, Part I-III. Field Museum of Natural History, Chicago, Ill.

MEEK, Ella Tourner. 1915. Seth Eugene Meek. Curtis-Johnson Printing Co., Chicago, Ill., pp. 53.

SCHULTZ, Leonard P. 1950. "Samuel Frederick Hildebrand" in *Copeia*, 1: 2-7. The American Society of Ichthyologists and Herpetologists. Ibid.

SMITHSONIAN INSTITUTION. 1912. "Expeditions Organized or Participated in by the Smithsonian Institution in 1910 and 1911" in *Smithsonian Miscellaneous Collections*, 59(11). Washington, D.C.

1913. "Explorations and Fieldwork of the Smithsonian Institution in 1912" in *Smithsonian Miscellaneous Collections*, 60(30). Ibid.

15. JAMES ZETEK: BARRO COLORADO BIOLOGICAL STATION (1923-1953),
p. 170

CHEESMAN, Evelyn. 1921. "Nature Reserve on the Panama Canal" in *The Daily Telegraph*, London, August 23.

FAIRCHILD, Graham B. 1979. "La Entomología en Panamá durante la primera mitad del siglo" in *Revista Médica de Panamá*, 4(3): 195-210. Academía Panameña de Medicina y Cirugía, Panamá, Panamá.

GOLDMAN, E. A. and James Zetek. 1926. "Panama" in Victor E. Shelford (ed.): Naturalist's Guide to the Americas, pp. 612-622. The Williams & Wilkins Company, Baltimore, Maryland.

GROSS, Alfred O. 1926. "Barro Colorado Biological Station" in *The Smithsonian Report*, pp. 327-342. Smithsonian Institution, Washington, D.C.

KELLOG, Vernon. 1926. "Barro Colorado Island Biological Station" in *Science*, LXIII (1637): 491-493. The American Association for the Advancement of Science, Washington, D. C.

MADDEN-HOBSON, Dorothy. 1947. "Jungle in the Tropics" in *Year Book of the Indiana Audubon Society*, pp. 22-25.

McEVOY, J. P. 1955. "Barro Colorado, Tropical Noah's Ark" in *The Reader's Digest*, May.

OCAÑA, Gilberto. 1981. "La misión del Smithsonian Tropical Research Institute en Panamá y en el trópico" in *Revista Medica de Panamá*, 6(1): 3-12. Academía Panameña de Medicina y Cirugía. Ibid.

RODRÍGUEZ, Carmen. 1949. "Arcadia tropical" in *Épocas* (octubre), pp 23-24. Panamá, Panamá.

SCOULLAR, William T. (ed.). 1916/1917. El Libro Azul de Panamá; relato e historia sobre la vida de las personas más prominentes. El Bureau de Publicidad de la América Latina, Panamá.

SNYDER, Thomas E., Wetmore, Alexander, and Bennet A. Porter. 1959. "James Zetek 1886-1959" in *Journal of Economic Entomology*, 52(6): 1230-31. The Entomological Society of America, Baltimore, Maryland.

STEVEN NEBINGER, Elizabeth. 1930. "Barro Colorado Island" in *Junior League Magazine*, 16(8) (May): 42-43. Kansas City, Kansas.

THE PANAMA CANAL NATURAL HISTORY SOCIETY. 1933. Memoirs. Balboa, Canal Zone. The Star & Herald Co., Panamá.

UNITED STATES. CANAL ZONE BIOLOGICAL AREA, BARRO COLORADO ISLAND. Reports//Canal Zone Biological Area. 1925-1965. Smithsonian Institution, Washington, D.C.

WARREN, Adrew and Nancy Andrew. 1953. "A visit to Barro Colorado Island" in *The Scientific*

Monthly, LXXVII(5): 227-232. The American Association for the Advancement of Science, Washington, D.C.

WETMORE, Alexander. 1945. "The Canal Zone Biological Area" in *Science*, 102(2634): 27. The American Association for the Advancement of Science, Washington, D.C.

WONG, Marina and Ventocilla, Jorge, with Oris Acevedo. 1995. (2nd edition). A Day on Barro Colorado Island. Smithsonian Tropical Research Institute, Panama.

ZETEK, James. 1917. Los moluscos de la República de Panamá. *Revista Nueva*, 1-2 (July-August): 1-69. Imprenta Nacional, Panama.

1923. "The Panama Canal species of the genus Anopheles" in *Proceedings of the Medical Association*, 13: 29-54. Colón, Panamá (Mount Hope).

1939. "Barro Colorado Island is proving ground for scientists" in *The Star and Herald*, Panama, August 15.

16. C. W. POWELL'S ORCHID GARDEN AT CERRO ANCÓN (1910-1926), p. 184

DWYER, John. 1964. "Panama, Plant Collection and the Missouri Botanical Garden" in *Annals of the Missouri Botanical Garden*, LI(1): 109-117. St. Louis, Missouri.

D'ARCY, William and Correa, Mireya (eds). 1985. La Botánica e Historia Natural de Panamá. Missouri Botanical Garden, St. Louis, Missouri. 455 pp.

D'ARCY, William. 1987. Flora of Panama. Checklist and Index, Part I. Missouri Botanical Garden, St. Louis, Missouri.

LOVE, Robertus. 1927. "How a fishing trip resulted in a wonderful tropical station for Shaw's Garden" in *The St. Louis Globe-Democrat Magazine*, May 22, pp.4-5. St. Louis, Missouri.

MISSOURI BOTANICAL GARDEN. 1937. "Contributions toward the Flora of Panama: based upon collections from the Missouri Botanical Garden Tropical Station, Balboa, C.Z." in *Annual Report*, 24: 175. St. Louis, Missouri.

OLIVER, Grey. 1925. "Panama orchids are numerous and beautiful" in *The Panama Times*, April, pp. 24-25, Panama.

RADER, Hattie Belle. 1927. "Powell's New Orchid Garden" in *The Panama Times*, March 19, Panama.

STANDLEY, Paul C. 1924. "Orchid collecting in Central America" in *Annual Report of the Board of Regents of the Smithsonian Institution*, pp. 353-366. Smithsonian Institution, Washington, D.C.

1927. "The Powell Orchid Garden in Panama" in *The Panama Times*, March 26, Panama.

Star and Herald. 1927. "Charles Powell, orchid expert is dead". August 19, Panama.

17. FRANK M. CHAPMAN: FROM BANKER TO A STUDENT OF NATURE IN PANAMA (1912-1935), p. 190

AMERICAN MUSEUM OF NATURAL HISTORY, The. Archives, Library. Correspondence of F. M. Chapman from and to Barro Colorado Island, 1926-1938. New York, N.Y.

BARTON, D. R. 1940. "Apostle of the Birds" in *Natural History*, pp. 48-51 (Jan.). New York, N.Y.

CHAPMAN, Frank Micheler. 1895. *Handbook of Birds of Eastern North America*. D. Appleton and Company, New York, N.Y.

1917. The Distribution of Bird-Life in Colombia. A Contribution to a Biological Survey of South America. The American Museum of Natural History, New York, N.Y. 729 pp.

1926. The Distribution of Bird-Life in Ecuador. A Contribution to a Study of the Origin of Andean Bird-Life. Bulletin of the American Museum of Natural History. Ibid. 784 pp.

1929. My Tropical Air Castle: Nature Studies in Panama. D. Appleton and Company. Ibid. 417pp.

1932. "In an Eden Where Man Befriends Beast" in *The New York Times Magazine*, December. New York, N.Y.

1938. Life in an Air Castle: Nature Studies in the Tropics. D. Appleton Century Company, New York, N.Y. 243pp.

KING, William C. 1948. Biographical Memoir of Frank Micheler Chapman 1864-1945. National Academy of Sciences, Washington, D.C.

18. LUDLOW GRISCOM AND HIS STUDIES ON THE BIRDS OF PANAMA (1917-1927), p. 201

AMERICAN MUSEUM OF NATURAL HISTORY, Archives. Unpublished reports of F. M. Chapman. New York, N.Y.

DAVIS, William E. 1994. Dean of Birdwatchers: A Biography of Ludlow Griscom. Smithsonian Institution Press, Washington, D.C.

GRISCOM, Ludlow. 1924. "Bird hunting among the wild Indians of Western Panama" in *Natural History*, XXIV(4): 505-519. American Museum of Natural History, New York, N.Y.

1925. "Benson in Panama" in *Natural History*, XXV(5): 493. Ibid.

1927. "An Ornithological Reconnaissance in Eastern Panama in 1927" in *American Museum Novitates*, 282. Ibid.

1927. "Undescribed or Little Known Birds from Panama" in *American Museum Novitates*, 280. Ibid.

1935. "The Ornithology of the Republic of Panama" in *Bulletin of the Museum of Comparative Zoology*, LXXVIII(3): 261-294. Harvard University, Cambridge, Ma.

19. PAUL C. STANDLEY AND THE FLORA OF PANAMA'S INTEROCEANIC REGION (1923-1925), p. 209

CALDERÓN, S. 1926. Datos sobre el viaje botánico de los Profesores Paul C. Standley y Samuel J. Record a Costa Rica y Guatemala en 1925-1926. Dirección General de Agricultura, Laboratorio: Sección Botánica. Imprenta Nacional, San Salvador, El Salvador.

DWYER, John D. 1964. "Panama, Plant Collection and the Missouri Botanical Garden" in *Annals of the Missouri Botanical Garden*, 51: 109-117. St. Louis, Missouri.

ESCOBAR, Novencido. 1987. Op.cit.

POPENOE, Wilson. 1964. "Paul C. Standley - An Appreciation" in *Ceiba*, 10(1). Escuela Agrícola Panamericana, Tegucigalpa, Honduras.

STANDLEY, Paul C. 1928. Flora of the Panama Canal Zone. Smithsonian Institution, United States National Museum. Contributions from the United States National Herbarium, 27. 500pp. U.S. G.P.O., Washington, D.C.

1927. "The Flora of Barro Colorado Island, Panama" in *Smithsonian Miscellaneous Collections*, 78(8). Smithsonian Institution, Washington, D.C.

1927. "Two new trees of the family Rubiaceae from Panama" in *Tropical Woods*, 11 (September): 25-26. Yale University School of Forestry, New Haven, Connecticut.

1927. "An Enumeration of the Sapotaceae of Central America" in *Tropical Woods*, 4 (December): 1-15. Ibid.

1924. "Orchid collecting in Central America" in *Annual Report of the Board of Regents of the Smithsonian Institution*, pp. 353-371. Smithsonian Institution, Washington, D.C.

1927. "Poisonous trees of Central America" in *Tropical Woods*, 9 (March): 3-7. Ibid.

WILLIAMS., Louis O. (ed.) 1963. Homage to Standley. Papers in Honor of Paul C. Standley. Chicago Natural History Museum, Chicago, Ill. 115pp.

     1963. "Paul Carpenter Standley: 1884-1963" in *Taxon*, XII,7 (Aug.-Sept.): 245-47. International Association for Plant Taxonomy, Utrecht, The Netherlands.

WOODSON, Robert E. 1963. "My Debt to Paul C. Standley" in *Homage to Standley*, pp. 33-35, op.cit.

20. THE EXPEDITIONS OF GEORGE PROCTOR COOPER TO THE FORESTS OF BOCAS DEL TORO AND CHIRIQUÍ (1926-1928), p. 219

COOPER, George Proctor. 1928. "The Forests of Western Panama" in *Tropical Woods*, 16 (Dec.): 2-9. Yale University School of Forestry, New Haven, Connecticut.

     1928. "Contributions to the Arborescent Flora of Western Panama" in *Tropical Woods*, 16 (Dec.): 9-35. Ibid.

     1928. "Some interesting trees of Western Panama" in *Tropical Woods*, 14: 1-8. Ibid.

HART, J. H. 1886. A Botanist Ramble in Central America; or, a Trip in the Mainland. Kingston, Jamaica.

STANDLEY, P. C. 1927. "New trees collected in Panama by George P. Cooper and George M. Slater" in *Tropical Woods*, 10: 47-51. Ibid.

     1935. "A new Sterculia from Panama" in *Tropical Woods*, 44 (Dec.): 25-26. Ibid.

21. PAUL ALLEN'S BOTANICAL AND FORESTRY STUDIES IN PANAMA (1934-1947), p. 227

ALLEN, Paul. H. 1939. "Notes from the Missouri Botanical Garden Tropical Station, Balboa, Canal Zone" in *Missouri Botanical Garden Bulletin*, XXV(6): 114-122. St. Louis, Missouri.

     19XX. "Collecting in Darien" in *Missouri Botanical Garden Bulletin*, XXVII(3) (March): 85-93. Ibid.

     1942. Poisonous and Injurious plants of Panama. (Unpublished manuscript.) Archives of the Smithsonian Tropical Research Institute, Panama.

     1956. The Rain Forest of Golfo Dulce. University of Florida Press, Gainesville, Florida.

     1964. "The timber woods of Panama" in *Ceiba*, 10(2): 17-61. Escuela Agrícola Panamericana, Tegucigalpa, Honduras.

DWYER, J. 1964. "Panama, Plant Collection and the Missouri Botanical Garden" in *Annals of the Missouri Botanical Garden*, 51: 109-117. St. Louis, Missouri.

POPENOE, W. 1964. "Paul H. Allen, botanist and plants man" in *Ceiba*, 10(2): 1-14. Escuela Agrícola Panamericana, Tegucigalpa, Honduras.

MORTON, C. V. 1942. "New Gesneriaceae from Panama" in *Annals of the Missouri Botanical Garden*, 29: 35. Missouri Botanical Garden, St. Louis, Missouri.

WILLIAMS, L. and H. P. Allen. 1980. Orchids of Panama. A Facsimile Reprint of the Orchidaceae. Missouri Botanical Garden, St. Louis, Missouri.

22. ALEXANDER WETMORE AND THE BIRDS OF PANAMA (1944-1966), p. 235

COOPER, V. and W. Cox. 1990. Guide to the Papers of Alexander Wetmore, Circa 1898-1979. *Guides to Collections*, 11. Archives and Special Collections of the Smithsonian Institution, Washington, D.C.

OENSER, Paul H. 1980. "In Memoriam: Alexander Wetmore" in *The Auk*, 97(3): 608-615. The American Ornithologists' Union, Lawrence, Kansas.

OLSON, Storrs. 1976. Collected Papers in Avian Paleontology Honoring the 90th Birthday of Alexander Wetmore. *Smithsonian Contributions to Paleobiology*, 27: I-XXII. Smithsonian Institution, Washington, D.C.

    1966. Collecting Itinerary of Alexander Wetmore in Panama, 1944, 1946-1966. Smithsonian Institution, Washington, D.C. (unpublished manuscript).

SMITHSONIAN INSTITUTION, Archives. The Alexander Wetmore Papers, 1898-1976. Washington, D.C.

THE PANAMA CANAL REVIEW. 1954. "Famed Authority Describes Panama As a Paradise For Ornithologists." Balboa, C. Z. Panama, March: 5-6.

WETMORE, Alexander. 1926. "Observations on the Birds of Argentina, Paraguay, Uruguay and Chile" in *Smithsonian Institution, United States National Museum*, Bulletin 133. Washington, D.C.

    1927. "Our Migrant Shore Birds in Southern South America" in *Technical Bulletin*, 26. United States Department of Agriculture, Washington, D.C.

    1956. "The Muscovy Duck in the Pleistocene of Panama" in *Wilson Bulletin*, 68(4): 327. Wilson Ornithology Society, Lawrence, Kansas.

    1965. "The Birds of the Republic of Panama" in *Smithsonian Miscellaneous Collections*, 150, Part I. Smithsonian Institution, Washington, D.C.

    1968. "The Birds of the Republic of Panama", 150, Part II. Ibid.

    1972. "The Birds of the Republic of Panama", 150, Part III. Ibid.

    1984. "The Birds of the Republic of Panama", 150, Part IV. Ibid.

23. STUDIES BY ALEXANDER WETMORE ON THE BIRDS OF PANAMA'S PACIFIC ISLANDS (1944-1956)
p. 247

BOVALLIUS, Carl Erik Alexander. 1972. Viaje al Istmo, 1881-1883. (Traducido del sueco por Abel Lombardo Vega). Ministerio de Educación, Panamá. 107 pp.

CLARK, A. H. 1946. "Echinoderms from the Pearl Islands, Bay of Panama, with a revision of the Pacific species of the genus encope" in *Smithsonian Miscellaneous Collections*, 106(5). Washington, D.C.

CASTROVIEJO, S. (ed.) 1997. Flora y Fauna del Parque Nacional de Coiba (Panamá). Agencia Española de Cooperación. Madrid, Spain.

COCHRAN, D. M. 1946. "Notes on the Herpetology of the Pearl Islands, Panama" in *Smithsonian Miscellaneous Collections*, 106(4). Ibid.

DAMPIER, William. 1697. A New Voyage Round the World. Dover Publications, Inc., New York, N.Y., 1968.

EARLANSON, C. O. 1946. "The Vegetation of San Jose Island, Republic of Panama" in *Smithsonian Miscellaneous Collections*, 106(2). Ibid.

JOHNSON, I. M. 1949. "The Botany of San Jose Island (Gulf of Panama)" in *The Arnold Arboretum*. Harvard University, Cambridge, Ma.

MORRISON, J. P. F. 1946. "The Non-marine Mollusks of San Jose Island, with Notes on those of Pedro Gonzalez Island, Pearl Islands, Panama" in *Smithsonian Miscellaneous Collections*, 106(6). Ibid.

SMITHSONIAN INSTITUTION, Archives. (The) Alexander Wetmore Papers, 1898-1976. Ibid.

WETMORE, Alexander. 1946. "The Birds of San Jose and Pedro Gonzalez Islands, Republic of Panama" in *Smithsonian Miscellaneous Collections*, 106(1). Ibid.

    1952. "The Birds of Taboga, Taboguilla and Urava, Panama" in *Smithsonian Miscellaneous Collections*, 121(2). Ibid.

1956 "The Birds of Coiba Island, Panama" in *Smithsonian Miscellaneous Collections*, 134(9). Ibid.

1959 "The Birds of Isla Escudo de Veraguas, Panama" in *Smithsonian Miscellaneous Collections*, 139(2). Ibid.

24. EUGENE EISENMANN BRANDON: LAWYER AND STUDENT OF THE BIRDS OF PANAMA (1939-1981)
p. 253

BUCKLEY, P. A., M. S. Foster, E. S. Morton, R. S. Ridgely and F. G. Buckley F. 1985. "Neotropical Ornithology" in *Ornithological Monographs*, 36. The American Ornithologists' Union, Lawrence, Kansas.

DELGADO, Francisco. 1985. "A New Subspecies of the painted parakeet (Pyrrhura Picta) from Panama" in Neotropical Ornithology: *Ornithological Monographs*, 36: 16-20, op. cit.

EISENMANN, Eugene. 1950. "Some notes on Panama birds collected by J. H. Batty" in *The Auk*, 67: 363-366. The American Ornithologists' Union, Lawrence, Kansas.

1951. "Northern birds summering in Panama" in *Wilson Bulletin*, 63: 181-185. Wilson Ornithology Society, Lawrence, Kansas.

1952. "Annotated list of birds of Barro Colorado Island, Panama Canal Zone" in *Smithsonian Miscellaneous Collections*, 117: 1-62. Smithsonian Institution, Washington, D.C.

1955. "The Species of Middle American Birds" in *Transactions of the Linnaean Society of New York*, VII: 1-128. New York, N.Y.

1956. "Notes on the Birds of the province of Bocas del Toro, Panama" in *The Condor*, 59(4): 247-262. Santa Clara, Cal.

1967. Species whose collection can contribute materially to ornithology. The Florida State University, Center for Tropical Studies, Albrook AFB, Canal Zone, 14pp. Panama.

1976. "Early memories of a bird student in Panama" in E.A. Fidanque, R. De Lima, V. E. Sasso, E. D. L. Perkins and J. Melamed (ed.): A Hundred Years of Jewish History in Panama, 1876-1976, pp. 386-391. Commemorative Edition of the Centennial of Kol Shearith, Israel. Panama, Panama.

EISENMANN, E. and H. Loftin. 1967. A list of birds known from the Cerro Campana Area, Panama. The Florida State University, Center for Tropical Studies, Albrook AFB, C. Z. 7pp. Panama.

1967. Checklists of birds known from the vicinity of the Heurtematte - La Jagua Field Station. The Florida State University, Center for Tropical Studies, Albrook AFB, C. Z. 9pp. Panama.

1972. Birds of the Western Chiriqui Highlands-Panama. Florida Audubon Society Field Check List. Russ Mason's Flying Carpet Tours, Kissimmee. Florida. 34pp.

GRAHAM, Frank. 1986. "Eisenmann's Monument" in *Birdland Audubon Magazine* (January), pp. 40-42.

HOWELL, Thomas R. 1985. "Eugene Eisenmann and the Study of Neotropical Birds" in *Neotropical Ornithology. Ornithological Monographs*, 36: 1-4.

RIDGELY, Robert .S. and John A. Gwynne, Jr. 1976 (2nd edition). A Guide to the Birds of Panama with Costa Rica, Nicaragua, and Honduras. Princeton University Press, Princeton, N.J.

UNITED STATES. CANAL ZONE BIOLOGICAL AREA, BARRO COLORADO ISLAND. Reports//Canal Zone Biological Area. 1925-1940. Smithsonian Institution, Washington, D.C. 1948. Annual Report. Smithsonian Institution, Washington, D.C.

WILLIS, Edwin O. and Eisenmann, Eugene. 1979. A Revised List of Birds of Barro Colorado Island, Panama. Smithsonian Institution Press, Washington, D.C. 31 pp.